June 1991 he and their part in their part in their part wes in court, arguing that while they in no way condoned Blake's espionage activities for either side, they were right to help him because the forty-two-year sentence he received was inhuman and hypocritical. Despite a virtual direction from the judge to convict, the jury found them not guilty on all counts.

Michael Randle has taken a keen interest in developments in Eastern Europe. In 1956 he undertook a march from Vienna to Budapest with leaflets expressing support for Hungarian passive resistance to the Soviet occupation, though he was prevented from entering Hungary by Austrian border guards. In 1968 he jointly coordinated for War Resisters International simultaneous international protests in Moscow, Budapest, Sofia and Warsaw against the Soviet-led invasion of Czechoslovakia. In the 1970s and 1980s he collaborated with the Czech dissident Jan Kavan, then living in London, smuggling literature and equipment to the democratic opposition in Czechoslovakia.

He has a degree in English from London University (1966) and an M.Phil in Peace Studies (Bradford, 1981). From 1980 to 1987 he was coordinator of the Alternative Defence Commission, contributing to its two major publications, *Defence without the Bomb* (1983) and *The Politics of Alternative Defence* (1987). He has contributed articles and reviews to *Peace News*, *New Society*, the *Guardian* and other newspapers and journals. He is also the author of several books: *The Blake Escape: How We Freed George Blake – and Why* (co-author with Pat Pottle, 1989); *Alternatives in European Security* (co-editor with Paul Rogers, 1990); and *People Power: The Building of a New European Home* (1991). From 1988 to 1990 he was coordinator of the Bradford-based Social Defence Project.

He married his wife Anne in 1962; they have two grown-up sons.

MICHAEL RANDLE

Civil Resistance

FontanaPress

An Imprint of HarperCollins*Publishers*

Fontana Press
An Imprint of HarperCollins*Publishers*
77–85 Fulham Palace Road
Hammersmith, London W6 8JB

A Fontana Press Original
First published 1994

2 4 6 8 9 7 5 3 1

ISBN 0-586-09291-9

Set in Linotron Baskerville

Printed and bound in Great Britain by
HarperCollins Manufacturing Glasgow

To Anne Randle,
and to the men and women of the jury
at No. 1 Court at the Old Bailey,
17–26 June 1991,
without whose independence and courage
the writing of this book would have been delayed
by several years.

ACKNOWLEDGEMENTS

I wish to express my particular thanks and gratitude to the Joseph Rowntree Charitable Trust who provided me with a grant to carry out the research for this book. Special thanks are due also to Ian Paten, former editor of Paladin Books, who first suggested my writing this book; to the series editor, Justin Wintle, for his suggestions and corrections; and to Anne Randle for her help and patience during an exceptionally busy year. I am grateful to Mrs Paula Alderson, widow of the late Mr Stanley Alderson, for giving me access to his unpublished manuscript *Non-Violence and the Citizen*. My thanks, too, to my colleagues on the Social Defence Working Group – Howard Clark, Christina Arber, Owen Greene, Bob Overy, Carol Rank, Andrew Rigby, Walter Stein and Tim Wallis-Milne – who, in the course of many meetings and discussions over the last several years, have contributed to, and helped clarify, my ideas on civil resistance.

My intellectual debt to the pioneers of non-violent theory, especially those writing in the post-World War II period, is self-evident in the text. Notable among these are Gene Sharp, Adam Roberts, Theodor Ebert, April Carter, George Lakey, Jacques Semelin, Christian Mellon and Jean-Marie Muller. I have been influenced, too, by the contribution to the concept of civilian defence by Anders Boserup, Andrew Mack, Gene Keyes, Lennart Bergfeldt and Alex Schmid, and to Steven Huxley, who has subjected the literature on non-violent resistance to a critical appraisal in his book on Finnish resistance to Russification at the turn of the century, *Constitutional Insurgency in Finland*. Chapter 2 in particular owes much to the overview of the development of passive resistance by

Huxley in that book. I am grateful to Gene Keyes, Lennart Bergfeldt and Bob Overy for sending me copies of their Doctoral theses entitled respectively *Strategic Nonviolent Defense in Theory: Denmark in Practice*; *Experiences of Civilian Resistance: The Case of Denmark 1940–1945*; and *Gandhi as an Organiser*. Naturally I take full responsibility for the views expressed in the book and for any mistakes it contains.

My thanks finally to friends and colleagues in the Department of Peace Studies at Bradford University, in War Resisters International, and in the broader peace and non-violence movement who have played so large a part in shaping my ideas and convictions.

CONTENTS

Introduction

When tens of thousands of people took the to streets of Manila in the Philippines in February 1986 and succeeded in overthrowing the corrupt oligarchy of Ferdinand Marcos, a new term entered the vocabulary of political discourse: People Power.

It was chiefly the term that was new. Mass civil resistance aimed at achieving a variety of political and social objectives became a significant force during the nineteenth century. It played in some cases a crucial role in struggles against colonial rule, dictatorship, coups and foreign occupation in the present century. Nevertheless, the events in Manila caught the public imagination in a special sense, perhaps because of the dramatic confrontation between the army on the one side supporting dictatorial rule, and unarmed civilians on the other insisting on democratic political change.

No one in 1986 expected, or could have predicted, that within a few years people power would be largely responsible for the transformation of the world's political geography and the pattern of international relations. Yet such is the case. Future historians may well regard the revolutions in Eastern Europe in 1989 among the major turning points in human history, comparable in importance to the Russian Revolution of 1917, and the French Revolution of 1789. Not only did they end Soviet domination in the region, they removed once and for all the political underpinnings of the Cold War. In large measure, too, they contributed to the final collapse of the Leninist model of communism in the Soviet Union itself and the break-up of the Soviet state.

Soviet developments began with the coming to power of

Gorbachev in 1985. Gorbachev's initial aim was reform within a continuing Marxist-Leninist political and social order. His importance as the facilitator of change can hardly be exaggerated, but it was the overthrow of the old regimes in Eastern Europe, and the pressures which this set off within the Soviet Union, that turned a programme of reform into a thoroughgoing revolution.

Clearly there has been a negative side to these developments. As with the collapse of any empire, the dissolution of the Soviet state and sphere of influence has brought new tensions and instabilities. The most tragic and menacing development has been the war and atrocities in former Yugoslavia. There is also, at the time of writing, a state of undeclared civil war between the neighbouring states of Armenia and Azerbaijan, and the threat of further violence both within and between a number of former Soviet republics. Some of the autonomous regions within the Russian republics and elsewhere have also begun to demand independence, threatening the further splintering of the old Union. Rocketing prices, unemployment, increasing homelessness are some of the problems confronting the former communist states, and as yet there is no consensus as to what kind of alternative social and political system is now required.

Hardly less momentous in its political implications than the collapse of autocratic communism in the Soviet Union and Eastern Europe has been the disintegration of the apartheid system in South Africa, and the prospect of majority rule in the near future. Though it was not achieved without bloodshed (most tragically in the clashes between the Zulu-based Inkatha movement and supporters of the African National Congress), civil resistance, coupled with international pressure, was central to the struggle. The demonstrations and riots in the black townships threatened general disorder, while the strikes and threatened strikes by COSATU (the Congress of South African Trade Unions) reminded the white population and government of their ultimate dependence on black labour. The opposition of the Churches to apartheid, and the active involvement of leading churchmen such as Desmond Tutu and Alan Boesak, added to the moral stature of the anti-apartheid campaign and helped to undermine the entrenched prejudices of the majority of the white population.

Elsewhere in the 'Third World', civil resistance has contributed significantly to the retreat of dictatorships and right-wing military regimes – in Chile, for example, and in much of Central and South America, in the Philippines, mentioned earlier, in Thailand, and in South Korea. True, there have also been setbacks and failures, most notably in China. Thus it is important to try to analyse the conditions in which civil resistance is likely to succeed at any given moment, and the tactics and strategy which could help to make it more effective.

The end of the Cold War has opened up the possibility of major arms reductions and the realisation within a reasonable time-span of global nuclear disarmament. But while there have been welcome international agreements to reduce both conventional and nuclear forces, the competition to sell strategic weapons continues, even to despotic regimes in the Middle East where war is a constant threat. At the nuclear level, even when the new agreement on strategic arms reductions comes into force, it will leave the US and Russia with the capacity to destroy each other – and much of the rest of the world – several times over. There is now a real opportunity to realise the dream of global nuclear disarmament. But if it is not seized, nuclear proliferation seems unavoidable. Civil resistance by the Western peace movements, and by human rights and peace movements in the East, helped to bring about the end of the division of Europe and the Cold War. It may be necessary again to pressure governments to seize the opportunities which now exist.

Civil resistance has been seen by some of its adherents as providing – at least potentially – an alternative to war and military defence. It has been used increasingly as a means of struggle against injustice, oppression and foreign domination where in the past a war of liberation would have seemed the only option. To that extent at least, it has shown that it can be a 'functional equivalent of war'. Moreover, in Czechoslovakia in 1968, mass civil resistance was used – with at least partial success – to oppose the invasion of Soviet and Warsaw Pact forces and demand the reinstatement of the legitimate government.

So far no state has thought it advisable to rely solely for defence on the capability of its citizens to resist invasion and occupation, or coups d'état, by non-violent means. Sweden, however, after successive studies, adopted this in 1986 as a complementary strategy. Others have given serious consideration to it in this capacity, most recently the former Soviet Baltic republics.

The potential of civil resistance as a form of alternative defence merits particular attention at a time when international war has become so destructive, and when there is a debate going on about the restructuring of global security in the post-Cold War era. Nuclear disarmament, and the drastically reduced levels of conventional armament which one assumes must accompany it, would also require an evaluation of alternative ways of preventing and solving conflict – but also, where conflict is unavoidable, of conducting it. The potential of 'defence by civil resistance' or 'civilian defence' is considered in some detail in Chapters 5 and 6.

The book traces the development of civil resistance, as an idea and as a social phenomenon, from its beginnings in the early nineteenth century to the present day. It is not a history of civil resistance as such – that would be beyond the scope of a work of this length; rather, it draws upon that history to show how civil resistance has developed, and to consider the role it might play in the future.

Although the main focus is on civil resistance in relation to macro-politics and strategy, we should not overlook its contribution to the politics of everyday life. Thus, since the postwar resurgence of civil resistance in Western Europe and the United States, a wide range of groups and campaigns have resorted to it, from the homeless who have squatted in empty houses, to women who have blocked busy roads to enforce their demand for pedestrian crossings. Nor indeed is there a sharp dividing line between the political and social struggles of everyday life and the broader struggles for emancipation. At both levels, the issue is how people are to take greater control over their lives. Indeed, it may well be that the eventual political outcome in Eastern Europe and the former Soviet republics, and in other countries which have recently ousted dictatorial governments, will hinge on how successfully the formalities of parliamentary democracy are matched by genuine democratic control at the grass roots. Civil resistance does not guarantee such control. It is a crucial weapon in the hands of those seeking to achieve it.

Civil resistance is a topic of outstanding social and political importance. I hope the present book, in sketching its development and analysing some of the issues it raises, will contribute to a better understanding of its mode of operation and its potential for shaping a freer and more equitable society and international system.

Chapter 1

Civil Resistance and *Realpolitik*

'Power', according to Mao Tse-Tung's famous dictum, 'comes out of the barrel of a gun.' In much the same vein, Stalin is said to have retorted when warned of the strength of Catholicism in Eastern Europe: 'How many divisions does the Pope have?'

Brezhnev had cause to reflect bitterly on those words of his predecessor as he faced the problem of Solidarity in Catholic Poland in 1980–1. Nor did the problem disappear with the imposition of martial law in December 1981 and the banning of the Solidarity movement. Indeed, the emergence of the movement can be seen in retrospect to have signalled the beginning of the end for communist power not only in Poland, but throughout Eastern Europe, and finally in the Soviet Union itself.

But Stalin and Mao were being disingenuous. Had they relied on the gun alone rather than upon a whole gamut of persuasive, manipulative and coercive strategies, neither would have achieved top leadership positions within their respective communist parties, or retained them to become two of the most powerful political leaders of the twentieth century. This is not, of course, to deny that violence, and the threat of violence, frequently plays a key role in regulating power relationships, especially those between the state and the citizen, and between one state and another. It is to recognise first that violence is not the only kind of coercive sanction available, and second that other factors can be important, even decisive.

Not only does the crude equation of power and violence fail to explain the relatively non-violent overthrow of dictatorial regimes of left or right over the last decade or so, it does not even explain the success of other revolutions and anti-colonial struggles where armed force did indeed play a major role. For if power came simply from the barrel of a gun, the enormous disparity in the modern era between the means of violence available to the state and the population would make successful rebellion highly improbable, and the very attempt to rebel an improbable and foolhardy adventure.[1] But rebellions are undertaken, and do succeed. Moreover, it is sometimes repressive and authoritarian regimes that prove most vulnerable. How is one to account for this?

The short answer is that a government is only as powerful as its ability to command the loyalty and obedience of key state institutions – the army, the police, the civil service and, beyond that, to secure the cooperation or at least the compliance of the majority of the population. Other things being equal, the greater the degree of voluntary cooperation the government enjoys, the more secure it will be. Conversely, a government that relies to a major extent on naked violence to secure the reluctant compliance of the population is particularly vulnerable to sudden overthrow precisely because its power base within society is so narrow. Even Machiavelli, the founding father, so to speak, of *realpolitik*, emphasised the underlying weakness of rulers who rely solely on coercion and violence.

In her seminal work *On Violence*, the American political scientist Hannah Arendt insists that power is rooted in voluntary cooperation. It refers, she says, 'to the human ability not just to act but to act in concert. Power is never the property of an individual; it belongs to a group and remains in existence only so long as the group keeps together.'[2] This capacity to 'act in concert' makes civilisation, makes society itself, possible.

The relationship of violence to power is a complex one. Hannah Arendt goes so far as to claim that violence is not only different from power – in the sense in which she defines it – but its very antithesis. This somewhat overstates the position. Even in societies which do not have any kind of central authority, sanctions play a role in maintaining group cohesion and establishing the norms of social behaviour.[3] It is true, however, that violence is the extreme and exceptional sanction, for were it not so the group would soon tear itself apart. Inducements, such as the fulfilment of basic physical and social needs which require working in cooperation with others, and sanctions, such as verbal censure, social ostracism, economic penalties – indeed all the myriad routine pressures of everyday life towards group conformity – count for far more.

But if the ultimate *source of power* is the group acting in concert, the institutions which coordinate and direct group activity can place enormous power in an executive or leadership structure. This is true even of many institutions within civil society, such as trade unions, political parties, Churches. It is true in a special sense of governments, which have the coercive institutions of the modern state at their disposal, and access to human and material resources unrivalled by any other corporate body. Governments, corporations, classes, individual leaders within movements and institutions, are powerful in so far as they command the loyalty of large numbers of people and can induce them to act in concert for a given end. The base of power lies within society, but it is the individuals and organisations who have the capacity to wield that power which we normally think of as powerful.

Power may be invested in a leadership in a purely voluntary way, as for instance when an individual is chosen to speak and act in a certain way on behalf, say, of a trade union branch or political movement. The lines of power in such a case are open and transparent. But power may also take the form of *domination*, that is to say *power over* others. Probably all governments to some degree, and dictatorial governments in the extreme, exercise power in this sense. It is a common feature too of hierarchical institutions within society, from the corporate firm to the patriarchal family. Manipulation and sanctions of various kinds are by definition associated with domination. Nevertheless, even the most arbitrary government requires a minimum of group loyalty to maintain its position and ensure that its commands are enforced.

In exercising control over state institutions, and over society as a whole, governments rely not only on sanctions on the one

3

hand and the freely given cooperation of their committed adherents on the other, but on another key element in power relationships – *authority*. Authority denotes the capacity to command obedience to orders, or the acceptance of one's judgement, not because of the threat of sanctions but because of position or status. The cultural norms and traditions of a society determine, at least partially, where authority resides and how absolute it is. Governmental authority depends critically on the strength of its claim to *legitimacy* in the eyes of the population, and its assumed right to command obedience within the limits of a given constitutional or traditional framework. In a parliamentary system, the government claims its legitimacy from the outcome of an election. It may nonetheless forfeit that legitimacy if it is regarded as having defaulted on its responsibilities, or if it acts outside the rules of the constitution, or uses its power in ways that are widely considered as unacceptable.

Third parties can be an important prop – or conversely a significant threat – to the power of governments or other groups. Thus a government depends to a greater or lesser extent not only on the cooperation of its own citizens but on that of other states with which it has diplomatic and trading relationships, and increasingly of other outside institutions and associations. Hence, in the case of a major confrontation with a section of its own population, a government is likely to expend a great deal of energy trying to convince the outside world of the legitimacy of its case. Its opponents, as resources permit, will attempt to do likewise. Similarly in disputes between groups within society, it will be important to both sides to enlist and retain public support.

Sensitivity to the reactions of third parties, and of its own power base, can act as a constraint on the use by a dictatorial government of extreme violence against its own subjects. This is one reason why publicity can be a lifeline for those seeking to challenge arbitrary power. Both internal and international pressure, for instance, contributed to the gradual undermining of the apartheid regime in South Africa and to General Pinochet's loss of authority in Chile. At the beginning of Pinochet's period of rule, after the coup d'état of 1973, he was able to round up and massacre hundreds of his political opponents, and to imprison and torture many more. By the time he was forced to resign his dictatorial powers, this was no longer a real option.

Dictators are often more aware than their critics of the fact that they cannot rule by violence and terror alone. This is demonstrated by the lengths to which they go to silence dissent and impose uniformity of thinking on the population through propaganda and indoctrination. Not that one should underestimate the effectiveness of a combination of verbal assault and the threat of dire punishment in repressing opposition. Ultimately, however, these methods breed cynicism and stagnation. The slogans will be faithfully repeated in public, but laughed at in the privacy of the home or the company of trusted friends. The stagnation of economic and cultural life, and endemic corruption in the administration, is frequently the outcome when a government relies primarily on violence and terror to maintain its position. Open defiance may be too costly, but there is no longer the will among the population to make things happen. There is a genuine dissipation of power in the sense defined by Arendt. One of the incentives for de-Stalinisation, following the death of the dictator, was probably the need to get the economy and society moving again. Unfortunately the reforms did not go far enough, and were ultimately halted and partially reversed when Brezhnev replaced Khrushchev as Soviet leader.

When disaffection is sufficiently widespread among the population, it is liable to spread to the army, the police, and other public servants who can never be entirely immunised against the current of opinion and feeling in society as a whole. One then has a potentially revolutionary situation. The disparity between the means of violence available to the government and its opponents diminishes, and the balance of power may shift decisively in favour of the latter. In some instances a bloody revolution or civil war results. In others the old leadership is overthrown in a coup staged by disaffected officers who are more in tune with what is happening in society, and may wish to avoid large-scale bloodshed, or perhaps to forestall a more thoroughgoing revolution. Sometimes the regime or polity under attack disintegrates altogether as its sources of power are removed. In still other instances, the government, realising the game is up, resigns and negotiates a peaceful transfer of power to its opponents. Disintegration and/or negotiated transfers of power occurred throughout most of Eastern Europe in 1989. Only in Romania was the change accompanied by organised violence when the *Securitate* forces loyal to the deposed dictator staged a bloody last-ditch stand against the army. It is not a coincidence that the *Securitate* was manned primarily by former inmates of state orphanages whose contacts with the general population had been deliberately kept to a minimum.

Such a progression from dictatorship to democracy is not, of course, inevitable. It is not historically determined. Stalinism in its extreme form prevailed until the dictator's death, and was not finally eradicated until the collapse of communism in the Soviet Union in 1991. It took the death of Salazar in Portugal, and of Franco in Spain, to open up the way to parliamentary democracy in those two countries. Thus it is important not to overstate the 'voluntarist' basis of state and government power. Under highly repressive regimes, the choice open to the individual in normal circumstances is a stark one: either comply (or at least go through the motions of complying) or face the loss of the means of livelihood, imprisonment, perhaps torture and death. The regime may be vulnerable to *collective* defiance, and may ultimately provoke it. But historically the erosion of dictatorial power to the point at which insurrection becomes a real possibility, and a significant threat, has frequently taken years or even decades. One of the major political challenges of our time is to develop methods and techniques whereby the citizen, ideally in cooperation with the international community, can more swiftly and effectively bring dictators to heel, and prevent coups d'état or slides to autocratic rule. Stated more generally, the task is to ensure that state power is brought and remains under democratic control. The further task beyond that is to develop an effective method of contention and resistance to empower groups, sections and classes within the community suffering disadvantage and discrimination.

Democratic constitutions are designed to control state power though a system of checks and balances. These characteristically involve the notional separation of executive, legislative and judicial functions, and the requirement to hold general elections at regular intervals. Often there is also a written constitution which sets out the functions of various branches of government and may include a Bill of Rights guaranteeing certain fundamental rights for all citizens. Where there is a written constitution, laws and directives can be challenged in the courts and declared void if they are judged to be in breach of the constitution.

These are important, but not sufficient, safeguards. They do not obviate the need for a further remedy in the hands of the population in the case of an abuse of power by the executive – or, of course, the violent overthrow of the constitution. Hitler, after all, came to power by constitutional means, proceeding thereafter by the use of street violence and state power to dismantle the democratic safeguards against dictatorial rule. The high-sounding declarations embodied in the constitutions of the Soviet Union and the 'people's democracies' in Eastern Europe did not prevent the horrors of Stalinism or the modified forms of autocracy which succeeded it. The framework of constitutional rule remained, but it was largely devoid of content.

Even in well-established parliamentary democracies, however, the power of the executive may be extended incrementally to the detriment of genuine democratic control. Already, with the advent of the modern party system, the notion of an independent legislature holding the executive in check is largely fictional in many Western countries. The independence of the judiciary, too, may be eroded in practice by the way judges are appointed and through various Establishment pressures. Thus the character of the Supreme Court in the United States was radically altered by the appointments made during the Reagan and Bush administrations. This resulted in a Supreme Court which reversed previous decisions that the use of the death penalty was unconstitutional, and in a spate of executions in the early 1990s. Similarly, during the Thatcher years in Britain, when Hailsham was Lord Chancellor, the judiciary became markedly more conservative.

A government may also circumvent the law by misusing the

intelligence and security services. It is now clear that both the CIA in the United States and MI5 and MI6 in Britain have engaged at times in illegal and wholly indefensible activities against their own citizens and those of other states, sometimes on their own initiative, sometimes with the connivance, and under the direction, of government ministers. Finally, even a democratically elected government and parliament can introduce laws, or pass enactments, which discriminate against, and deny the fundamental rights of, individuals or whole sections of the community. Britain's discriminatory immigration laws are a case in point. The internment of 'enemy aliens' in wartime is another example. Even more scandalous was the internment in the US of thousands of American citizens of Japanese origin during World War II.

The power of the state *vis-à-vis* the citizen has increased exponentially with the evolution since the nineteenth century of the modern state bureaucracy, making it all the more necessary to re-examine the adequacy of traditional safeguards against the abuse of state power. The modern state is a potentially dangerous instrument in any hands. In the hands of Hitler and Stalin, it enabled the construction of tyrannies without parallel in previous history.

In classical constitutional theory, the ultimate sanction of the citizens faced by a wholesale abuse of power is armed rebellion. As noted earlier, one of the serious problems with that solution is the disparity in the means of violence available to the state as against that at the disposal of its rebellious subjects. Only when the government is already seriously weakened and can no longer depend on its army and security services have the insurgents a realistic chance of succeeding.

Guerrilla warfare has been proposed, in such extreme circumstances, as a technique of armed struggle which could overcome the imbalance of military force between the two sides. It was a particularly favoured solution in some circles during the 1960s and 1970s following the successes of guerrilla warfare in a number of 'Third World' countries – China, Cuba, Algeria, Vietnam, Zimbabwe. It has indeed significant points in common with the notion of civil resistance discussed in this book, notably in its emphasis on the importance of the political struggle and the need to undermine the opponent's power. Yet a prolonged guerrilla war can have dire consequences for a society, particularly perhaps in a highly urbanised society. In such a setting, where there is no clear battle line between the two protagonists, and where the urban guerrilla operates in effect in the disguise of civilian dress, severe repression by the state's forces is virtually inevitable. (There may even be an intention to provoke repression as a means of politicising the population.)

Urban guerrilla warfare is likely also to be deeply divisive. As the security forces increase their precautions against attack, the temptation is for the guerrilla to shift to the softer target of 'collaborators'. But since large numbers of people are inevitably drawn into some degree of cooperation with the *de facto* authority, the front line comes to be drawn deeper and deeper within the community. At this stage, guerrilla warfare tends to become increasingly indiscriminate and to spill over into outright terrorism. That progression is indeed tragically apparent in the Provisional IRA campaign in Northern Ireland since 1970.

Finally, the expectation, or hope, that guerrilla warfare would have a decentralising effect politically in the post-revolutionary society has not been borne out in practice. Indeed, Gene Sharp has argued that it would have the opposite effect because of the centralising impetus of the military struggle,[4] especially in the latter stages of a guerrilla campaign when, according to the prescription of Mao, Guevara and other exponents, it takes on the character of full-scale conventional warfare. Centralisation, however, in the case of countries like China, Vietnam and Cuba, is also traceable to the political ideas of the revolutionaries.

Civil resistance is a method of collective political struggle based on the insight that governments depend in the last analysis on the cooperation, or at least the compliance, of the majority of the population, and the loyalty of the military, police and civil service. It is thus grounded in the realities of political power. It operates by mobilising the population to withdraw that consent, by seeking to undermine the opponents' sources of power, and by enlisting the support of third parties. Its methods range from protest and persuasion to social, economic and political non-cooperation, and finally to non-violent intervention.[5] Demonstrations, vigils, the organising of petitions are some of the characteristic actions associated with protest and persuasion. Strikes, go-slows, boycotts, civil disobedience are among the methods of non-cooperation. And sit-ins, occupations and the creation of parallel institutions of government are among the methods of non-violent intervention.

Two important characteristics of civil resistance, as defined here, are that it is *collective* action, and that it avoids any systematic recourse to violence. Thus it is differentiated from individual dissent on the one hand and forms of collective resistance involving military action on the other. This is not to imply that civil resistance requires the acceptance of a pacifist or non-violent ethic, but simply to distinguish it as a social phenomenon from armed insurrection, guerrilla warfare, or conventional war. Whether it is ever practicable or desirable to combine civil resistance with military and paramilitary action is a separate question which we will consider later.

Civil resistance needs to be placed within the broader concept of *non-violent action*. The latter includes acts of individual resistance, such as conscientious objection; transnational initiatives, such as the non-violent direct action by Greenpeace to prevent nuclear tests in the Pacific, whale-hunting, or the dumping of toxic wastes; and the imposition of economic and diplomatic sanctions by individual states or organisations, such as the European Community or the United Nations. Evidently, civil resistance conducted inside a particular country may be combined with other forms of non-violent action. Indeed, assistance from third parties, in the form for instance of sanctions by international bodies, can be crucial to the success of the internal resistance.

The goals of civil resistance may be reformist, such as the removal of a particular injustice, or the amendment of a particular law. Gandhi's campaigns in South Africa on behalf of the Indian community, the suffragette campaign in Britain in the early years of this century, the civil rights movement in the United States in the 1950s and 1960s, and the anti-poll tax campaign in Britain in the early 1990s are examples of such reformist campaigns. Sometimes the methods of protest and persuasion – now the common currency of every democratic society – will be all that is necessary or appropriate in such campaigns. But more severe pressure may be necessary and legitimate. Moreover, apparently reformist demands may have much more sweeping political implications, for instance entailing the resignation of a government pledged to resist them.

The goals may be more encompassing and even revolutionary from the start. They may be aimed at the overthrow of a particular government or *de facto* authority, or the demise of a whole political and social system. The goals of the non-violent insurrections in Eastern Europe in 1989 were revolutionary in the sense that they sought systemic political and social change. Sometimes, however, even there, the initial demands were related to civil rights, or the protection of the environment, and escalated into a full-scale confrontation with the regime. It is a characteristic of regimes which outlaw any open expression of dissent that they rapidly lose their authority if they are successfully defied even over an issue that does not in itself directly challenge their right to govern.

The methods of civil resistance may be employed in confrontations between different interest groups within society. Many of the characteristic weapons of civil resistance, such as strikes and boycotts, were forged in the labour movement in the struggles with employers in the nineteenth century, or in struggles between landlord and tenant. Such disputes between different groups or sections of society may draw in the state authorities on one side and develop into full-scale political and social confrontations. The British General Strike of 1926 is an example of this.

This study focuses on civil resistance in specifically political contexts, and, within that, pays particular attention to confrontations aimed at ending dictatorial, arbitrary or foreign-imposed rule. The reason for this is firstly that cases in which the resistance

11

confronts the full force of state power demonstrate most effectively its potential and limitations; and, secondly, that the problem of providing effective remedies against the extreme abuse of state power is a central political issue of our times. In a later chapter we will also be considering the notion of 'defence by civil resistance' or 'civilian defence' (also called variously 'civilian-based defence', 'social defence', 'popular non-violent defence') in which a state or society would prepare systematically for civil resistance as a substitute, in part or in whole, for military defence.

The actors, then, in the kind of civil resistance mainly considered here are the government – or some other official authority – on the one side, and a movement or organisation of civil society on the other. It can also, however, involve the contention of rival claimants to state power, for instance where an existing legally appointed government coordinates resistance to an attempted coup or foreign occupation. Thus Yeltsin and the Russian Parliament acted as a centre for resistance against the anti-Gorbachev coup in the Soviet Union in August 1991. An even clearer case was the resistance to the attempted Kapp putsch against the Weimar Republic in Berlin in 1920, where the legitimate Ebert government withdrew first to Dresden, then to Stuttgart, and directed a successful campaign of total non-cooperation against the putsch.

In a confrontation between state authorities and a civilian-based movement, each side will seek to undermine the power base of the other. For, as noted earlier, power structures are not unique to governments and state institutions; they permeate every institution of civil society – the family, the trade union, peace, civil rights or environmental movements. The elements of such power within the institutions of civil society are not different in kind from those analysed earlier except that the sanction of violence may be absent altogether or mediated through the courts. Thus within, say, a civil rights campaign, the cohesion and commitment at the base is the original, the defining source of power. The power and authority of its leadership – whether formal or informal – will depend on the degree to which it is regarded as legitimate and/or effective. Its leverage may also be enhanced by the support of third parties. Indeed, in a confrontation with the state, success or failure may hinge on winning over initially neutral or uninvolved parties – political groups, Churches, sections of the media, and perhaps international bodies and foreign governments.

The organisational structure of civilian organisations may, of course, be kept deliberately informal and as non-hierarchical as possible to ensure that all important decisions are made by the membership as a whole rather than a leadership élite or the bureaucracy. Yet some delegation of decision-making is probably inevitable once the group gets beyond a certain size, and this may be particularly important in a situation of conflict where quick decisions have often to be made. Moreover, an *informal* leadership tends to emerge in every organisation, comprising people with greater experience, knowledge or commitment than the majority of members.

As the earlier discussion indicated, psychological and moral factors are crucial elements in the kind of political warfare which civil resistance represents. 'Moral factors' here have the double sense of factors affecting morale, and factors having to do with moral and ethical issues. An important part of the explanation for the dramatic collapse of communist power in Eastern Europe is that communist parties and governments lost their morale and self-confidence. But this in turn was due in large measure to the dissipation of that sense of having an historic mission which fired the leaders of the October Revolution in Russia, and some at least of the communist leaders and governments in Eastern Europe after World War II. Similarly, the European colonial powers in the inter-war and postwar years lost faith in their 'civilising mission' -- instructed largely, it must be added, by the civil or armed resistance of their imperial subjects.

This is not to suggest that the protagonists with justice on their side necessarily carry the day. Nevertheless, in the political and ideological battle aimed at winning support from third parties, and strengthening and extending one's own power base, the central argument is almost inevitably cast in moral terms. The side that wins that argument stands greatly to strengthen its hand.

The moral question also permeates the debate over means. For those engaging in civil resistance, as much as for the government side, the question of means is a crucial moral-cum-strategic issue. It relates not only to the question of whether or not to use violence against persons or property, but to the issue of which non-violent sanctions it would be legitimate and politic to employ in any given situation. Thus, in a parliamentary democracy, while non-violent obstruction and civil disobedience may sometimes be justified, these are not methods to be embarked upon lightly. If they are used in circumstances where they cannot be justified, and especially where they are widely regarded within the society as unacceptable, they are unlikely to be effective. Moreover, the disapproval of the public will strengthen the government's hand in using force to repress its opponents.

The dynamic inter-relationship between power, coercion and authority is demonstrated by events in Thailand in the spring of 1992, events which also provide an interesting example of civil resistance in action. A summary of what occurred may help to clarify some of the rather abstract distinctions set forth in this chapter.

During April and May of 1992 a pro-democracy movement gained strength in Thailand. This followed a coup d'état in February of the previous year by an army general, Suchinda Kraprayoon, who declared himself Prime Minister. A coalition government formed after elections in March 1992 continued to accept his premiership. The larger background to the movement was decades of domination of political life in Thailand by the military, which continued even during the period of civilian rule that preceded the coup. The protesters demanded not only the resignation of Suchinda, but also changes in the constitution to ensure that future prime ministers could only be chosen from among elected MPs, and to curtail the powers of the military-dominated Senate.

The demonstrations were met with repression and massacre. On two successive nights, Monday, 18 May and Tuesday, 19 May, as some of the protesters began looting and rioting, the army opened fire indiscriminately. At least one hundred people were killed (some reports suggest a much higher figure) and several hundred injured. Over 3000 were arrested. The massacres and the brutal handling by the army of those arrested were shown on Thai television, but far from cowing the population this appeared to strengthen the determination to see Suchinda removed.

After two nights of massacre and mass arrests, the declaration of a state of emergency, the imposition of a dusk-to-dawn curfew, and the banning of gatherings of more than ten people, it seemed reasonable to assume that the demonstrations would come to an end, at least for the time being. Instead the protesters once again took to the streets in their tens of thousands on the Wednesday evening, barricading themselves into the university area.

At this point Thailand's king, Bhumibol Adulyadej, intervened. Calling for national reconciliation, he prevailed upon Suchinda to release the opposition leader, Chamlong Srimuang, from prison, and summoned both men to his presence. Thai television showed them shuffling on their knees before the king, and that evening Suchinda ordered the release of more than 3000 people arrested during the demonstrations and agreed to support the changes in the constitution demanded by the protesters. Chamlong for his part appealed to demonstrators to call off their protests. These, however, continued, and on Sunday, 24 May, Suchinda resigned. Next day the Thai Parliament agreed to amend the constitution to restrict eligibility to the premiership to elected MPs, and to curtail the Senate's powers. Subsequently a civilian prime minister, Anand Panyarachun, was appointed by Parliament pending a general election.[6] The election duly took place on 13 September.

The *power* of the opposition was demonstrated by its ability to bring tens of thousands of people onto the streets, including many in Thailand's rising middle class. It was met with the naked *violence* of the military-dominated government which might well have destroyed it, at least in the short term. But two days of massacres, beatings and mass arrests failed to deter the opposition. The brutality of the repression, and the courage and persistence of the demonstrators, began to undermine the

15

authority of the military-backed government. Some cabinet ministers made statements distancing themselves from the repression, and there were rumours too of troops stationed in other parts of the country starting to move towards the capital to back the demonstrators' demands. Finally the king exerted his own extraordinary authority in the context of Thai society to bring the immediate crisis to a halt.

The popular power which ended, temporarily at least, the military-dominated rule did not arise purely spontaneously. It was preceded, as one leading opposition activist and theoretician, Sulak Sivaraska, has recalled, by years of organisation and the study of methods of non-violent action.

> We cooperated with other Buddhists, with Christians, with Muslims, internationally, to learn how to resist non-violently. I joined non-violence trainings in Mexico and Philadelphia, and other trainers came to Thailand. This sort of thing was going on for 15 years. So when the demonstrations came this time, it was this hard core that has been trained for so long that took charge, very modestly, behind the scenes, and used fasting, prayer and so on. That's why it was very, very effective; for so long they held the people to peaceful behaviour. That's why the government and the military became very upset, they wanted to break it and they didn't know how to break it. They used their own gangsters disguised as demonstrators, throwing bricks, throwing bottles, and that's how the violence started.[7]

Whether or not the looting and rioting that accompanied the demonstrators was the work of government *agents provocateurs*, as Sulak contends, it was marginal to the political outcome – though of course it did provide the pretext for the massacres and mass arrests. What counted politically was that upward of 100,000 people took to the streets, brought the capital and other major cities to a standstill, and refused to be cowed or intimidated until they had won their immediate demands.

Of course, things might easily have turned out differently, and for a time it seemed almost inevitable that they would. The parallels with Tiananmen Square almost four years earlier are obvious. Nor should the grim lessons of previous struggles to establish a stable democracy in Thailand be overlooked. In 1973 a student-led revolt brought down the two-man military rule which had been in power for ten years. Three years later, however, amid further student demonstrations, one of the deposed leaders was brought back and a terrible revenge wrought on the protesters. Whether or not something similar happens again will depend in part on how far the opposition in Thailand retains its capacity to mobilise mass opposition, and in part on the evident determination of the international community to apply severe sanctions in the event of another attempted military takeover.[8]

Hannah Arendt predicted that in a head-on clash between violence and power, the outcome would hardly be in doubt. 'If Gandhi's enormously powerful and successful strategy of non-violent resistance had met with a different enemy – Stalin's Russia, Hitler's Germany, even pre-war Japan, instead of England – the outcome would not have been decolonisation, but massacre and submission.' But she goes on to add, perceptively: 'To substitute violence for power can bring victory, but the price is very high; for it is not only paid by the vanquished, it is also paid by the victor in terms of his own power.'[9]

What the Thai example shows, as did the overthrow of the Shah of Iran in 1979, is that in favourable circumstances the authority of a government which resorts to naked violence may be eroded so rapidly that it loses the ability to command the instruments of state violence. When that occurs, people power can prevail over state violence, even in the short term. Under still more favourable circumstances, the army and police may refuse from the start to carry out orders to massacre civilians, as happened in the victory of people power in the Philippines in 1986. In the former German Democratic Republic, too, there is clear evidence that Erich Honecker wished to suppress the mounting demonstrations in November 1989 by military force but simply lacked the authority to carry out this policy.

But victory in a campaign of civil resistance is no more assured

than in a military one. As in any war, the overall balance of
forces will affect the outcome. So too will the understanding,
organisation and strategy of those engaged in civil resistance.
These are among the issues we consider in greater detail in the
chapters that follow.

Chapter 2

The Evolution of Passive Resistance

There is nothing new under the sun. In 494 BC the Roman plebeians, aggrieved at their status and condition of life, withdrew to a hill above the city and refused to play their part in civic affairs until their grievances were met.[1] Centuries later, around the year AD 1600, women of the Iroquois Indian nation refused to have intercourse with their warrior husbands, and thus to bear them warrior sons, until they obtained the right to decide on whether or not the nation should go to war.[2] This echoed, albeit unconsciously, an idea put forward by the classical Greek dramatist Aristophanes in his play *Lysistrata*.

Numerous other examples can be cited to show that the use of non-cooperation as a means of applying pressure against individuals and groups is not peculiar to any period or civilisation. This is hardly surprising. Most of the tasks essential to keeping a society functioning require cooperation. In egalitarian tribal societies without a central system of authority, the withdrawal of that cooperation is one of the most drastic sanctions used to deter or punish offenders, and maintain social cohesion.[3] In post-tribal societies, with divergent socio-political and interest groups, non-cooperation becomes an effective means of promoting the claims of one group against another or against central authority. Finally, once societies or states have developed a marked degree of interdependence, non-cooperation in the shape of trade embargoes and the like become an obvious means of applying pressure short of war, or as a prelude or accompaniment to it.

It scarcely needs saying, however, that human beings have emotional and psychological needs as well as purely physical

19

ones. Love and social approval are essential to meeting these needs. The withdrawal of approval, particularly on the part of those we love or respect, constitutes a pressure that can be as strong or even stronger than physical deprivation. In stateless tribal societies, public censure, gossip, social ostracism rank alongside the withdrawal of physical cooperation as prime sanctions against individuals who contravene the social mores.[4] We can, indeed, view such sanctions as a species of non-cooperation at the emotional and psychological level. They clearly retain a considerable force even in more atomised modern society, exercising a pressure for group conformity which is far from being necessarily desirable. Some of the advocates of passive resistance in the nineteenth century saw themselves as the champions of 'moral force' as opposed to 'physical force'. In fact, as we shall see, both moral and physical pressure are normally brought into play in campaigns of civil resistance.

However, history does not quite repeat itself. Changed circumstances transform the manner in which people act together and the possibilities for them to do so effectively. In that sense, some social phenomena are new, even if prefigured at an earlier point in history. In tracing the evolution of an idea or movement, it is important to identify such moments of transformation.

The most direct antecedent of twentieth-century civil resistance is the collective organisation and action which emerged in Europe and North America from the late eighteenth century onwards – and also to some extent in countries whose economies and social structures were drastically altered by the impact of colonial and imperial expansion. Sometime in the early nineteenth century – or possibly as far back as the American colonists' agitation prior to the outbreak of the War of Independence – the term 'passive resistance' was coined to denote this innovative form of struggle.[5] A second antecedent, reaching much further back into history, and contributing indeed to the eighteenth- and nineteenth-century phenomenon of collective non-cooperation, is the tradition of individual dissent and disobedience.

*   *   *

The Evolution of Passive Resistance

The flourishing of collective political action in general in Europe in the nineteenth century, and of forms of passive resistance in particular, was due largely to the spread of industrial capitalism and to various social and political developments attendant upon it. Urbanisation and the rise of the factory system enhanced the possibilities of people acting in concert for the achievement of social and political goals. So too did increasing literacy, though this was still at a very low level throughout most of Europe until late in the century. At the same time, dislocation, impoverishment and exploitation made concerted action more necessary as far as the artisan and labouring classes were concerned. In Britain, which led the industrial revolution, self-organisation among these classes had by the late eighteenth century produced embryo political movements (for instance in the shape of the Corresponding Societies) and embryo trade unions (often disguised as Benefit Clubs and Friendly Societies to evade repressive laws). In Europe as a whole, it had produced by the mid to late nineteenth century powerful trade unions, and socialist, Marxist, anarchist and other radical movements and parties.

Industrial capitalism had also produced a new articulate manufacturing and professional class who demanded a say in the running of government. This emerging 'middle class', often in alliance with a more numerous artisan and working class or peasantry, championed the demand for liberal constitutional reform and the broadening of the electorate. Sometimes the result was violent revolution, notably in much of Europe in the period between the French Revolution of 1789 and the wave of revolutions that swept across the continent in 1848. But improved methods of organisation and mobilisation also opened up possibilities for mass non-cooperation and civil disobedience. Thus, in Britain, agitation under mainly middle-class leadership pressurised the government into passing the Reform Act of 1832. Although the Act excluded the working class from the electorate, it both provoked, and helped lay the groundwork for, an upsurge of working-class radicalism in the shape of the Chartist movement with its demands for universal suffrage, its mass demonstrations, and its threat of a general strike to enforce its demands. In other

European countries, too, even a limited extension of electoral politics served to establish the demonstration, the petition, the public gathering as accepted features of the political culture, and facilitated more radical forms of mass action for social and political goals.[6]

The eighteenth and nineteenth centuries also saw both the consolidation of the modern bureaucratic state and the rise of nationalist struggles. Nationalism was sometimes stimulated when the middle class found its political aspirations thwarted by existing dynastic or imperial arrangements. Thus nationalist struggles tended to overlap with liberal constitutionalist struggles aimed at broadening the franchise and ending absolutist forms of government. Both were spearheaded by the middle class, though with the support of other classes with different priorities and a more radical agenda.

Civil resistance, then, in the sense of organised *collective* non-cooperation, evolved from the late eighteenth century onwards in the course of various emancipatory struggles: for workers' rights; for national liberation; for liberal constitutionalism; or for revolutionary social and political goals. It was nourished by an older tradition of conscientious dissent and disobedience which has continued to maintain a life of its own down to the present time. I include in the latter the tradition of pacifism which expressed itself chiefly in the refusal to bear arms or to pay taxes for military purposes. Gandhian non-violence in the present century can be seen as an attempted fusion of these strands in European resistance culture coupled with traditions of non-violence and cultural and social resistance in India and elsewhere. The focus in this book on the European and North American antecedents of civil resistance prior to the present century stems in part from my belief that these were of seminal importance, in part from my own limited knowledge of other traditions.

It is necessary to sound a caveat here concerning the moral and political thrust of passive/civil resistance. It has been crucial certainly to many emancipatory struggles, but on occasions it simultaneously helped to establish or consolidate the domination of a particular class or linguistic group. Thus there were often chauvinistic and even racialist overtones in much nineteenth-century linguistic nationalism. Moreover, the assertion of the political aspirations of one group within a particular territory might be at the expense of another at a time when national boundaries in Europe were still in the process of being defined. For example, the Hungarian passive resistance against Austria in the mid-nineteenth century, while clearly an emancipatory struggle in so far as it was directed against Austrian absolutism, also consolidated Magyar domination over the Slav and Romanian population who predominated in part of the territory.[7] Struggles for liberal reforms, too, helped to establish and consolidate middle-class hegemony, though, as noted above, they also facilitated organisation and agitation for radical change.

It is important to make this observation to avoid the pitfall of assuming that a struggle conducted without violence must necessarily be for a just cause, or that, even when it is, there will be no moral ambiguities about any ensuing victory. Collective struggle without violence can produce domination as well as liberation. It may be a useful and necessary exercise to evaluate civil resistance purely as a technique of struggle. But when it comes to applying it, the moral and political goals and likely consequences must be the prime consideration in the debate if one is to minimise the risk of multiplying injustice rather than reducing it.

Before considering passive resistance as it emerged in the late eighteenth and early nineteenth centuries, it will be useful to outline briefly the heritage of dissent and resistance which nurtured it.

Disobedience and rebellion: the European heritage

The right, the duty even, to break the law in obedience to conscience is a recurrent theme in the Graeco-Roman and Judeo-Christian traditions. In the *Antigone* of Sophocles, the heroine defies what she sees as an outrageous and immoral order by King Creon that her brother Polynices' body should remain unburied because he had led a foreign army against his own city-state of

Thebes. The drama, in a sense, was played out for real in Roman persecutions of the early Christians who refused to worship the emperor or to serve in the army.

Christians were not the only people to find the commandment to worship the Roman emperor-gods unacceptable. The Jewish historian Flavius Josephus (AD 37–95?) records an occasion during the reign of the emperor Caligula (AD 37–41) in which the Jewish community successfully resisted the Emperor's order that his statue should be erected in the Temple at Jerusalem. 'Many ten thousands of Jews', the historian records, petitioned the Roman governor in Syria charged with enforcing the Emperor's command, and stated their resolve to die rather than to 'permit such things as are forbidden us to be done by the authority of our legislator, and by our forefathers' determination that such prohibitions are instances of virtue.'[8]

Within the Christian tradition, the obligation laid upon the individual to disobey laws or commands regarded as sinful was bound up with another which softened its provocative edge – the obligation of obedience to civil authority, enunciated by St Paul in the New Testament. The effect of this double principle was to forbid rebellion even against an unjust state, but to enjoin disobedience at the point at which the state made demands on the individual which conflicted with Christian morality. The distinction was doubtless lost, however, on a Roman governor faced with a whole Christian community refusing to bear arms. Individual acts of disobedience taken by a sufficient number of people united in a common belief have the force of collective action.

In Christian medieval Europe, the Pauline doctrine of civil obedience conflicted with the Germanic feudal tradition which gave barons the right forcibly to remove a king who ruled unjustly. Moreover, insurrection and revolution were commonplace in the Italian city states, and the papacy itself, now as much a temporal as a spiritual authority, often encouraged rebellion.

St Thomas Aquinas in the thirteenth century laid the groundwork for a shift away from the Pauline doctrine. Influenced by Aristotle and other classical philosophers whose writings had reached Europe via Moslem Spain, he propounded a theory of natural law, based on rationality and the common good, against which all man-made laws were to be measured. Unjust laws, Aquinas argued, were, strictly speaking, not laws at all, but acts of violence. If rulers acquired power by violence or corruption, then – unless subsequently legitimised by public consent or superior authority – it was permissible to overthrow them. This was a theory which lent itself to civil disobedience, even to violent rebellion. Later, however, Aquinas backed away from it, fearing no doubt the social consequences of a private right to depose or kill tyrants. While individual disobedience continued to be a Christian duty in circumstances where obedience would mean acting immorally, rebellion aimed at overthrowing an unjust ruler could only be legitimately undertaken, Aquinas argued, by properly constituted authority.[9]

The fourteenth-century English religious reformer and biblical scholar, John Wyclif, went further. 'There is no unconditional and eternal heritage of secular dominion, no human title to possession can secure such; only he who stands in grace is the true lord,' he declared; 'mortal sin disqualifies the sinner from administering God's fief.'[10] In other words the ruler who falls from grace forfeits his claim to authority. John Huss (1373–1415), the Bohemian religious reformer, adopted Wyclif's 'doctrine of lordship', arguing nonetheless that it did not justify violent rebellion. His death at the stake in 1415 triggered the fifteen-year-long Hussite insurrection, though his ideas and teachings were more accurately reflected in the practice of the pacifist Bohemian Brethren.

The Protestant Reformation of the sixteenth century broadened the potential for dissent. Not that this was the intention of its most representative figure, Martin Luther, who vehemently upheld the duty of passive obedience to authority, 'whether it act justly or unjustly'. Disobedience, he stated, was 'a greater sin than murder, unchastity, theft and dishonesty'.[11] Moreover, the initial impact of the establishment of nationally based Churches was to strengthen the hand of those monarchs who claimed to exercise both spiritual and temporal authority free from papal interference. But as religious dissent proliferated, and dissenters challenged the absolutist claims of national monarchies – as Luther had earlier challenged papal claims – it eventually became apparent that a degree of religious toleration was the alternative to national disunity and perhaps civil war. Toleration came slowly and unevenly, but where it did, it opened up space for dissenters to organise and to propagate their ideas.

John Calvin (1509–64), in Geneva, also insisted on the duty to obey the civil authority, though he conceded the possibility of legitimate resistance by 'lesser magistrates' (authorities) to impious government. His co-religionists in Scotland and France, faced with a totally different political situation, took up this sub-theme in Calvin's teaching and placed it in the centre of their own. Knox, in exile and under sentence of death in his own country, boldly asserted that where rulers failed in their duty to uphold morality and true religion the people had not only a right but a duty to resist. The doctrine that men owed a duty of obedience to a king who disobeyed God's laws was blasphemy. 'For it is no less blasphemy to say that God hath commanded kings to be obeyed when they command impiety, than to say that God by his precept is author and maintainer of all iniquity.'[12]

The French Huguenots also faced a strong Catholic monarchy determined to crush them, and it was one of their number, Mornay, who wrote a powerful and influential tract in support of the right to resist – the *Vindiciae contra Tyrannos* (1579).[13] It was republished many times in England and elsewhere whenever there was a crisis in the relationship between the Crown and the people.[14] Nevertheless, its spirit was not democratic but aristocratic; as in Aquinas, the right to resist resided not in the private individual but in duly constituted authority. It asserted the rights of towns, provinces, classes against the claims of absolutist royal power. The same position was taken by the spiritual leader of the French Huguenots, Beza, who succeeded Calvin in Geneva.

In addition to these two main branches of Protestantism, other sixteenth-century religious-cum-political movements, such as those of the Anabaptists and Mennonites, went much further in defying the established temporal and spiritual authorities.

These two particular movements also advocated a return to the communist and pacifist principles of the early Christians. The seventeenth century saw a proliferation of such radical sects and movements, particularly during the period of the English Civil War which produced the Levellers, Diggers, Quakers, Ranters and others. The Levellers demanded universal suffrage and equality before the law. The Diggers, or True Levellers, sought to establish a commonwealth in which there would be complete equality and all property would be held in common. Their resistance often took the form of what, in today's parlance, would be termed non-violent direct action. Thus the Diggers squatted on common land at Weybridge in Surrey and on various other sites in the country which they proceeded to dig up and cultivate (hence their name). Christopher Hill has shown that they represented only the tip of an iceberg of radical dissent, and that True Levellers were felt to be a particularly dangerous threat because of the number of their supporters and sympathisers within the army ranks.[15]

The seventeenth-century philosopher whose writings in defence of the English Revolution became a cornerstone in liberal constitutionalist thought was John Locke. He was one of several political thinkers to advance the notion of a 'social contract' between rulers and ruled. Government was essential to provide certain vital benefits for society, such as the impartial judgement of disputes, the power to enforce decisions, and the ability to defend society against outside threats. The king who failed to live up to his responsibilities was in effect reneging on the contract with society and thereby forfeited his legitimacy. In the extreme case he could be resisted and overthrown.

> The end of government is the good of mankind; and which is best for mankind, that the people should be always exposed to the boundless will of tyranny, or that the rulers should be sometimes liable to be opposed when they grow exorbitant in the use of their power, and employ it for the destruction, and not the preservation, of the properties of their people?[16]

Moreover, for Locke, as much as for Knox or Mornay in the previous century, the right to resist implied the right when necessary to use violence. Locke sarcastically dismisses the notion that force by an opponent could be resisted in any other way, and concludes: 'he therefore that may resist must be allowed to strike'.[17] This did not mean, however, that either Locke, or those in the Whig/constitutionalist tradition following him, were unaware of other ways of applying pressure to achieve political change. On the contrary, recourse to military force was seen as the ultimate sanction to be applied only when other means were unavailing or clearly inappropriate. Steven Huxley has argued that this is why, in the constitutionalist tradition, no sharp conceptual distinction was drawn between violent and non-violent types of resistance.[18]

However, a tradition of vigorous resistance which nevertheless excluded a resort to violence on moral and religious grounds flourished during the seventeenth century amongst the Quakers and other radical sects. The Quakers denounced the abuses of their day in the most forthright terms, combining this with a blunt refusal to comply with laws they regarded as immoral. This posed a direct challenge to authorities, and resulted in hundreds of Quakers and members of other puritan sects being imprisoned. If the Quakers at that time formulated no theory of collective civil disobedience as a means of coercing the authorities, seeing their disobedience, as the early Christians had done, as a matter of individual conscience, they nevertheless evolved through practice an extremely powerful campaigning technique which was responsible for important reforms.

In North America in the seventeenth century, Quaker defiance of an edict by the colonial government prohibiting public assembly faced the authorities with a choice of making mass arrests or backing down. They chose the latter course. The Quakers waged a similar successful campaign in America against the payment of tithes to the Established Church.[19] In England, in 1670, William Penn and William Mead put up a spirited defence at the Old Bailey against a charge of causing a riotous assembly for preaching on Sunday in the city of London. They were acquitted by a jury who made legal history by defying the Recorder's direction to find the two men guilty and resisting his efforts to browbeat them by having them 'locked all night without meat, drink, fire or other accommodation ... [or] so much as a chamber pot, though desired'.[20] A plaque commemorating the courage of the twelve members of the jury is now displayed in the main lobby of the Old Bailey.

The point to stress here is that this Quaker tradition of public action and campaigning, which has continued down to the present time by them and other groups, was genuine *resistance*. It was different in kind from the non-resistance of the pre-Protestant era and of some of the more quietist sects, such as the Mennonites, whose impulse was to retire altogether from public life. A tradition of conscientious dissent and disobedience, sometimes combined with absolute pacifist principles, continued into the nineteenth and twentieth centuries, inspiring the work of reformers like the anti-slave campaigner, William Lloyd Garrison, and some of the influential advocates of passive resistance, most notably Thoreau and Tolstoy.

Collective non-cooperation – the birth of passive resistance

With non-cooperation, theory largely followed practice. Its potential was discovered as it were piecemeal by trial and error. There was little systematic discussion of it prior to the late eighteenth century with the publication of William Godwin's *Enquiry Concerning Political Justice*. As noted above, in the nineteenth century, demonstrations, marches, strikes, sometimes civil disobedience, and other forms of collective action were developed both by radical reform movements and the growing proletariat created by industrial capitalism. Movements for national autonomy or total independence also frequently found that the most effective method of struggle open to them was passive resistance. Finally, from around the mid-century onwards, socialist, anarchist and syndicalist movements frequently placed the general strike at the heart of their strategy to overthrow the capitalist system. It will be convenient, therefore, to review in tandem the development of the theory and practice of collective non-cooperation down to the turn of the present century.

Pre-eighteenth-century contributions

There are relevant insights into the power of collective non-cooperation prior to Godwin. Niccolò Machiavelli (1469–1527) noted the vulnerability of rulers in the face of defiance by their agents and the general population during a period of transition from a 'civil principality' to absolute rule:

> Principalities usually come to grief when the transition is being made from limited power to absolutism. Princes taking this step rule either directly or through magistrates. In the latter case their position is weaker and more dangerous, because they rely entirely on the will of those citizens who have been put in office. And these, especially in times of adversity, can very easily depose them either by positive action against them or by not obeying them.[21]

Elsewhere Machiavelli warns that the ruler 'who has the public as a whole for his enemy can never make himself secure; and the greater his cruelty, the weaker does his regime become'.[22] Nevertheless, it seems that Machiavelli expected that the refusal of agents and people to obey orders would be the prelude to conspiracy or violent insurrection rather than that non-cooperation would of itself bring about a tyrant's downfall. His work is mainly directed to advising princes on statecraft, including the judicious use of deceit, repression and military force to retain power. However, another sixteenth-century writer/statesman, Etienne de la Boëtie (1530–63), does give more serious consideration to non-cooperation as a mode of coercive political action. The theme of his *Discours de la Servitude Volontaire* (literally 'Discourse on Voluntary Servitude') is that the power of tyrants comes from the voluntary cooperation and 'servitude' of the people; if that is withdrawn, the tyrant will be powerless:

Resolve not to obey, and you are free. I do not advise you to shake or overturn him [the tyrant] – forbear only to support him, and you will see him, like a great colossus from which the base is taken away, fall with his own weight and be broken in pieces.[23]

But La Boëtie makes the mass withdrawal of cooperation sound rather too simple; after all, servitude under tyranny was no more 'voluntary' in Renaissance Italy than it is today. In fact, in an earlier passage in the essay, La Boëtie acknowledges: 'It often happens we are obliged to obey by force.' In that case, he says, we ought to 'bear the evil patiently, and reserve ourselves for a future and a better fortune'.[24] There is little prospect held out here that non-cooperation could be sustained and brought to a successful conclusion in the face of violent repression.

A more important point is that La Boëtie's essay was not part of, and did not give rise to, a debate at the time about the possibilities of non-cooperation.[25] It was valued as an indictment of tyranny rather than a novel prescription for overturning it. It was not published until 1574, after La Boëtie's death, and then in plagiarised and incomplete form without acknowledgement of its authorship, and used by French Huguenots, Scottish Calvinists and Dutch Protestants as a propaganda tract against Catholic absolutism. Not until 1727 was it published under La Boëtie's own name and included in a collection of the works of his friend and contemporary, Montaigne. It was first published in English in 1735.[26] However, as we shall see, its importance lies not in the influence it had in its own time, but on writers and theorists in the nineteenth and twentieth centuries who rediscovered the work.

Radical and early working-class movements

Godwin's treatment of non-cooperation is altogether more substantial and of its time. The *Enquiry Concerning Political Justice* was published in 1793 during the period of heated debate in England on the French Revolution. It may well have been intended, like

Paine's more famous essay, as a riposte to Burke's *Reflections on the French Revolution*, and has become a classic of libertarian/anarchist literature. If obedience is withdrawn, Godwin argues, the fabric upon which unjust government, encroachment on freedom and subjection are built falls to the ground.[27] He does not altogether rule out recourse to violent resistance, but sees this as a very last resort, not to be embarked upon without the prospect of success and even then only 'where time can by no means be gained, and the consequences instantly to ensue are unquestionably fatal'.[28] A revolution without violence, he maintains, would lead to the 'euthanasia of pernicious government'.[29]

Godwin's book enjoyed immense popularity in the years immediately following its publication, particularly in élite literary circles, but also among the groups of artisans and workers who clubbed together to buy it.[30] But by the closing years of the century, things had changed dramatically. Many of the poets and literary figures – Southey, Coleridge, Wordsworth – recanted their earlier radicalism, while repressive legislation, such as the Two Acts of 1795–6 and the Seditious Societies Act of 1799, was used to suppress the Corresponding Societies and other radical and reformist groups.

In the post-Napoleonic War period there was a renewed interest in his ideas, thanks largely to the work of the poet Shelley – and to the notes by the radical journalist/publisher Richard Carlile in his pirated edition of Shelley's *Queen Mab*.[31] Godwin's ideas continued to influence the socialist and labour movement through such nineteenth-century reformers as Robert Owen, the utopian socialist, Francis Place, a founder-member of the London Correspondence Society in 1792, and William Thompson, the early socialist economist. Godwin's wife, Mary Wollstonecraft, was also an important figure in her own right. Her book *A Vindication of the Rights of Women*, published in 1792, applied Enlightenment ideas to the position of women in society and marked a crucial moment in the long and continuing struggle for women's rights. Her demand for women's suffrage was taken up by the Chartists in the 1830s, but was not fully realised until 1928 after many years of agitation and the major civil resistance and civil disobedience campaigns of the suffragettes in the early years of this century.

Shelley – who eloped with and eventually married Godwin's daughter by Mary Wollstonecraft – adopted Godwin's ideas with enthusiasm, and gave them poetic expression in such works as *Queen Mab*, *The Revolt of Islam* and *Prometheus Unbound*. One poem is particularly interesting in the context of the present discussion. *The Mask of Anarchy* was written in response to the Peterloo Massacre of 1819. This occurred when a large, orderly crowd, including many women and children, who had gathered in St Peter's Field, Manchester to hear the radical orator Henry Hunt, was attacked by yeoman cavalry and hussars. Eleven people were killed and hundreds injured in what became known as the 'Battle of Peterloo' – an ironic reference to Waterloo. The poem combines a scathing polemic against the postwar reaction and tyranny in Britain with an explicit advocacy of non-violent resistance to overcome it. The polemic is well exemplified in the early stanzas:

> I met Murder on the way –
> He had a mask like Castlereagh[32] –
> Very smooth he looked, yet grim;
> Seven blood-hounds followed him:
>
> All were fat; and well they might
> Be in admirable plight,
> For one by one, and two by two
> He tossed them human hearts to chew
> Which from his wide cloak he drew.

Later Shelley presents his vision of peaceful resistance which would defeat tyranny:

> Let a vast assembly be,
> And with great solemnity
> Declare with measured words that ye
> Are, as God has made ye, free – ...
>
> And if then the tyrants dare
> Let them ride among you there,

Slash, and stab, and maim, and hew, –
What they like, that let them do.

With folded arms and steady eyes,
And little fear, and less surprise,
Look upon them as they slay
Till their rage has died away.

Then they will return with shame
To the place from which they came,
And the blood thus shed will speak
In hot blushes on their cheek.

Every woman in the land
Will point at them as they stand –
They will hardly dare to greet
Their acquaintance in the street.

And the bold, true warriors
Who have hugged Danger in wars
Will turn to those who would be free
Ashamed of such base company . . .

Rise like Lions after slumber
In unvanquishable number –
Shake your chains to earth like dew
Which in sleep had fallen on you –
Ye are many – they are few.

Taken literally, Shelley's vision may seem removed from reality.
As a metaphor for the public revulsion to the Peterloo Massacre
and its political consequences, it was extraordinarily accurate.
For Peterloo, more than any other single event, established the
right to public demonstration in nineteenth-century England.[33]
Clearly there was by this time a deepening understanding of the
possibility of non-cooperation and civil disobedience as a method
of resistance and contention. In Britain, for instance, after
Peterloo, attempts by the government to gag the press by the
infamous 'Six Acts' were countered – with eventual success – by
a veritable campaign of defiance in which hundreds of radical
journalists, printers and distributors spent terms in prison.
Edward Thompson graphically describes the process:

There is perhaps no country in the world in which the contest for the rights of the press was so sharp, so emphatically victorious, and so peculiarly identified with the cause of the artisans and labourers. If Peterloo established (by a paradox of feeling) the right of public demonstration, the rights of a 'free press' were won in a campaign extending over fifteen or more years which has no comparison for its pigheaded, bloody-minded, and indomitable audacity. Carlile (a tinsmith who had nevertheless received a year or two of grammar school education at Ashburton in Devon) rightly saw that the repression of 1819 made the rights of the press the fulcrum of the Radical movement. But, unlike Cobbett and Wooler, who modified their tone to meet the Six Acts in the hope of living to fight another day (and who lost circulation accordingly), Carlile hoisted the black ensign of unqualified defiance and, like a pirate cock-boat, sailed straight into the middle of the combined fleets of the State and Church. As, in the aftermath of Peterloo, he came up for trial (for publishing the Works of Paine), the entire Radical press saluted his courage, but gave him up for lost. When he finally emerged after years of imprisonment, the combined fleets were scattered beyond the horizon in disarray. He had exhausted the ammunition of the Government, and turned its *ex officio* informations and special juries into laughing-stocks. He had plainly sunk the private prosecuting societies, the Constitutional Association (or 'Bridge-Street Gang') and the Vice Society, which were supported by the patronage and the subscriptions of the nobility, bishops and Wilberforce.

Carlile did not, of course, achieve this triumph on his own. The first round of the battle was fought in 1817, when there were twenty-six prosecutions for seditious and blasphemous libel and sixteen *ex officio* informations filed by the law officers of the Crown. The laurels of victory, in that year, went to Wooler and Hone, and to the London juries which refused to convict.[34]

In the economic and social struggle, too, the strike more and more replaced machine-breaking, rick-burning and similar actions as the chief weapon of working-class protest and resistance. The timing of this shift in organisation and methods of action varied from one country to another, starting earlier in those countries such as Britain and France where capitalist industrialisation first took root. The significance of this shift is discussed in more detail later.

Nationalist and constitutionalist campaigns

Etymologists have traced the first written use of the term 'passive resistance', and its German equivalent, '*passiver Widerstand*', to 1819, the year in which Shelley wrote *The Mask of Anarchy*.[35] It was applied mainly to constitutionalist and nationalist struggles rather than to those of the working class, and it sometimes denoted peaceful pressure within the law rather than civil disobedience and mass non-cooperation. In 1848, the year of revolution in Europe and 'the birth of nations', the President of the Prussian National Assembly, Hans Victor von Unruh, called publicly for a campaign of passive resistance to oppose the dissolution of the Assembly by the Crown.[36]

At this period, passive resistance became the centre of heated political debate. Marx, in an article in *Neue Rheinische Zeitung* in December 1848, denounced it as a means used by the bourgeoisie against the revolution.[37] His disciple, Ferdinand Lassalle, in a speech in Dusseldorf in 1849, described the passive resistance of the National Assembly as a betrayal; passive resistance was a contradiction, resistance that was no resistance, a product of the bourgeoisie's recognition of the need for resistance coupled with its fear to act accordingly.[38] What Marx and Lassalle were attacking, however, was not mass non-cooperation by the population as a whole but the exercise of legal and parliamentary pressure on the authorities by a middle class whom they suspected of wanting to avoid unleashing all-out revolution. Marx waxed sarcastic too about the constitutional pedigree on which the Prussian National Assembly was basing its claims.

Closely related to constitutionalist struggles, and based on an appeal to the same fundamental principles, were nineteenth-century nationalist struggles. Without renouncing violence under all circumstances, the leaders of these struggles increasingly recognised the possibilities of passive resistance. The prototype here was the resistance in the late eighteenth century in Britain's American colonies in the decade that preceded the outbreak of hostilities in 1775.[39] The campaign began with the defiance of the Stamp Act in 1765 – an Act which imposed duties on a range of paper goods including legal documents and newsprint. Resistance took the form of petitions, tax refusal, the social boycott of stamp-tax agents, the publication of newspapers without payment of the duty, and the non-importation and non-consumption of British goods. Most of the agents resigned as a result of this pressure, and it was already a dead letter by the time of its repeal in March 1776.

The Townshend Acts of 1767, which imposed duties on a wide range of goods, met with similar resistance. The Acts were repealed in 1770, except for the tax on tea. The Tea Act of 1773, designed in part to secure the enforcement of the tax on tea while at the same time strengthening the commercial position of the East India Company, was countered with a campaign to get the tea agents to resign. It also provoked the famous Boston Tea Party in which merchants dumped a cargo of tea in Boston harbour in December 1773.

The British government responded by passing the Coercive Acts. These virtually closed down Boston harbour, granted exceptional powers to the governor of Massachusetts, and gave governors in all states the right to billet soldiers in certain circumstances in unused buildings. The Acts were aimed primarily at punishing the state of Massachusetts but – as Edmund Burke warned the colonists – they represented a threat to all the colonies. However, beginning in 1773 prior to the Boston Tea Party, the elected assemblies in the various colonies had begun establishing 'correspondence societies' to coordinate their response to British measures, and by the time the Coercive Acts were passed they were ready to mount a united resistance. The First Continental Congress, which took place in September 1774, brought together representatives of all the state assemblies and adopted a detailed programme of non-cooperation known as the Continental Association. In addition to the economic measures, courts were closed, taxes refused, British governors openly defied and extra-legal Provincial Congresses convened to oversee the enforcement of the Association's measures. In April 1775 the first shots of the War of Independence were fired, but as John Adams – who succeeded George Washington as President – wrote in 1815:

> A history of military operations from April nineteenth, 1775 to the 3rd of September, 1783, is not a history of the American Revolution . . . The revolution was in the minds and hearts of the people, and in the union of the colonies; both of which were substantially effected before hostilities commenced.[40]

Nevertheless, the American War of Independence overshadowed the campaign of non-cooperation that had preceded it. Far more influential as a model of passive resistance for nationalist/constitutionalist goals was that conducted by Hungary against Austria from 1849 to 1867. Its aim was the restoration of the constitution which was suspended by Austria in 1848 and which had recognised Hungary's status as an autonomous kingdom within the Habsburg Empire. Led by a Hungarian landowner and politician, Franz Deák, the resistance took the form mainly of a boycott by Hungarian MPs of the Imperial Parliament in Vienna and non-cooperation by Hungarian county councils in carrying out Austrian policies. But it included also resistance at popular level, including tax refusal, a boycott of government employment and positions, social boycotts of Austrian troops and agents, and a range of symbolic actions, protests and demonstrations. In 1867, the campaign – in conjunction to be sure with other factors, including Austrian weakness after its defeat by the Prussians at the Battle of Sadowa in the previous year – resulted in a compromise agreement which met the essential Hungarian demands.[41]

The Hungarian campaign influenced all subsequent passive resistance campaigns in the nineteenth century for constitutionalist and nationalist goals, and indeed, by way of Gandhi, those in the present century. It was the prototype for the Finnish passive resistance to attempted Russification from 1899 to 1906. This resistance was ignited by a new Russian military law in 1899 increasing the length of military service, drafting Finns into Russian units or placing Russians in charge of Finnish ones. At the same time, the power of the Finnish Diet was reduced to that of a provincial assembly. The Finns refused to implement the law and there was widespread resistance to conscription. In 1903 the constitution was suspended, and in the following year the Russian governor Bobrikov was assassinated. There is evidence that the resistance had begun to lose momentum by this time, but it received unlooked-for assistance in the shape of the 1905 revolution in Russia, and the Empire-wide general strike. The embattled Tsar repealed the conscription law, and in 1906 the Finnish Diet was re-established on a more democratic basis.[42]

In Ireland, the Hungarian resistance caught the imagination of Arthur Griffith, a founder-member of, and key figure in, Sinn Fein (founded in 1905). In 1904, in a series of witty, polemical articles in the *United Irishman*, Griffith outlined the course of the Hungarian resistance and advocated a campaign along similar lines in Ireland. Irish parliamentarians, he argued, should boycott the British Parliament and demand the restoration of the constitutional position as of 1782 when Britain had conceded Irish parliamentary independence. The articles were published in a penny-pamphlet form later that year under the title *The Resurrection of Hungary: A Parallel for Ireland*.[43] As an historical account it has been severely criticised, one critic likening it to 'a fairy tale'.[44] In fact it was not so much a fairy tale, more a propaganda tract. As such it was immensely successful, enjoying a wide circulation and being republished in 1912 and again in 1918. (The 1918 edition included a reference to the Finnish resistance as providing another example of a successful campaign.) It was also translated into a number of Indian languages and widely distributed within India.[45] Gandhi cited the Hungarian campaign and recommended the Transvaal Indians in South Africa to pursue a similar course of action, relying almost certainly on Griffith's account.[46]

But Ireland had its own history of passive resistance, and some critics of Griffith's tract argue that he would have done better to have turned to that rather than trying to force parallels with a Central European country whose politics he only half understood. In the eighteenth century, the Dean of St Patrick's Cathedral, Jonathan Swift, had recommended his fellow countrymen to 'burn everything English but her coal', and proposed a system of Dual Monarchy in which Ireland's only connection with England would be through the Crown. Daniel O'Connell in the nineteenth century brilliantly exploited the organisational possibilities open to him in the (highly restricted) electoral system of the period. His election as member for County Clare in 1828 faced the British government with the choice of declaring the election void (on the grounds that Catholics were not eligible to become MPs) or to change the law. Fearful of provoking a full-scale insurrection, they chose the latter course, and the Relief Bill was passed the following year. O'Connell's campaign became a model for reformist organisation and agitation in Britain. For instance, Thomas Attwood's Political Union, which spearheaded the campaign for the Reform Act of 1832, was consciously modelled on the Catholic Association.[47]

O'Connell's efforts to secure greater independence for Ireland, however, were unsuccessful. Like Swift, he was prepared to settle for a system of dual monarchy with England. He proposed the setting up of a Council of Three Hundred to act as the *de facto* government of Ireland, and toyed with the notion of a boycott of Parliament. Thomas Davis, another major figure in the Irish national movement in the first half of the nineteenth century, was also prepared to settle for a dual monarchy. While not renouncing the use of force, he appears to have envisaged active non-cooperation as the principal means of applying political pressure.[48] In the early 1880s, the National Land League under the leadership of Michael Davitt and Charles Stuart Parnell conducted a vigorous campaign against exorbitant rents and evictions – leading on occasions to violent confrontations despite the efforts of the leadership to avoid this. Rent refusal, and the complete ostracisation of anyone who attempted to farm land from which others had been evicted, formed the core of the struggle. The word 'boycott' was coined in this period following the ostracisation of a certain Captain Boycott, the agent of an absentee English landlord.[49] The Sinn Fein movement itself produced one major essayist committed on principle to the rejection of violence. This was Robert Lynd (1879–1949), an Ulster-born writer who contributed to the journal *Sinn Fein* and insisted that a non-violent struggle would maintain the unity of the country and prove more difficult than armed rebellion for the British to suppress.[50]

The 1916 rebellion in Ireland and the subsequent guerrilla war of 1919–21 resulted in the subordination of civil resistance to the military struggle. Nevertheless, many of the specific measures advocated by Griffith were implemented, including the establishment of an Irish National Assembly, *Dail Eireann*, in Dublin in 1919 following Sinn Fein's massive victory at the polls. Moreover, in January and June of the following year, Sinn Fein won similarly impressive victories in the elections to the municipal, county and rural district councils, and by the autumn, on the advice of *Dail Eireann*, the majority of councils outside north-east Ulster had severed their connections with the existing British-administered Local Government Board. The British system of justice was also largely supplanted by the 'Dail Courts', and by July 1921 there were an estimated 900 such Parish Courts and seventy District Courts in operation.[51] Thus, if Ireland had become largely ungovernable – by Britain – in 1920–1, this was due not only to the armed rebellion but to the establishment of a parallel structure of government, law and administration.

The degree of interaction between the Irish and Indian independence struggles is striking. The influence within India of Griffith's history of the Hungarian resistance within India has been mentioned. But Griffith for his part took a keen interest in the Indian nationalist movement and exchanged information with several Indian patriotic journals. He regarded the Indian Swadeshi movement – which amongst other things propagated a boycott of British manufactures – as the equivalent of Sinn Fein. In 1907, the future Indian Prime Minister, Jawaharlal Nehru, visited Dublin during a vacation from his Cambridge studies and wrote to his father that Sinn Fein was similar to the advanced section of the Indian National Congress.[52]

Clearly, then, there was a cross-fertilisation of ideas between various movements for national independence from at least the period of the Hungarian struggle onwards, leading to the adoption of passive resistance as an important, if not the central, strategy in independence struggles.

Utopian and revolutionary projects

The notion of a general strike that would overturn the capitalist order was a recurrent one among European radical and revolutionary movements in the nineteenth century. The Chartists had dreamed of it in the 1830s and 1840s, though never came close to implementing it. Richard Tucker, the American anarchist whose writings were influential in both his own country and Europe, was one of the theorists to place the general strike at the centre of his proposed strategy. Though supporting violence in self-defence, he attacked Lassalle's critique of passive resistance as 'the resistance that did not resist'. On the contrary, Tucker argued, it was the most effective weapon in the hands of the working class.[53] In Italy from around 1900, syndicalism was a growing force in the working class, and in 1904 Italian workers staged the first more or less successful general strike in history in protest against the killing of workers and peasants in the south and in Sardinia.[54] Georges Sorel, the major theorist of syndicalism, though a passionate advocate of revolutionary violence, also regarded the general strike as the crucial revolutionary weapon.

The general strike that came closest to realising its revolutionary objective took place across the Russian Empire in 1905. It broke out in January 1905 as a result of the 'Bloody Sunday' massacre of over 100 unarmed demonstrators in St Petersburg,

and strikes, demonstrations, and sometimes armed clashes paralysed the country for most of that year. In October, the Tsar
announced major concessions to the protesters, including the
establishment of an elective legislature. The attempt by the
Bolsheviks and Mensheviks in Moscow to turn the strike into
an armed uprising in December 1905 can be seen in retrospect
to have been a cardinal blunder, enabling the Tsar to crush
the insurrection. Twelve years later, in the February revolution,
strikes, mutinies, mass desertions and demonstrations finally
brought about the end of Tsarist rule.

The nineteenth-century writer who was more directly in the
non-violent tradition and close to individualist anarchism in his
political outlook was the American writer Henry David Thoreau.
Thoreau engaged in personal civil disobedience by refusing to
pay his poll tax to the state of Massachusetts over a period of six
years on the grounds that it supported slavery and an unjust war
against Mexico. His essay on civil disobedience, first published
in 1859 under the title *Resistance to Civil Government*, was occasioned
by his arrest and overnight imprisonment for his tax refusal. (To
his annoyance, a friend paid his fine to secure his release.) It
was reprinted after his death under the title by which it is now
generally known – *On the Duty of Civil Disobedience.*[55]

Thoreau argues for selective civil disobedience on grounds of
principle. He had paid his highway tax because he was 'as desir-
ous of being a good neighbour' as he was 'of being a bad subject'.
He withheld paying the poll tax, not because of any particular
item in the tax bill, but 'to refuse allegiance to the State, to
withdraw and stand aloof from it'.

In defending his action on grounds of conscience, Thoreau is
in the mainstream tradition of radical dissent. However, in denying that he owed any allegiance to the American state while it
went on behaving as it did, and in refusing to pay taxes to it, he
took his defiance further than most. The crucial point, though,
is that he propounded the notion that conscientious law-breaking
was politically effective – more so than voting, or engaging
in propaganda campaigns, or attempting to work through
constitutional methods to change the laws.

Cast your whole vote, not a strip of paper merely, but your whole influence. A minority is powerless while it conforms to the majority; it is not even a minority then; but it is irresistible when it clogs by its whole weight. If the alternative is to keep all just men in prison, or give up war and slavery, the State will not hesitate which to choose. If a thousand men were not to pay their tax-bills this year, that would not be a violent and bloody measure, as it would be to pay them and enable the State to commit violence and shed innocent blood. That is in fact the definition of a peaceable revolution, if any such is possible. If the tax-gatherer, or any other public officer asks me, as one has done, 'But what shall I do?' my answer is, 'If you really wish to do anything, resign your office.' When the subject has refused allegiance and the officer has resigned his office, then the revolution is accomplished.[55]

In this passage, Thoreau appears to recognise the coercive implications of mass defiance and resignations by government officials. Yet his appeal is essentially to the individual conscience, and he looks to the moral impact of civil disobedience rather than its coercive potential:

I know this well, that if one thousand, if one hundred, if ten men, whom I could name – if ten *honest* men only – ay if *one* HONEST man, in this state of Massachusetts, *ceasing to hold slaves*, were actually to withdraw from this copartnership, and be locked up in the county jail therefor, it would be the abolition of slavery in America.

It is possible that Thoreau was familiar with La Boëtie's essay on Voluntary Servitude. His close friend Ralph Waldo Emerson certainly knew of it, and dedicated a poem to its author. However, there is no direct evidence on this matter.

One can easily see why Tolstoy saw in Thoreau a kindred spirit. He praises Thoreau's 'admirable essay' and the example he set in going to prison for refusing to pay taxes to the state.[56]

Tolstoy's entire emphasis is on individuals acting according to conscience, regardless of consequences. The 'golden rule' that one should do to others as one would have them do to oneself, or at least that one should not do to others what one would not have them do to oneself, was embodied, he believed, in the teachings of all the great sages and inscribed in the human heart. That is why non-Christians who heeded the dictates of conscience would also be led to an uncompromising rejection of violence. However, the principle was most perfectly expressed in the teachings of Christ. 'We must take the Sermon on the Mount,' he wrote, 'to be as much a law as the theorem of Pythagoras.'

Tolstoy rejected both Church and State. The one corrupted Christ's teaching, the other was an institution based on murder and exploitation. War, whether defensive or offensive, he denounces as murder and contrary to God's law. Tolstoy is no less opposed to patriotism, which he rejects as an expression of egoism and self-aggrandisement, and as the cause of war. To the argument that the patriotism of an oppressed people should be judged in a different light, he replies that it is even more dangerous since it is rooted in bitterness and more likely to give rise to war. One does not require patriotism, he argues, in order to oppose the subjugation and exploitation of people; Christ's teaching already implies this, and if all would follow that teaching such abuses would come to an end. It is ironic in the light of this that Tolstoy should have such a profound effect on one of the twentieth century's representative nationalist leaders, M. K. Gandhi.

As one would expect, Tolstoy has no time for the tactic of political assassination pursued by some anarchists at that period. He opposes assassination, however, not only on moral but also on political grounds. 'How,' he asks, 'can an organised body of Anarchists, . . . quietly considering means of improving the condition of the people, find nothing better to do than to murder people; the killing of whom is as useful as cutting off one of the Hydra's heads?'[57] It is not the czars, emperors or kings, he states, who are the cause of oppression and war, even though they do organise them. 'But it is those who have placed them in, and

45

support them in, a position in which they have power over the life and death of men. Therefore it is not necessary to kill Alexanders and Nicholases ... but only to leave off supporting the social condition of which they are the product.'[58] The passage is reminiscent of La Boëtie's argument and may owe something to it as Tolstoy had certainly read *On Voluntary Servitude*.

Tolstoy was not interested in changing political institutions as such. 'Christian doctrine, in its true sense,' he states, 'never proposed to abolish anything, nor to change any human organisation. The very thing which distinguishes Christian religion from all other religions and social doctrines is that it gives men the possibilities of a real and good life, not by means of general laws regulating the lives of all men, but by enlightening each individual man with regard to the sense of his own life.'[59] Nonetheless, he did believe in the power of public opinion, always provided people would speak the truth as they perceived it. He praised the work of the anti-slavery campaigner William Lloyd Garrison, citing at length in his essay 'The Kingdom of God is within you' Garrison's proclamation on non-resistance sent to the Society for the Promotion of Peace in 1838.[60] He also had a shrewd notion of how to arouse public opinion, and successfully pleaded the cause of a persecuted Christian pacifist sect in Russia, the Doukhobors, writing letters to the foreign press and making statements on their behalf until they were given permission to emigrate *en masse* to Canada.

Tolstoy also took a keen interest in Gandhi's passive resistance campaign in South Africa and the two exchanged several letters. But Tolstoy's understanding of passive resistance is entirely that of the individual refusing out of personal conviction to engage in war or exploitation, or to pay taxes to a state which is responsible for such things. Gandhi, a keen reader of Tolstoy's moral and political essays, was no less concerned with right action. However, he combined this with a gift for organisation, and an intuitive understanding of the responses of the Indian masses, that made him an outstanding political leader of a kind that Tolstoy neither wished to be nor was capable of being.

The Evolution of Passive Resistance

Steven Huxley sums up the evolution of passive resistance in the nineteenth century as follows:

> Throughout Europe in the nineteenth century passive resistance developed into an articulated doctrine and concrete practice of struggle for various groups and classes. For the rising bourgeoisie it was a suitable approach to the defense and achievement of their interests against both the old regime and the masses. For 'the masses' it was a mode of struggle against oppression. For nationalists it was a weapon highly compatible with economic development and cultural self-assertion; in other words, it was a way to independence. For socialists and anarchists it was the means of contention most in harmony with their ideals, as well as being the most suitable weapon for their struggle.[61]

Where are we to place passive resistance in the broader context of emancipatory struggle in eighteenth- and nineteenth-century Europe and North America? The work of Charles Tilly and his co-workers helps us to do this. In *The Rebellious Century: 1833–1933*, they examine the incidence of major collective violence in France, Germany and Italy during this period, and relate it to a changing pattern of collective organisation and action. They draw an important distinction between *competitive, reactive* and *proactive* conflict.[62]

Competitive conflict is a more common feature of the pre-industrial era. It is rooted in organisation at the communal level and expressed in such things as feuds and brawls between rival villages, competing groups of artisans and the like; soccer violence between rival football supporters would be a present-day example. Charles Tilly and his co-authors note that competitive violence declined dramatically with the centralisation of state power in the course of the nineteenth century, partly because the setting for power struggles moved from the local to the national level.

Reactive conflict arises out of resistance to the claims of the centralising state (allied to an expanding industrial capitalism), and is typified by tax rebellions and riots, violent resistance to conscription, machine-breaking, the occupation of enclosed land, and so forth. Here too the organisational base is at the communal level, and again the incidence of reactive struggle declined as the power of the central state increased and the legitimacy of its claims became more widely accepted.

Proactive conflict is defined by the fact that at least one group is 'making claims for rights, privileges or resources not previously enjoyed.'[63] It is rooted in *associational* forms of organisation – more open and bureaucratised than the communal forms, aiming at national or international outreach, and usually with a public programme and distinct ideology. Confrontations with authority tend here to result from relatively brief coordinated mass actions and shows of strength such as demonstrations, marches and strikes.

In practice, of course, the distinctions are not always so clear-cut; nor are there distinct periods separating the prevalence of one form of action over another. Clearly, however, the proactive forms of struggle, and associational forms of organisation, are the characteristic modern forms, and they emerged as something new on the social and political scene in Europe in the course of the late eighteenth and nineteenth centuries.

Charles Tilly and his collaborators note, in relation to all three forms, that when violence occurs it does so as a consequence of collective action that is not of itself violent. To quote the authors: 'practically no common forms of collective action which we have encountered are intrinsically violent.'[64] The bulk of collective violence 'emerges from much larger streams of essentially non-violent collective action', and is then frequently the result of a 'forcible reaction of a second group – often of specialized repressive forces in the employ of governments – to the non-violent collective reaction of the first'.[65]

A further important finding is that the vast majority of instances of collective political action – demonstrations, strikes, tax refusals, resistance to conscription – 'did *not* end in violence.'[66]

Thus out of 20,000 strikes which took place in France from 1890 through 1914, only 300 to 400 produced any violence beyond the scale of minor pushing and shoving. From 1915 through 1935, the figure is 40 or 50 violent strikes out of 17,000. . . . The violent events did not begin much differently from the non-violent ones; for the most part, the presence or absence of resistance by a second party determined whether violence (in our sense of damage or seizure over resistance) resulted. Many of the Italian land occupations of the nineteenth century went on peacefully; the violence typically began when landlords, troops, or mafiosi arrived to expel the occupiers from the land.[67]

The criteria which the Tilly group employs do not distinguish between violence on the part of the police or army from that on the part of protesters. Thus a strike or demonstration in which the protesters maintained a completely non-violent discipline would register as an occasion of major political violence if the police or army killed or wounded more than a certain number of people or inflicted serious damage to property. This is a serious disadvantage when it comes to assessing the relative merits of violent and non-violent action in achieving the desired ends.

However, the Tilly group sees no sharp distinction between violence and non-violence. The fundamental strategic choice, they argue, 'is not between violent and non-violent means. It is between different forms of collective action which vary in the probability that they will lead to violence.'[68] Elsewhere they conclude: 'No tragic chasm separates violence from non-violence, in 1968 or 1768.'[69]

This conclusion is questionable. On pragmatic as much as moral grounds, organisers of mass demonstrations often go to great lengths to ensure that protesters avoid violence, even in the face of attacks by the police, precisely because the chasm between violence and non-violence can be tragic – in human terms and in terms of the effectiveness of the action. The non-violent discipline of protesters in the former GDR and Czechoslovakia in

1989, even in the face of police attacks, was probably crucial to their success. (However, the authors acknowledge that they were 'unable to put together anything like a comprehensive record of such everyday twentieth-century forms of collective action as the non-violent demonstration', adding that 'the history and sociology of the demonstration as a distinctive modern form of action remain to be written'.[70])

Governments have frequently provoked violence among protesters to provide themselves with a cover for using extreme violence on the streets, or introducing draconian laws. The history of nineteenth-century radical and working-class agitation in Britain reveals the lengths to which governments were prepared to go using *agents provocateurs* to *instigate* violence during strikes and demonstrations, and even to foment uprisings which they knew were foredoomed to failure. G. D. H. Cole and Raymond Postgate record the activities of the government spy Oliver who travelled from town to town in 1817 posing as a representative of the 'Physical Force Party', urging groups of labourers and artisans to take up arms and assuring them that their district was almost alone in not being ready to take action. In the main he was unsuccessful, but he did persuade a small group of framework knitters in desperate straits to gather whatever arms they could and march towards Nottingham until intercepted by a party of soldiers. Thirty-five of the insurgents were tried for high treason, of whom twenty-three were convicted. Four of them were hanged. Of the others, eleven were transported for life, three others for fourteen years, and the rest to various terms of imprisonment.[71]

However, the main conclusion the Tilly group draws about the effectiveness of violence in the historical process is crucial. The presence or absence of violence, they conclude, makes very little difference to the historical outcome, '*but the collective action which leads to violence is the very stuff of history*' (emphasis added).[72] What counts is not the presence or absence of violence, but whether or not there was collective action. 'Groups which did not develop the capacity to strike, to demonstrate, to turn away the tax collector lost power – or never gained it.'

It will be clear from this that the modes of action characteristic of passive resistance correspond to those of collective action, sometimes of the reactive type of struggle, more often of the pro-active type as defined by the Tilly group. In this sense passive resistance, even if not always so called, can be seen as ranking alongside, but in contrast with, premeditated armed rebellion, at the heart of a tradition of eighteenth- and nineteenth-century European resistance culture.

Where the collective action was met by violence or repression on the part of the authorities, the protesters and their leaders still had a choice whether or not to retaliate, if only in the very limited sense of using violence in self-defence. The emphasis in the evolving tradition of passive resistance during the nineteenth century was on avoiding retaliatory violence. Only in the twentieth century, however, under Gandhi's leadership, was an explicit concept of non-violence, which included the willing acceptance of suffering at the hands of the opponent, erected into a cardinal principle of this type of action. As we shall now see, as Gandhi developed his ideas on non-violence he sought to distance his methods from those of passive resistance, and evolved a new vocabulary in which to express them.

Chapter 3

Satyagraha to People Power

The aim of this chapter is to provide a summary overview of the development of civil resistance in the present century and to deal with several campaigns in various political contexts in sufficient depth to bring out some of the key issues and controversies raised by this kind of action.

The figure whose actions and ideas have most crucially influenced the development of civil resistance in the twentieth century is Mohandas K. Gandhi – 'Mahatma' Gandhi. In the early years of the century in South Africa, and in subsequent campaigns in India up to his death in 1948, Gandhi combined an ethical commitment to non-violence with an uncanny political acumen and outstanding qualities of organisation and leadership. His most crucial contribution to the liberation struggle in India was to awaken the Indian masses to a realisation of their own power, and to forge a link between them and the educated political élite of the Congress party. Non-cooperation and civil disobedience were the weapons of India's millions, and provided the nationalist movement with a disruptive and potentially coercive sanction short of armed rebellion to back up its demands.

But though the Gandhian influence has been predominant for much of the century, other traditions played their part. The 1905 general strike across the length and breadth of the Russian Empire demonstrated the revolutionary potential of mass non-cooperation, but was not linked to any doctrine of non-violence; neither were the strikes, demonstrations and mass desertions that finally brought revolution to Russia in March 1917 (the 'February Revolution'). The suffragette campaign in Britain, too, in the period leading up to the First World War, was not Gandhian in origin or ethos, though it employed many of the same methods, including notably civil disobedience and hunger strikes. It was Gandhi who was influenced by some of these events rather than exerting an influence upon them.

Some of the subsequent instances of civil resistance, especially in Europe in the inter-war years, also harked back to an older European heritage. In 1920 an attempted pro-monarchist putsch in Berlin led by a right-wing landowner was defeated within days by a general strike in the city, and a policy of total non-cooperation at every level of society. In 1923, when French and Belgian forces occupied the Ruhr to enforce war reparations by the seizure of coal supplies, they were met with a campaign of passive resistance which included strikes by miners and rail-waymen, non-cooperation by civil servants, even the refusal of shopkeepers to serve the occupying forces. The resistance eventually crumbled in the face of hunger, rising unemployment and hyper-inflation, and was officially called off by a newly appointed German government led by Gustar Streseman in September. It nevertheless achieved some positive results. A US commission set up to mediate adjusted the war reparations claims in Germany's favour, and made the execution of its provisions dependent upon the restoration of the economic and political unity of the German Reich. The last provision was intended to forestall what many regarded as France's real objective in invading the Ruhr, namely to detach the whole of the Rhineland area from Germany and create a French client state.[1]

During World War II, there was widespread civil resistance in occupied Europe, especially in Western and north-western Europe, and this too owed little to the Gandhian tradition. It ranged from actions such as the wearing of symbols to the publication of underground newspapers, go-slows and obstruction, and intermittent mass action in the form of strikes and demonstrations.[2]

In the Netherlands in 1940, students in Delft and Leiden struck in protest at the dismissal of Jewish professors. There were major industrial strikes in Amsterdam, Hilversum and other cities in

February 1942, again in protest against the treatment of Jews, and in April and May 1943 several hundred thousand took part in a strike against a German order that Dutch ex-servicemen should report for internment in Germany. In September 1944 railway workers struck in a move timed to coincide with Allied parachute landings at Arnhem and Nijmegen.

In Norway, forty-three organisations with a total of 750,000 members formed a Coordinating Committee to resist the Quisling government's attempt to bring any one of them under Nazi control. In 1942 teachers successfully defied an attempt to introduce the teaching of Nazi doctrines in the schools, and led to the abandonment by Quisling of the attempt to create a Nazi-style corporate state in Norway.

In Denmark – which was invaded ostensibly to preserve its neutrality and was therefore permitted to retain its own government – a 'people's strike' in Copenhagen in August 1943 led to the resignation of the government and the imposition of direct German rule. In October of the same year a massive clandestine rescue operation led to the smuggling of ninety-five per cent of the Jewish population to safety in Sweden. Strikes, demonstrations and sabotage continued thereafter, culminating in a general strike in Copenhagen in June 1944.

In France, in response to a broadcast appeal from General de Gaulle, there were mass demonstrations in both the occupied and unoccupied zones on May Day 1942 and again on 14 July. There were also extensive strikes in June 1942 in opposition to the attempts to coerce people to work in factories in Germany, and again in February 1943 when the Vichy government passed a decree introducing labour conscription to meet German demands for more workers in their factories. In France too, as in the Netherlands, Italy and elsewhere, there were campaigns of strikes, sabotage and obstruction in the latter part of the war timed to coincide with Allied offensives.

Gandhi, however, exerted a major influence upon many of the postwar liberation movements. Thus some of the key figures in the generation of postwar African leaders – including Kwame Nkrumah of Ghana, Kenneth Kaunda of Zambia and Julius

Nyerere of Tanzania – modelled their campaigns explicitly on Gandhian lines. In Ghana and Zambia especially, civil resistance, and the threat of it, played a significant role in the independence struggles. The campaigns that took place in South Africa in the post-World War II period – the 1946 campaign by the Indians in Natal, and the Defiance of Unjust Laws campaign jointly launched by the African National Congress and the South African Indian Congress in 1952 – were also Gandhian in conception.[3] However, some of the liberation movements which were initially strongly influenced by Gandhian ideals gradually distanced themselves from the commitment to non-violence, and developed a more pragmatic strategy in which sabotage and even armed rebellion were combined with civil resistance. This was the case most notably with the African National Congress and the Pan-Africanist Congress in South Africa.

Gandhi's influence is unmistakable in the civil rights campaigns in the United States in the 1950s and 1960s (discussed in more detail later), and those of the radical wing of the nuclear disarmament movement in Britain, the United States and Western Europe. The Direct Action Committee against Nuclear War in Britain arose out of an attempt in 1957 by a Quaker, Harold Steele, to sail into the British nuclear testing zone at Christmas Island in the Pacific as a form of non-violent intervention. In the following year, a crew comprising members of the Committee for Non-violent Action (CNVA) in the US made two attempts to sail into the US testing zone at Eniwitok in the *Golden Rule*.[4] Later that same year, Earle and Barbara Reynolds and their family, together with Nick Mikami from Hiroshima, attempted to sail their ketch, *Phoenix*, into the prohibited zone. While these expeditions did not realise their immediate objective they were widely publicised and played an important role in mobilising opposition to nuclear weapons. The Direct Action Committee organised the first Aldermaston March in Britain in 1958, and adopted the now universal nuclear disarmament symbol. By the early 1960s the peace campaigns had reached the proportions of a mass movement involving hundreds of thousands of people in many countries. In 1961 in Britain, thousands took part in sit-down demonstrations in city centres or bases organised by the Committee of 100 and the Direct Action Committee Against Nuclear War. Mass demonstrations and civil disobedience were features also of the anti-Vietnam war movements in the United States, Western Europe and elsewhere in the latter 1960s and early 1970s, and here too the Gandhian heritage is evident in many of the protests and demonstrations, even if they now tended to have a more militant and strident tone. Within Vietnam, guerrilla warfare was the main instrument of national struggle. Nevertheless, there too civil resistance played a significant role, particularly during the 1963 campaigns by Buddhists and students against the US-backed government of Ngo Dinh Diem in South Vietnam.

The peace movement of the 1950s and 1960s had a strongly internationalist emphasis. Not only was there international representation on marches and demonstrations within particular countries, but increasingly campaigning groups within different countries worked together on specifically transnational actions, such as the Sahara Protest Team against French atomic weapons tests in 1959–60, and the San Francisco–Moscow March of 1960–1. In January 1962, the World Peace Brigade was set up at a conference in Beirut with the aim of providing a more permanent organisational base for projects of this kind. (See the section below on Transnational Non-violent Action.)

From the 1960s onwards, stimulated no doubt by the examples of Gandhi, Martin Luther King, and the anti-nuclear and antiwar movements, civil resistance techniques were used with increasing frequency for a whole range of issues and at a variety of levels – from small local campaigns to those involving thousands or tens of thousands of people. In France, starting in the late 1950s, there was mounting opposition to the war in Algeria, with demonstrations sometimes taking the form of sit-downs in front of trains taking soldiers to the war. In 1961 an attempted military coup by French generals in Algeria against the policies of General de Gaulle was defeated by non-cooperation, and a display of national unity called for by de Gaulle and by the trade unions and major political parties. In Northern Ireland from the mid to late 1960s, civil rights campaigners challenged the endemic discrimination in the Province. The subsequent, and continuing, tragedy in the area should not be allowed to obscure the important achievements of the civil rights movement in mobilising large numbers of people for a time across the old nationalist/unionist divide and forcing the authorities to introduce reforms in local government elections, and to end many discriminatory practices.[5] 1968 also saw student and left-wing unrest, amounting at times to quasi-insurrections, in the United States, Britain, West Germany, Italy, and – most spectacularly – France. Vietnam, at this point, had become the catalyst for a thoroughgoing critique of Western capitalist society, and a younger generation rediscovered Marxist and anarchist ideas.

A rejection of capitalism, however, did not imply an endorsement of the 'actual existing socialism' in the Soviet Union and Eastern Europe, and for the young rebels the alienation from the Soviet model was deepened when Soviet and Warsaw Pact tanks rolled into Warsaw in August 1968 to put an end to the reforms of the Prague Spring. In Czechoslovakia itself, thousands of people poured out onto the streets to confront the oncoming tanks, and they maintained a remarkable civil resistance to the occupiers until Dubcek and the other leaders had been released and re-installed in office. However, the Czechoslovak leadership had been pressurised in Moscow into making concessions, including the re-introduction of censorship, and this enabled the Soviet leaders to apply 'salami tactics' over the following months to secure their removal and institute a wholesale purge of the Party. In the still longer perspective, however, the invasion, and the heroic non-violent resistance it encountered, undermined still further the credibility and authority of Communist Party rule in Eastern Europe.

From the mid to late 1960s, and into the early 1970s, there was a distinct shift among anti-Vietnam campaigners and radical youth and leftist movements in the West towards a romantic notion of revolutionary violence, epitomised in the cult of Che Guevara. Some of the demonstrations took on a more aggressive, macho style in which punch-ups and fist-fights with the police were sometimes seen as evidence of determination rather than as a breakdown of discipline. A minority, like the Weathermen in the States, the Angry Brigade in Britain, the Red Army Faction in West Germany and the Red Brigades in Italy put their commitment to 'urban guerrilla warfare' into practice with the sabotage of buildings and in some cases kidnappings and bomb outrages. In the 1970s the male macho style of leadership and demonstrations came under attack from the resurgent women's movement, many of whose groups developed alternative non-hierarchical approaches to organising and brought new vigour and imagination to non-violent protest.

During the 1970s, too, environmental issues became a major focus of public concern, and here again various forms of non-violent action were commonly employed, from large-scale occupations and sit-downs at nuclear power plants, or at the sites scheduled for building such plants, to daring and imaginative non-violent intervention by teams of Greenpeace volunteers. In some of the major civil disobedience demonstrations, such as those at Seabrook in the United States and Torness in Scotland, non-violent discipline was strengthened through on-site role play and other forms of training.

The 1980s saw the rise of a new mass peace movement. By now the notion of using non-violent direct action on a variety of issues had become more common and more widely accepted in many countries than had been the case in the 1950s and early 1960s. This facilitated the use of civil disobedience on a far larger scale, including by the mainstream organisations like the Campaign for Nuclear Disarmament (CND) in Britain, which had firmly rejected it in the earlier period. Women this time around played a major part, organising national and transnational campaigns. In 1981, some 40,000 women surrounded the Greenham Common base in Berkshire, and women took the initiative in organising some of the international marches and setting up peace camps at the proposed missile sites, such as that at Comiso in Italy. Demonstrations were on a truly massive scale, bringing millions of people onto the streets of Europe and exerting tangible pressure on the governments of the countries concerned.

Although the movement failed to prevent the deployment of the new generation of Euromissiles, it can claim some credit for bringing the superpowers to the conference table, eventually to sign an agreement to remove them. There was also an important exchange of ideas and information between a section of the Western peace movement and the human rights and peace groups in Eastern Europe, extending to the organisation of several joint projects. Moreover, the mass demonstrations of the early 1980s, often highly innovative and imaginative in form, were widely reported in Eastern Europe and had the unintended consequence of encouraging imitation.

Outside Europe, there were particularly vigorous campaigns in the US (spearheaded by the Freeze Movement), Canada, New Zealand, Australia and the South Pacific area. In New Zealand, the campaign won an outstanding political success with the election of David Lange as prime minister of a Labour government pledged to keep New Zealand as a nuclear-free zone and to prohibit visits by British and American warships. There was also strong opposition in New Zealand, Australia, the island chains of Micronesia and Polynesia, Vanuatu, Fiji and other territories in the Pacific to continued French nuclear testing. In 1985 the members of the South Pacific Forum signed the Treaty of Rarotonga, an expression of their opposition to nuclear tests and their desire for a nuclear-free Pacific.[6]

Meanwhile, elsewhere in the world, from 1979, and through the 1980s, civil resistance achieved strategic successes to the point of transforming the international scene. In 1979 in Iran, despite massacres by the Shah's military forces, followers of Ayatollah Khomeini and others took to the streets literally in their millions and forced the resignation and flight of the ruler. The spirit of this unarmed insurrection was the very opposite of non-violent, and the regime which took over was authoritarian and fanatical, yet the power of total non-cooperation to undermine an armed and determined autocracy had again been demonstrated. During the 1980s mass action overturned the Marcos regime in the Philippines and the Duvalier dictatorship in Haiti, and brought democratic reform in Korea, Chile and elsewhere in Latin

America. In the West Bank and the Gaza Strip, too, Israeli rule was seriously challenged by the *Intifada* after twenty years of occupation. By the early 1990s the apartheid system in South Africa was visibly crumbling under the combined assault of riots and disorders in the black townships, guerrilla attacks, campaigns of non-cooperation, and international sanctions and boycotts at both official and unofficial levels.

Some of the successes, to be sure, were short-lived. In Haiti, the success of people power in 1986 in forcing 'Baby Doc' Duvalier to flee into exile was followed by a further period of military rule and political repression. In December 1990 a left-wing priest, Jean-Bertrand Aristide, was elected President, but he too was overthrown in another army coup. A general strike and civil disobedience, coupled with the imposition of sanctions by the United States, failed to restore the legitimate government, though, in July 1993, in face of continuing international pressure and sanctions, the military rulers in Haiti gave an undertaking that they would allow Aristide to return to the country and resume his role as its president. In other cases civil resistance failed to achieve success at least in the short to medium term. In Fiji, a coup in May 1987 removed the elected government of Dr Bavadra which drew much of its support from the Indian population, and a further coup in September of that year consolidated military rule at a time when a compromise political settlement seemed within reach. While there was some civil resistance to the coups, the racial divisions between Indians and indigenous Fijians, stirred up by the pro-coup parties and factions, prevented a united resistance.[7] In China, the massacres in Tiananmen Square and elsewhere in Beijing in June 1989 dashed any immediate hope of democratic reform in that country, and again underlined the fact that civil resistance provides no easy solutions.

Yet it was in the communist countries of the Soviet bloc that people power achieved its most telling and strategically important victories. Civil resistance was an important element in the revolts in East Germany in 1953, in Hungary in 1956, in the recurrent crises in Poland, and of course in the opposition to the Soviet-led intervention in Czechoslovakia. There was also a continuing, low-level cultural resistance to the imposed regimes which progressively undermined their authority and legitimacy. The establishment of Solidarity in August 1980, and its rapid growth to become by far the most powerful political force in Poland, can be seen in retrospect to have been the turning point in the fortunes of Communist Party rule – and Soviet hegemony – in Eastern Europe. In the mid to late 1980s, the Gorbachev reforms in the Soviet Union on the one hand and the clear signal that the Soviet Union was no longer prepared to intervene militarily to save embattled Communist Party governments in Eastern Europe eased the way for the 1989 revolutions. Gorbachev's reform programme was itself a response to an economic and political crisis within the Soviet bloc to which the recurrent revolts and challenges – and especially the emergence of Solidarity in Poland – had made a fundamental contribution.

Gorbachev was not prepared to use force to maintain Communist Party rule in Eastern Europe, but he did use it spasmodically in several of the Soviet republics in a vain attempt to maintain the integrity of the Soviet Union. In April 1989, demonstrators in Tbilisi, Georgia were attacked by Soviet (chiefly Russian) troops, and a number of people killed or seriously injured. There was a further bloody repression in Baku, Azerbaijan, in January of the following year leading to demonstrations by an estimated 750,000 people at the funerals of those who had been killed. But there was also a crucial display of people power in Moscow in February 1990 in support of Gorbachev's proposal to end the Communist Party's monopoly of power. One hundred and fifty thousand people attended a demonstration in Moscow, constituting the largest demonstration since shortly after the Russian Revolution of 1917. In October 1990, the Parliament of the Russian Federation declared that Soviet laws would apply to its territory only after it had ratified them. Then, in January 1991, while the rest of the world was preoccupied with the Gulf War, Soviet special forces, presumably acting under orders from Moscow, occupied the television and radio stations in Vilnius, Lithuania, and the Interior Ministry in Riga, Latvia, in attempts to bring the republics to heel. In both cities, civilians formed physical and human barricades around the Parliament buildings in response to public radio appeals. Five people were killed and fourteen wounded when Soviet forces attacked the Parliament building in Riga.

Nevertheless, all-out confrontation between the centre and the republics was avoided, and the latter steadily increased their relative strength and independence. It was in fact the plan to sign a new Union Treaty that sparked off the attempted coup to oust Gorbachev and re-establish central control under hardline communist leadership. This was defeated in a new and extraordinary demonstration of people power, discussed in more detail later in this chapter.

How much direct influence Gandhian ideas of non-violent action exercised in these events in Eastern Europe and the Soviet Union is difficult to judge. In a very broad sense, of course, the experience of Gandhi's campaigns in South Africa and India has become part of a worldwide pool of knowledge. In Poland in the 1970s, the Catholic monthly *Wiez* published in translation accounts of the campaigns of Gandhi, Luther King and Brazilian trade unionists, and in 1977 a group which embarked on a public hunger strike in protest against the arrest of nine KOR (Committee for the Defence of Workers) members made specific reference to the tradition of Gandhi and Luther King.[8] Following the imposition of martial law, Lech Walesa referred on a number of occasions to Gandhi and non-violence, and in 1984 underground publishing groups produced Polish editions of some of the writings of two leading Western exponents of non-violent action, Jean-Marie Muller (France), and Gene Sharp (USA).[9] The Freedom and Peace group (*Wolnosc i Pokoj* – WiP), founded in 1985, had close links with the Western peace movement and identified itself unambiguously with the non-violent approach. In East Germany, Christian church groups actively promoted non-violence; so too did some of the Prague students in Czechoslovakia's Velvet Revolution. Overall, however, the restraint of the demonstrators probably owed more to an understanding of the fact that a bloody uprising could be disastrously counter-productive and might just be the development that would after all trigger Soviet intervention. In Romania, of course, there was serious bloodshed, though only after Ceausescu had fled from Bucharest and the *Securitate* attempted a violent counter-revolution.

In the case of the Baltic republics, there is clear evidence that the civil resistance to the attempted Soviet clamp-down in January 1991, and again at the time of the August coup, was influenced by Gene Sharp's writings on civilian-based defence.[10] We consider the developments in the Baltics both prior to and following their independence later in this chapter. Meanwhile, in the rest of this chapter, we examine in somewhat greater detail several representative civil resistance campaigns in various contexts.

Liberation struggles

India

The simple version of Gandhi's achievement in India is that he won the nation's independence by his leadership and organisation of non-violent action against British rule. The campaigns did make, of course, a vital contribution to the independence struggle. But it is important to place them in an historical context and to see how they interacted with constitutional and other pressures for reform.

Gandhi's first campaigns in India following his return there from South Africa in 1915 focused on a number of local issues. At the same time he began putting into practice his ideas on a constructive programme aimed at self-reliance. The principal campaigns at a national level in which he was involved were those against the Rowlett Acts of 1919 (anti-terrorist laws which placed severe restrictions on freedom of speech and assembly), and in support of the Khilafat movement in the same year (a campaign for the Sultan of defeated Turkey to be permitted to retain the guardianship of the Muslim holy places); the non-cooperation campaign of 1920–2; the civil disobedience campaigns of 1930–1, and 1932–3; the campaign of individual civil disobedience in 1940; and the Quit India campaign of 1942. He devoted equal, if not greater, energy to the cause of Hindu–Muslim unity, putting his life on the line on several occasions as a result of fasting or direct intervention in trouble spots, and on the constructive programme which he regarded as an integral part of the campaign for *swaraj* – a term denoting both self-government and self-reliance. Not all these campaigns were successful; some, in Gandhi's own estimation, were disastrous failures. Overall, however, they made a vital contribution to the independence movement.

The setting in which Gandhi took on the role of a national leader was framed by the Lucknow Pact in 1916, in which the National Indian Congress and the Muslim League agreed to cooperate in pursuit of an agreed programme of constitutional reform, and the 1917 Montagu Declaration. This promised 'increasing association of Indians in every branch of the administration and the gradual development of self-governing institutions, with a view to the progressive realisation of responsible government in India as an integral part of the British empire.'[11] The Government of India Act in 1919 – generally referred to as the 'Montagu-Chelmsford Reforms' – was presented as the first stage in the implementation of this policy. It reformed the franchise so that about one in ten of the Indian male population gained the vote, established separate communal electorates for Muslims and other religious minorities, and increased the powers of the Provincial Legislatures. However, certain key areas, such as foreign affairs, the currency, and criminal law, remained in the hands of the colonial government in Delhi.[12]

Despite his reservations about the Act, Gandhi initially favoured Congress's cooperation with it. In the same year, however, he led a campaign of defiance against the newly passed Rowlett Acts. This brought outbreaks of violence and culminated in the massacre by forces under the command of a British officer, Colonel Dyer, of nearly 400 unarmed demonstrators at Jallianwalla Bagh in Amritsar. It was this massacre, and official British reaction to it, that finally made Gandhi disillusioned with the British Empire. At the same time his support for the Khilafat movement increased his influence among the leaders of India's

Muslim community and gave him the stature of a national figure.

The 1920–2 campaign of non-cooperation was conducted against the British *raj* as such and was aimed at achieving *swaraj* within one year. It enjoyed the backing of both the Indian National Congress and the Khilafat movement, and was planned to take place in distinct phases of increasing assertiveness. The first phase (from August 1920 to October 1921) comprised a 'triple boycott' of the Provincial Councils, schools and law courts, a massive recruiting and fund-raising drive, and the introduction of spinning-wheels into the villages (the Bezwada programme), and finally a complete boycott of foreign cloth. Coupled with a reform of the Congress constitution, the Bezwada programme transformed Congress – as Gandhi intended that it should – from an élite pressure group into a mass movement.

The second phase comprised 'individual' civil disobedience, the withdrawal of civilians from government employment, and a campaign for Indians to withdraw from the military and the police. The third phase was to comprise 'assertive' civil disobedience, starting in Bardoli, where Gandhi felt the people were most ready to undertake it, and followed by other areas, provided that strict conditions had been fulfilled, including the adoption of *swadeshi* (use of home-produced articles, particularly clothing), a commitment to non-violence and communal unity. A particularly important feature of this campaign was the integration of the 'constructive programme' – production of home-spun cloth and work at the village level – and non-cooperation.[13]

The campaign gained mass support, involving hundreds of thousands in acts of non-cooperation and defiance that often linked national and local issues. But outbreaks of violence in some areas led Gandhi to postpone the phase of mass civil disobedience and finally to abandon it altogether. He first postponed the launch of mass civil disobedience in Bardoli when serious rioting accompanied the visit of the Prince of Wales to Bombay in November 1921. Nevertheless, 'defensive' civil disobedience – the defiance of bans imposed by many of the Provincial governments on political meetings and the outlawing of the Congress and Khilafat committees in November 1921 – resulted in the arrest of over 30,000 volunteers and the imprisonment of many prominent Congress leaders.

Alarmed by the extent of the protests, the Viceroy, Lord Reading, indicated that, provided Congress would call off the non-cooperation, the government was prepared to lift the ban on the two organisations, to release those imprisoned as a result of the campaign, and to convene a Round Table Conference on the constitution. This offer marked a significant success for the campaign, but to the consternation of many of his colleagues in Congress, Gandhi refused the offer on the grounds that the amnesty did not cover some of the Khilafat volunteers who had called for resignations from the Army. In February 1922, the postponed mass civil disobedience was due to be launched in Bardoli. Before this could take place, however, a massacre of twenty-two policemen in Chauri Chaura in the United Provinces finally decided Gandhi to cancel civil disobedience altogether for the time being. Gandhi himself was arrested in March, and Congress subsequently resumed cooperation with the new constitution.

Following a period of two years' imprisonment for incitement (1922–4), Gandhi was not pre-eminent in Congress politics until 1928. Instead his energies were concentrated on the constructive programme, his work for the Harijans (Untouchables), and on behalf of Hindu–Muslim unity. In 1924 he undertook a three-week fast in an effort to stem communal violence after 150 Hindus had been killed in riots in Kohat.

Gandhi was attracted back into national politics by the growing disillusion of the Congress politicians with the working of the 1919 constitution, the high-handedness of the Simon Commission entrusted to review its workings, and his concern about the growing disunity of the Indian population. In 1929, Congress voted for the first time for complete independence, a boycott of the legislature and of a British-sponsored Round Table Conference, and for civil disobedience at the discretion of the All India Congress Committee. Many both inside and outside Congress were ready at this juncture to support violence, as is indicated by the narrow majority in Congress for a motion condemning a bomb attack on the Viceroy's train.[14] Much therefore depended on whether or not Gandhi could produce a sufficiently imaginative and challenging form of civil resistance to meet the emotional as well as the political needs of the moment.

Gandhi's response was the famous Salt March. In March 1930, with eighty of his most trusted followers, the sixty-one-year-old leader set off on the 240-mile walk from Ahmedabad to the sea at Dandi. There he openly defied the salt-tax law by making salt from evaporated sea water. In one sense it was gesture politics, and was viewed with considerable scepticism by some of the sophisticated Congress politicians. The gesture, however, touched exactly the right chord among the mass of the Indian population – or at any rate the Hindu part of it – and marked the beginning of a nationwide campaign of civil disobedience. This involved chiefly salt-tax defiance and the boycott of foreign cloth, but encompassed also a social boycott of government servants, resignations from government posts, and refusal to pay land revenue. Jails were filled as a total of 60,000 resisters were imprisoned during the period of the campaign.[15] Those imprisoned, however, represented only a fraction of the people who boycotted foreign cloth, contributed funds to the campaign, or participated in other ways. Women too played an active part in the campaign, participating in the running of the Congress organisation, and in picketing and civil disobedience. In Gujarat, Gandhi's home base, the British administration virtually collapsed, and most Provincial governments came under severe pressure. The main disappointment, however, from Gandhi's and Congress's standpoint, was the low level of Muslim participation outside the Frontier region. The hopes of achieving Hindu–Muslim unity in a common action had not been realised.

The 1930 London Conference, though boycotted by Congress, reiterated Britain's commitment to granting India Dominion status. Gandhi and the members of the Congress Working Committee were released from prison, and early in 1931 Gandhi and the Viceroy, Lord Irwin, reached an agreement – the Gandhi–Irwin Pact – under which Congress would suspend civil disobedience whilst the government would withdraw the special powers designed to deal with it and release all civil disobedience prisoners. In September, Gandhi attended the Second Round Table Conference in London as the sole representative of Congress – a move designed principally to conceal the rifts within the organisation. The conference itself ended in deadlock, mainly over the issue of Congress's claim to represent all Indians, including Muslims, and of separate electorates for Untouchables and other minorities.[16] However, Gandhi recognised the importance of enlisting support among the British electorate and lost no opportunity to visit universities, schools, religious groups and leaders, and ordinary working people, including notably some of the Lancashire cotton workers who had been adversely affected by the *swadeshi* campaign and the boycott of foreign cloth.

Soon after his return to India, Gandhi was re-arrested and, rather half-heartedly, Congress renewed the civil disobedience campaign. This time around it was less successful, and did not take root to the same extent among the rural population. Gandhi himself, however, was able to influence the British government's constitutional proposals when, in September 1932, he undertook a 'fast unto death' inside prison as an expression of his opposition to the plan to grant Untouchables separate constituencies. This led to a compromise arrangement for the Untouchables agreed in discussions with their leader, Dr Ambedkar.

Gandhi was released in May 1933 on the eve of a fast of self-purification. Realising that mass civil disobedience was a spent force and unpopular with Congress, he sought ways to bring it to an honourable conclusion. It was followed by a period of 'individual civil disobedience', but this was never popular. Gandhi retired from Congress altogether in 1934, and the organisation re-engaged in constitutional politics. The new Government of India Act of 1935 devolved the government of the provinces almost totally into the hands of elected Indians, and in the 1937 elections Congress became the party of government in seven of the eleven provinces.[17] At the same time the election undercut Congress's claim to represent all Indians, Muslims as well as Hindus, though it revealed also the relative weakness at this stage of the Muslim League, which won only 109 of the 482 seats reserved for Muslims, gaining just under five per cent of the Muslim vote.[18]

Civil disobedience re-emerged on the political scene in India following the outbreak of the Second World War. In November 1939, Congress withdrew from Provincial government, and in 1940, under Gandhi's leadership, it launched a campaign of individual civil disobedience based upon an unequivocally pacifist slogan: 'It is wrong to help the British war effort with men or money. The only worthy effort is to resist all war with non-violent resistance.' At the end of the first phase of the campaign, many prominent Congress figures were in jail, including thirty-two former ministers, seven of whom had been Provincial premiers. By May 1941, 14,000 *satyagrahis* (non-violent resisters) were in jail, and by the end about 26,000 had been convicted according to government estimates.[19] Nevertheless, there was not the enthusiasm which had marked the 1920–2 and 1930–1 campaigns, and by mid-1941 the government regarded it as no longer posing an administrative problem.[20]

In 1942, following the collapse of a mission to India by Stafford Cripps, Congress launched a new mass campaign – the Quit India campaign. This was severely, and on the whole effectively, suppressed by the British government, whose hand was strengthened by the wartime presence of additional troops in India, and by the fact that it no longer had to worry, at a time of Britain's own national peril, about opposition at home or abroad. The members of the Congress Working Party were imprisoned until the end of the war, and this body, plus the All India Congress Committee, and the Provincial Congress Committees, were declared illegal. Gandhi himself was arrested before he and the Congress leadership could formulate a coherent strategy or communicate with the Provincial Congress Committees.[21]

In the postwar period, Gandhi again played a central role in the negotiations on the constitution for an independent India. He resolutely opposed partition to the end. However, the various negotiations that had taken place between him and the leader of the Muslim League, M. A. Jinnah – in April and May 1938 and again in September 1944 – produced only deadlock. In the July

1945 elections to the legislatures, Congress won ninety per cent of the non-Muslim vote, but the Muslim League had virtually a clean sweep of the special Muslim seats in the legislatures, and large majorities in Bengal and the Punjab. Partition at this point was almost inevitable.

Gandhi's last, most heroic contribution to Indian politics occurred in the immediate aftermath of independence, when he put his life on the line visiting areas stricken by the communal slaughter that marked the partition of the country. His personal intervention and 'penitential' fasts – in Calcutta in September 1947 and Delhi in January 1948 – had a dramatic impact and brought at least a temporary halt to rioting in the areas concerned. Lord Mountbatten, India's last Viceroy and first Governor-General, paid tribute to him following the Calcutta fast as 'My One Man Boundary Force'. Others, however, were less impressed. On 30 January Gandhi was assassinated by a fundamentalist Hindu angered by what he saw as Gandhi's undue deference and concessions to his Muslim fellow countrymen.

Even such a succinct exposition of Gandhi's career reveals the complex interaction in the Indian independence struggle between radical civil resistance and conventional politics. The mixed fortunes of the campaigns also demonstrate the importance of the broader context in which they were taking place, even when facing the same opponent. In the campaign of 1920–2, and again in 1930–1, the difficulty for the British authorities was that they could not act too violently or repressively against a non-violent movement without alienating the moderate Indian politicians whose cooperation they hoped to enlist, and without risking opposition at home and abroad. Thus the campaigns, precisely because they were non-violent as well as radically disruptive of the administration, exercised genuine pressure in the tough world of *realpolitik*. However, as noted above, at the time of the Quit India campaign Britain was less constrained and could act more ruthlessly in putting down the resistance.

How different, we may ask, was Gandhi's *satyagraha* from earlier passive resistance? The term *satyagraha* was coined in 1907 in an effort to find an *equivalent* in Gujarati and other Indian languages to the English term 'passive resistance', as the contemporary issues of *Indian Opinion* show.[22] However, from the early period of the South African campaign, Gandhi had put a much greater emphasis than previous practitioners of passive resistance on the notion of converting the opponent through voluntary self-suffering,[23] and on the principled rejection of any resort to violence. Later, he was to write: '*satyagraha* differs from Passive Resistance as the North Pole from the South. The latter has been conceived as a weapon of the weak and does not exclude the use of physical force or violence for the purpose of gaining one's end, whereas the former has been conceived as a weapon of the strongest and excludes the use of violence in any shape or form.'[24]

Despite his determination to distance *satyagraha* from passive resistance, Gandhi was well aware of historical and contemporary examples of the latter and, especially in the early days in South Africa, referred favourably to them in propagating his ideas. Thus in various issues of *Indian Opinion* he cited the example of the nineteenth-century Hungarian resistance to Austrian rule, the contemporary Sinn Fein struggle in Ireland, a Chinese boycott in 1905–6 of American goods in response to US anti-Chinese legislation, the boycott of British goods in Bengal in 1905 in protest against a British proposal of partition, the general strike in Russia in the same year – the 'Russian remedy', as he called it, which could be adopted in the struggle against tyranny[25] – and the campaign of the suffragettes in England.[26] Moreover, in expounding the workings of *satyagraha*, Gandhi did not solely emphasise the moral and psychological impact of voluntary suffering on the opponent, but insisted also on the dependence of governments on the cooperation of the population and the vulnerability of authority in face of sustained non-cooperation.[27] He freely acknowledged, too, that in presenting his proposal for non-cooperation to Congress he had emphasised the pragmatic argument on the grounds that otherwise it would not have been accepted.[28] It may also be the case, as Gene Sharp has suggested, that Gandhi himself was first led to adopt civil resistance in the South African campaign from the evidence of its practical effectiveness rather than reasoning 'from the ethical to the political'.[29]

Gandhi's own views on violence and non-violence were complex, and indeed shifted down the years. He drew a careful distinction between the moral obligations imposed on those who fully accepted the doctrine of *ahimsa* (non-violence) and those who did not. The former ought never to resort to violence, but must be prepared to lay their lives on the line if necessary in opposing injustice. The latter were not only entitled to use violence in extreme circumstances but had a positive duty to do so unless they too were prepared to adopt non-violent methods. Gandhi spoke admiringly too of the Polish resistance to Hitler's aggression in 1939. 'If Poland has that measure of uttermost bravery and an equal measure of selflessness, history will forget that she defended herself with violence. Her violence will be counted almost as non-violence.'[30]

Because many of Gandhi's colleagues and followers did not share his views on non-violence, his *satyagraha* campaigns were not in practice as far removed from previous passive resistance as he himself wished them to be. Nevertheless, they bore the stamp of his intense moral commitment and were frequently conducted with a remarkable and indeed unprecedented non-violent discipline. In this respect they were different and established a new pattern. Moreover, Gandhi's organising ability and strategic judgement honed the technique for future practitioners, including those who did not share completely, or share at all, his belief in non-violence.

South Africa 1946–92

Outside India itself, Gandhi's influence was particularly strong in Africa. The fifth Pan-African Congress which met in Manchester in October 1945 – organised by its founding father, the black American leader W. E. B. DuBois – brought together some of the new generation of African leaders, including Kwame

Nkrumah of Ghana and Jomo Kenyatta of Kenya.[31] For the first time since 1919, the African National Congress (ANC) sent representatives to the meeting, which demanded autonomy and independence for Africa and endorsed Gandhi's passive resistance as the only effective way of persuading alien rulers to respect the rights of unarmed subject races.[32]

In 1946 the Indian community in Natal engaged in a passive resistance campaign against the introduction of laws that restricted their right to own landed property and thus segregated them from the white community. Within a short period of the launching of the campaign, 600 resisters had been arrested, and by its close, 2000 had suffered imprisonment, among them an Anglican clergyman, Reverend Michael Scott, who was to become a major campaigner against apartheid and for the rights of Africans, and a prominent figure in the anti-nuclear war campaign in Britain in the late 1950s and early 1960s.[33]

In 1949 the ANC, strengthened by a vigorous new executive which included Walter Sisulu as Secretary-General, Nelson Mandela and Oliver Tambo, voted for a Programme of Action which would include 'strikes, civil disobedience, non-cooperation' to secure African demands.[34] Three years later, in 1952, the ANC and the South African Indian Congress jointly launched the Defiance of Unjust Laws Campaign in which over 7000 people in total defied apartheid laws. In October and November, however, there were serious riots in Port Elizabeth, Denver, Kimberley and East London, and although not connected with the defiance campaign, and condemned by its organisers, they had an adverse effect on the movement and gave the authorities ammunition to use against it.

The government also armed itself with new powers to control meetings, both public and private, and to restrict the activities of particular individuals. Most of the leaders, both African and Indian, were arrested in August 1952 and charged under the Suppression of Communism Act.[35] They were found guilty, and given prison sentences of a number of years suspended on condition that during the period of suspension they did not commit any further offences under the Act. A Criminal Law Amendment

Act increased the penalties for inciting or participating in civil disobedience, including lashes. In November, the Governor-General issued a proclamation dealing with the incitement of 'natives' which also placed severe restrictions on the holding of meetings of more than ten blacks in a 'native area'. This had the effect of pre-empting the ANC's plans to spread the campaign amongst rural Africans. By the end of the year, as a result of banning orders, arrests of leaders and internal dissensions within the black population, the campaign had lost momentum.

The longer-term resistance did of course continue. An important landmark here was the 1955 Congress of the People, an initiative launched by the ANC but supported by the major non-white and inter-racial political organisations. The Congress adopted a Freedom Charter setting out the terms for a future democratic South Africa. In the same year, African women took the lead in defying the pass laws,* and 20,000 of them converged on the Union Buildings in Pretoria. In December 1956 police made mass dawn arrests of active opponents of apartheid of all races, and 156 were charged in a Treason Trial which dragged on for over four years, resulting, however, in the acquittal of all defendants in March 1961. Meantime, in 1960, the newly formed Pan-Africanist Congress (PAC) – a breakaway organisation from the ANC – launched a civil disobedience campaign against the pass laws. Fifty thousand resisters presented themselves without passes at police stations in various locations in March 1960. This was the occasion of the Sharpeville massacre in which sixty-nine unarmed protesters were shot by South African police and 180 injured.

In the face of the increasing repression, the ANC in 1962 established a military wing, 'Umkonto we Sizwe' (Spear of the Nation), which initially limited itself to acts of sabotage against government buildings and installations, but later extended its activities

* The pass laws obliged 'non-Europeans' to carry one or more of up to twelve passes (permits) to reside in or visit given areas; they were a central weapon in the Nationalist government's attempt to enforce racial segregation – 'apartheid'.

to include attacks on the security forces. Other organisations, too, including the PAC, set up military wings during this period. Umkonto's armed struggle was eventually suspended in 1990 following the release of Nelson Mandela.[36] However, guerrilla warfare inside South Africa itself (as opposed to South-West Africa – Namibia) was not on a sufficient scale to pose a serious military threat to the white minority government. In general, strikes, demonstrations, boycotts, plus the formidable township insurrections on the one hand and moral pressure from leading South African churchmen such as Desmond Tutu and Alan Boesak on the other, have been the principal means inside South Africa of undermining the apartheid system. During the 1970s, too, the Black Peoples Convention, proponents of black consciousness, adopted a non-violent approach in its resistance to apartheid. Steve Biko, its best-known leader, died in police custody in September 1977 aged only thirty-one.

In addition to the internal opposition, South Africa came under increasing pressure from the 1950s onwards from the UN and other international bodies in the shape of embargoes, sanctions and sports boycotts. Its position was significantly weakened by the collapse of Portuguese colonialism in Angola and Mozambique in the 1970s, and the ultimate failure in 1979 of Ian Smith's attempt to maintain an independent white supremacist state in Southern Rhodesia. In 1990 it was forced by internal pressure from the SWAPO guerrilla movement, and external pressure from the UN, to cede independence to South-West Africa – Namibia. Step by step, too, the Nationalist government of President De Klerk, has, since 1989, been induced to scrap the apartheid laws and to accept the need to hold discussions with the ANC and others on a future democratic system for the country.

At the time of writing the question at issue is not whether white minority rule will end but how soon and in what manner. The clashes between the ANC supporters and the mainly Zulu followers of Chief Buthelezi's Inkatha movement (with encouragement and financial support from the government) have added a further tragic dimension to South Africa's problems. It is significant, however, that when the talks between Nelson Mandela and President De Klerk broke down after the Boibatong massacre in June 1992, the ANC resisted demands to renew the armed struggle and embarked instead on a campaign of 'mass action'. It is clearly in its ability to bring the South African economy to a standstill and cause serious disruption through strikes and other forms of civil resistance that the strength of the ANC lies.

Elsewhere in Africa, civil resistance and constitutional agitation often went hand in hand in the campaigns for independence. In Ghana, Kwame Nkrumah launched a 'Positive Action' campaign in 1949 which put pressure on the British authorities to speed up the moves towards independence. Civil resistance also played a significant role in the break-up of the Central African Federation in 1962 and the consequent achievement of independence by Zambia. In April 1962, all the main opposition parties boycotted the elections and in August of the same year Kenneth Kaunda of the United National Independence Party (UNIP) announced a plan to call upon all Northern Rhodesia's 11,000 civil servants employed by the Federal government to resign.[37] UNIP also made preparations for a general strike, and for a large international march which would proceed from Dar es Salaam in Tanganyika to the Northern Rhodesian border. These steps, however, proved unnecessary because Britain announced its intention to allow individual countries to cede from the Federation.

Overall, the pattern has been that in the majority of African colonies that did not have a large settler population, conventional political agitation – sometimes interspersed with more militant action such as boycotts, strikes and demonstrations – was sufficient to ensure a more or less peaceful transition to independence. However, in the Portuguese colonies of Angola and Mozambique, and in other countries where there was a large and well-entrenched settler population – Algeria, Kenya and Southern Rhodesia – guerrilla warfare rather than civil resistance provided the coercive force behind the independence movements.

Civil rights

The cross-fertilisation between the black American struggle against discrimination and the liberation movements in Africa is of long standing, and is epitomised in the crucial role played by W. E. B. DuBois in the development of the Pan-African Congress. It is not surprising, then, that in the United States, as in South Africa and elsewhere on the African continent, civil resistance should have been regarded as a crucial weapon in the struggle for civil rights. The difference in the political and legal context, however, between campaigns in the US and those either in South Africa or the colonies seeking independence, was that in principle the US constitution already guaranteed the basic rights of every citizen to 'life, liberty and the pursuit of happiness'. Thus direct action and civil disobedience in the streets and at the grass roots went hand in hand in the US with action through the courts, leading at times to the use of the military and police to enforce court decisions. The most dramatic example of this was in 1957, when President Eisenhower ordered Federal forces to Little Rock, Arkansas, where the local mayor had called out the National Guard to prevent school integration.

DuBois himself was one of the organisers and leaders of a silent march by 8000 blacks down Fifth Avenue in Washington, staged by the National Association for the Advancement of Colored People in June 1917, just after the first American troops had landed in Europe during World War I. Their ironic slogan was: 'Make America Safe for Democracy'.[38] In the 1920s and 1930s, A. Philip Randolph, President of the Brotherhood of Sleeping Car Porters, one of the most powerful black organisations in the US, and a Baptist minister and later Congressman, Reverend Adam Clayton Powell, ran successful campaigns against discrimination in public and private institutions. In 1941 the mere threat by Randolph that he would call for a mass march to the Lincoln Memorial in Washington to demand an end to discrimination in the defence industries was enough to prompt President Roosevelt to issue an executive order to meet this demand.

In 1942, under the direct inspiration of Gandhi's campaigns, a small inter-racial group, the Congress for Racial Equality (CORE), was set up in Chicago and employed tactics of non-violent direct action to enforce the desegregation of selected lunch counters, restaurants, swimming-baths and municipal buildings in a number of US cities. One of its organisers, Bayard Rustin, was to become a close associate of Martin Luther King and to play a prominent part in both the civil rights and peace movements. In 1947 Rustin was one of a small inter-racial team who undertook a 'Journey of Reconciliation' following a Supreme Court decision outlawing discrimination on interstate travel. They journeyed together on Greyhound and Trailways buses to test whether the law was being implemented. In North Carolina, Rustin and several others were sentenced to thirty days working on chain gangs for sitting together in the front of a bus.

However, the first civil rights campaign to have an impact nationally and gain worldwide attention was the Montgomery Bus Boycott, sparked off in December 1955 by the refusal of a seamstress, Rosa Parks, to vacate her seat at the front of a bus. Black community leaders, including the then twenty-six-year-old Baptist minister Martin Luther King, formed the Montgomery Improvement Association, to organise the boycott. After a year of campaigning, the protesters won their case when the Supreme Court ruled that segregation on intra-state buses was illegal. Subsequently, King, Rustin and other black leaders formed the Southern Christian Leadership Conference (SCLC) to apply the lessons of Montgomery throughout the South. In 1957, SCLC organised a 'Prayer Pilgrimage' to the Lincoln Memorial in Washington attended by 25,000 people.

January 1960 saw the first student sit-in at a lunch counter in Greensborough, North Carolina that had refused to serve a black agricultural student. The movement spread with extraordinary rapidity, aided by radio and television coverage. By March the sit-ins had spread to more than fifty cities. In April 1960 the Student Nonviolent Coordinating Committee (SNCC) was established to support the sit-ins, and the scale and militancy of the demonstrations grew. Within two years virtually all public facilities had been integrated.[39] 'Freedom Rides' by CORE volunteers in May 1961 to test another Supreme Court decision, this time banning discrimination in interstate bus *stations*, also won a signal victory. Following repeated assaults and arrests, and the bombing of one bus, the Attorney General, Robert Kennedy, ordered the Interstate Commerce Commission to force bus companies and railways to comply with the Supreme Court ruling.

The dramatic high point of the civil rights movement was the 1963 Civil Rights March on Washington for jobs and freedom, supported by the main civil rights organisations. A. Philip Randolph, who had threatened to hold such a march back in 1942, was one of the organisers; it was coordinated by Bayard Rustin. Over 200,000 gathered in front of the Lincoln Memorial in Washington to hear speeches by civil rights leaders and organisers, including Martin Luther King, who delivered his famous 'I have a dream' speech. It was the largest demonstration in US history up to that date, attended by 150 members of Congress and well-known singers, writers and other public figures.

Voter registration was another major issue taken up by the civil rights movement. This was aimed at overcoming the legal and technical obstacles placed in the way of black people exercising their voting rights. In 1964 a coalition of civil rights organisations sponsored the Mississippi Summer Project, bringing black and white students to Mississippi to assist in voter registration. Several volunteers lost their lives in racist attacks and murders. In 1965 a march from Selma, Alabama to the state capital, Montgomery, was halted and then attacked by state troopers. After legal battles, the protesters won a judgement in a US district court and were able to continue the march. In the meantime, however, three white Baptist ministers had been attacked by members of the Ku Klux Klan and one had died from his injuries. Then, several hours after the conclusion of the march, a thirty-nine-year-old woman from Detroit, Viola Liuzzo, driving demonstrators back to Selma, was shot and killed. President Johnson went on national television to denounce the murders. Later that year, Congress passed the Voting Rights Act which opened the way to increased black participation in the elections and a significant increase in the number of black candidates elected to Congress.

But while there were significant gains, discrimination in education, jobs, housing and pay continued, leading to rising frustration. In 1965 the black ghetto of Watts in Los Angeles erupted in seven days of looting and violence in which thirty-four people died. Over the next several years there were uprisings in more than a dozen US cities, including Chicago, Detroit, Atlanta and San Francisco. The non-violent philosophy of the SCLC came increasingly under challenge, notably from the dynamic Black Muslim leader, Malcolm X. King moved to Chicago, concentrating now on the issues of poverty and deprivation, and making plans for a Poor People's march on Washington to establish a 'tent city' near the Lincoln Memorial. He never lived to see it. In April 1968 he was struck down by an assassin's bullet in Memphis, Tennessee, where he had gone to lead demonstrations in support of a strike by garbage workers. The Poor People's march went ahead, but the tent city lasted less than two months and failed to secure the radical action needed to deal with the problems it was seeking to address.

The achievements of the black civil rights movement in the US provided an enormous fillip to the use of non-violent action by other peoples or sections of society facing prejudice or discrimination in one form or another. Increasingly since the late 1960s, for example, women in many countries have engaged in demonstrations and protests, like the suffragettes before them in the early years of the century, often combining this with action through the courts. So too have gay and lesbian movements, the 'Grey Panthers' in the US, indigenous peoples in northern Europe, the United States, Canada, and many Asian and Latin American countries.

Transnational non-violent action

The strongly internationalist emphasis of the peace and non-violent action movements has been noted earlier. This both encouraged, and was reinforced by, the overlap in ideas and

personalities between the peace, civil rights and anti-colonialist/
anti-apartheid movements. Reverend Michael Scott, who had
been arrested for civil disobedience in South Africa in 1946 and
had become a major figure in the anti-apartheid movement and
movement for colonial freedom, was an active member of both
the Direct Action Committee Against Nuclear War in Britain
and co-founder, with Bertrand Russell, of the Committee of 100,
which launched a major civil disobedience campaign in the early
1960s, involving tens of thousands of people, against the British
government's nuclear strategy.

Bayard Rustin is another representative figure. In 1938 he had
been an organiser with the Communist Youth League in the US,
but he resigned when it changed its position on the war, and
joined the Fellowship of Reconciliation. He was imprisoned for
twenty-eight months during the war as a conscientious objector,
and on his release in 1945 led the Free India Committee, being
arrested several times for sit-ins inside the British Embassy in
Washington. As noted earlier, he took part in the US in 1947 in
CORE's 'Journey of Reconciliation', which was jointly sponsored
with the pacifist Fellowship of Reconciliation, and in 1948, at
the invitation of the Congress Party, spent six months in India
studying the Gandhian movement.

Rustin's role in the civil rights movements of the 1950s and
1960s has already been mentioned. He was active also with the
US War Resisters League and War Resisters International, and,
from the late 1950s, with the Committee for Nonviolent Action,
which organised direct-action demonstrations against war preparations and cooperated closely with the kindred Direct Action
Committee against Nuclear War in Britain. During visits to
Britain in the 1950s, he gave encouragement and support to
younger peace activists wanting to introduce Gandhian-style
demonstrations and civil disobedience into the anti-war – and
subsequently anti-nuclear weapons – campaigns. He was one of
the main speakers in Trafalgar Square at the start of the first
Aldermaston March in 1958, and was involved in a number of
transnational projects, including the Sahara Protest Action in
Ghana in 1959–60 and the San Francisco–Moscow March in

1960–1 (see below). In his personal history, one can see how the traditions and experience of Gandhian civil rights and peace movements contributed to the flowering of civil resistance in the post-World War II period.

The transnational direct-action projects initiated by the peace movement were particularly productive in bringing together the various strands of a wider emancipatory movement. The Sahara Protest Project illustrates the point. As noted earlier, this was an attempt to send an international team assembled in Ghana, West Africa to the French atomic testing site at Reggan in the Algerian Sahara. The initiative was that of the Direct Action Committee in Britain, but the project was co-sponsored by the Committee for Nonviolent Action in the US, and the Ghana Campaign for Nuclear Disarmament. It brought together peace movement, black American and African campaigners. Among its organisers and participants were Bayard Rustin and another black American peace activist, Bill Sutherland (at that time advisor to the Ghanaian Finance Minister, K. A. Gbedemah), Ntsu Mokhehle, President of the Basotho Congress Party[40], and Michael Scott, whose work in and on behalf of South Africa was noted earlier. In fact, by the late 1950s Michael Scott was such a well-known campaigner for African freedom that on his arrival at Accra airport in November 1959 he was greeted as a national hero by the vast crowd who turned out to meet him and carried him shoulder high to the reception lounge.[41]

The team was halted on its first attempt by French authorities just inside Upper Volta (now Burkina Faso) and had its vehicles seized by French Customs officials. It made two subsequent forays into Upper Volta, on the second of which the team members were arrested and dumped back across the border at a remote crossing point. But speakers from the team addressed large open-air rallies on its journey through Ghana, and the project helped to consolidate African opinion against nuclear weapons. In April of the following year, at the suggestion of Michael Scott, the Ghanaian President, Kwame Nkrumah, called a pan-African conference in Accra against nuclear imperialism and colonialism which was attended by representatives of most of the independent African of the independent African countries at the time, a delegation from the Algerian Provisional government (including Frantz Fanon), and representatives of a large number of resistance movements from other parts of Africa. Among the international advisors with a particular interest in non-violent action who attended were Ralph Abernathy of the Southern Christian Leadership Council in the US, A. J. Muste, Michael Scott, April Carter, and Gene Sharp. The conference approved, amongst other things, plans to establish a 'Positive Action Centre' in Ghana to train people for further direct action against French tests and for anti-colonial struggles. But the training centre never materialised in its intended form, becoming instead a centre for the political training of members of the governing Convention Peoples Party.[42]

The Sahara Protest Expedition was only one of a number of transnational projects organised by the peace and allied movements in this period. The 1960–1 San Francisco–Moscow March involved a multinational team travelling 6000 miles, mostly on foot, across America and mainland Europe to Moscow.[43] The impact such projects were having led A. J. Muste, Bayard Rustin, Bill Sutherland, Jayaprakash Nayaran (a leading Indian Gandhian) and the Reverend Michael Scott, amongst others, to convene a conference in January 1962 in Beirut to establish the World Peace Brigade. Muste, Nayaran and Scott were its three co-chairmen, and its first project was one in support of the campaign for the break-up of the Central African Federation – widely regarded as a device for prolonging white domination in the area – and the granting of independence to Northern Rhodesia (Zambia). Rustin, Sutherland and another Indian Gandhian, Siddharaj Dhadda, attended a meeting of the Pan-African Freedom Movement of East and Central Africa (PAF-MECA) in Addis Ababa in February 1962 and won support for a plan for a march from Dar es Salaam in Tanganyika to the border with Northern Rhodesia. This was to coincide with a general strike in the latter country which Kenneth Kaunda and the United National Independence Party (UNIP) were already planning. UNIP, the Tanganyikan African National Union

(TANU – the party led by Julius Nyerere), **PAFMECA**, and the World Peace Brigade were represented on Africa Freedom Action, the body set up to organise the march. Rustin, Sutherland and others took up residence in Dar es Salaam to devote themselves to the work and to take responsibility for the international representation on the march. Africa Freedom Action undertook important campaigning work, but in the end the march itself, and the projected general strike, did not take place because the British authorities backed away from support of the Central African Federation and eventually accepted the right of individual countries to secede.

The World Peace Brigade undertook several other projects, including notably a Delhi–Peking Friendship March in 1963 aimed at promoting understanding between India and China during and after the brief border war between the two countries.[44] But the World Peace Brigade never developed a solid organisational structure and after a few years faded away.

Its demise did not mark the end of such transnational interventions. There is space here to mention just a few of these. In December 1966, an ad hoc group based in Britain, Volunteers for Peace in Vietnam, sent four well-known clergymen from Britain, West Germany, the US and Canada to the Democratic Republic of Vietnam (DRV – North Vietnam) to witness and report back on the US bombing campaign.[45] Some two years later, a larger team of seventy-three British peace activists travelled to Cambodia with the aim of sharing the hazards of the bombing with the people of that country and trying to deter the US from continuing its raids.[46]

'Support Czechoslovakia' in 1968 was a protest action organised by War Resisters International involving international teams demonstrating simultaneously in Moscow, Warsaw, Budapest and Sofia against the Soviet-led invasion of Czechoslovakia.[47] Another international project organised by an ad hoc pacifist group was 'Operation Omega' (1971), which combined protest against repression in East Bengal (now Bangladesh) by the Pakistani army with the delivery of high-protein food to refugees.[48]

In June 1972, in the spirit of Harold Steele's efforts in 1957,

and those of the crews of the *Golden Rule* and the *Phoenix* in 1958,
a Canadian-owned sailing vessel, the *Vega/Greenpeace III*, sailed
into the French nuclear testing zone at Mururoa Atoll and was
rammed and boarded by a French navy patrol ship.[49] In a subsequent protest voyage in 1981, the French Ecology Party's candi-
date in the presidential election sailed with the *Vega*, and won an
undertaking from the French authorities that the level of radiation
would be independently assessed provided he desisted from going
through with his plan. These initiatives galvanised opposition to
the tests in the South Pacific, and their effectiveness was in a sense
underlined when French secret service agents blew up another
Greenpeace protest ship, *Rainbow Warrior*, in Auckland harbour
in 1985, killing the Portuguese photographer who was on board
at the time.[50]

The ambition to create a permanent organisation for transnational non-violent intervention persisted. In 1981 a less
grandiose but more realistic version of the World Peace Brigade
was set up, mainly as a result of an initiative of some of those
who had been involved in the earlier project. This was the Peace
Brigades International (PBI), which initially focused its activities
on Central America, establishing a core group in Costa Rica in
1982 for training in non-violence. In 1983 it sent an international
team of nine to the border between Nicaragua and Honduras to
monitor violence by the Contras and carry out practical work,
and to prepare the way for a permanent presence by a US Christian group, Witness for Peace. In the same year it sent volunteers
to Guatemala to assist those campaigning on behalf of families
of people who had 'disappeared'. PBI volunteers have remained
in Guatemala, despite the fact that they received death threats
during 1989, had their house in Guatemala City damaged by a
grenade attack, and had three members badly injured in knife
attacks. Volunteers carrying out similar escort work in El Salvador that began in 1987 have encountered arrest and harassment
by the military police. The team was expelled in 1989 on the
grounds that it represented a threat to the state, but returned
later at the invitation of the government.[51] PBI also began sending
volunteers to Sri Lanka in 1989 to act as unarmed escorts

to lawyers working on behalf of people detained without trial.[52]

Civil resistance against dictatorship: Latin America, Iran, the Philippines

The question which remained unanswered by Gandhi's successes in South Africa and India, and by those of most of the other occasions of mass civil resistance discussed above, was whether this method could succeed against a dictatorship, or indeed any well-armed and ruthless opponent. The achievement of the Norwegian teachers and of other groups which proffered non-violent resistance to the Nazis in occupied Europe showed that *limited* victories were possible, but there was no expectation in these cases of being able to *overthrow* Nazi power or force it to end the occupation. The short answer seems to be that civil resistance can succeed against a dictatorship, though not necessarily at any given moment in time. Sometimes a lengthy period of low-profile campaigning is required, coupled preferably with international pressure. However, on occasion a determined and apparently unassailable opponent is toppled because the armed forces desert the regime in face of the unity and persistence of the population.

Chile and South Africa represent examples of the process of erosion. General Pinochet's seizure of power in a military coup in Chile in 1973, and his wholesale imprisonment, torture and execution of opponents or suspected leftists, suggested that nothing short of military force would remove him. Instead his authority and his power base in the middle class were undermined by the economic and political incompetence of his regime, by the persistent non-violent resistance of the mothers of the 'disappeared', by trade unions, numerous 'base groups' in the towns and villages, and by international pressure. In 1983, in the face of a deteriorating situation, Pinochet felt obliged to open a dialogue with the opposition. But protests continued, coupled with several bomb outrages, and in the following year he declared a state of siege. In 1986, 15,000 people were arrested in anti-government demonstrations, and there were widespread strikes even though these were illegal. A plebiscite in 1988, which Pinochet had called in an effort to bolster his position, backfired and set the stage for a return to democratic government. While Pinochet remained Commander-in-Chief (and therefore a potential threat to the new democracy), he agreed not to stand for the presidency.[53]

There have been similar successes for non-violent action, sometimes limited, sometimes far-reaching, elsewhere in Latin America at various times. In El Salvador in April–May 1944, the military dictator General Maximiliano Hernández Martínez was overthrown in three weeks of non-violent insurrection.[54] In Guatemala in June of the same year, the dictator General Jorge Ubico, who had ruled the country since 1931, was unseated by eleven days of strikes and protests, culminating in a complete shutdown of Guatemala City.[55] In Bolivia in 1977–8 a mass hunger strike, starting with four women and eventually involving 1200 people, opened up the latent divisions within the ruling clique and its supporters, and led to the release of the majority of the country's political prisoners, the lifting of a ban on trade unions, and other concessions. For various deep-seated political and economic reasons, it did not, however, lead to the establishment of a stable democracy.[56]

Uruguay's struggle for democracy has elements in common with that of Chile. The military seized power in 1973 and established one of the most brutal regimes in Latin America, banning all political and trade union activity, imprisoning 7000 people on political grounds (out of a total population of only three million), and making extensive use of torture. However, in 1980, faced with economic decline and political unrest, it sought a mandate for an authoritarian constitution based on the doctrine of national security. Like the Pinochet regime in Chile some years later, it received a resounding rebuff, with eighty-seven per cent of the electorate voting no. Military rule continued, but there was sufficient opening up of the situation to allow some political and human rights organisations to establish themselves, among them the Uruguayan branch of Service for Peace and Justice (SERPAJ), founded by a Jesuit priest, Luis Perez Aguirre. In

August 1983, following the arrest and torture of a number of students, three members of SERPAJ embarked on a public fast – in the presence of the international press. This acted as a catalyst for mass action. A day of protest called by SERPAJ on 25 August was a major success, taking the form of virtually the entire population of Montevideo entering their homes at an agreed time, turning off all lights and rattling pots and pans in concert. In November, 500,000 people – a sixth of the entire population of the country – took part in a mass demonstration against the government, followed in January 1984 by a general strike. Elections finally took place in November, marking the first step in the restoration of democratic government.[57]

The most dramatic examples of civil resistance bringing about the revolutionary overthrow of authoritarian regimes were in Iran in 1979 and the Philippines in 1986. In Iran, millions went on strike and took to the streets. Despite massacres of unarmed demonstrators, the protests continued. But unrest began to grow among the armed forces, and on 12 February, following violent clashes between the Imperial Guard and airmen at two airbases in Teheran, the army command declared its neutrality and ordered its forces back to barracks, thereby sealing the fate of the Shah's regime.[58]

In the Philippines, the US-backed regime of Ferdinand Marcos had by the early 1980s lost much of its support in its traditional power base in the middle class due to its corruption and inefficiency. Its credibility and moral standing suffered a further blow in 1983 when the opposition leader, Benigno Aquino, was shot down in full view of television cameras by Marcos's security forces as he stepped down from a plane bringing him back from exile in the US. The murdered man's widow, Corazón Aquino, won a dramatic victory in the presidential elections of 1986, but Marcos refused to accept the result and was confirmed as President by the National Assembly. The move was denounced by the Catholic bishops, and the Defence Minister, Juan Ponce Enrile, called upon the army and the people to recognise Aquino as President.[59] When Marcos sent units of the armed forces to attack Enrile's headquarters, tens of thousands of civilians, including nuns and

priests who had worked with the people in grass-roots movements, blocked the army's advance. The army refused to open
fire, and Marcos and his wife Imelda fled the country. The term
'people power' was coined to describe this extraordinary victory
of an unarmed revolt. That victory was possible because the
Marcos regime had lost all claim to legitimacy by his repudiation
of the election result, had lost its power base in the civilian population, and finally lacked the authority to command the obedience
even of the armed forces.

Civil resistance against military coups: the anti-Gorbachev coup, August 1991

All the cases discussed so far in this section of the chapter involved
civil resistance from below against an established authority.
However, civil resistance has also been used on occasions by
or on behalf of an existing legitimate government. This will be
discussed in more detail in the chapters on defence by civil resistance, but I conclude this chapter with a brief exposition of two
instances: the resistance to the attempted anti-Gorbachev coup
in the Soviet Union in August 1991, and the resistance to the
Soviet-led invasion of Czechoslovakia in August 1968.

The resistance to the anti-Gorbachev coup has parallels with
two other frequently cited cases where civil resistance thwarted
attempted coups: the Kapp putsch in Berlin in 1920, and the
overthrow of the Generals' Revolt in Algiers in 1961.[60] The anti-
Gorbachev coup collapsed even more swiftly and dramatically
than did these other failed attempts. The preliminary move
occurred at 4.50 p.m. on the evening of Sunday, 17 August when
the plotters arrived at the Crimean dacha where Gorbachev was
on holiday with his family, cut off the telephones, and demanded
that he transfer his powers to the Vice-President, Ganady
Yanayev. According to Gorbachev's own account, he told them
to 'go to hell'. Gorbachev was due back in Moscow the next day
to sign a new Union Treaty giving the Soviet republics a much
greater say in running their own affairs. The forestalling of that
event was one of the immediate aims of the coup. Ironically, its

effect was to precipitate the break-up of the Soviet Union.

Early on Monday morning, tanks and other military vehicles moved onto the streets of Moscow, and Yanayev broadcast an announcement that Gorbachev was indisposed and that he, Yanayev, was therefore taking over power as head of an eight-man committee. Other members of the committee included the heads of the three armed services, the Ministers of Defence and the Interior, and the head of the KGB. The speaker of the Soviet Parliament announced that it would meet in emergency session the following Monday to endorse the state of emergency, a move clearly aimed at giving the coup a façade of legitimacy.

The committee made it clear at once that it intended to brook no opposition. It declared an immediate six-month state of emergency in Moscow, Leningrad and other areas of the Soviet Union, and issued a decree banning protest strikes and demonstrations. It threatened to introduce curfews where it met resistance, and to dissolve local authorities which resisted its control. It also took over all television and radio stations in Moscow, and announced that only nine – pro-communist – newspapers would be allowed to continue publication. Thus the subsequent suggestion by some political commentators that the coup attempt was totally mismanaged does not stand up to examination. The coup failed not because the plotters failed to take all the obvious steps in its planning and execution, but because the opposition of the people was too powerful. The mistake was not in how the coup was conducted, but in the decision to attempt it in the first place.

The most spectacular early setback was the failure to arrest the Russian President, Boris Yeltsin. According to some sources, however, this was not due to any oversight or carelessness on the part of the plotters, but to the refusal of KGB officers sent to arrest or kill him to carry out the orders they had received. Similarly, troops flown in from Odessa to put down the street demonstrations staged a sit-down at Moscow airport and refused to proceed to the city.[61] No less ominously, from the plotters' point of view, was the positive response to Yeltsin's call for a general strike from the coalminers of the economically vital Kuzbass area and the Vorkuta region in the Arctic Circle.[62]

Having escaped arrest, Yeltsin at once repaired to the Russian Parliament building – as did hundreds of other deputies. In his finest hour, he strode down the steps of the building, climbed onto one of a few tanks lined up by their commanders to defend it against possible attack, and addressed the growing crowd of Muscovites assembled there, denouncing the coup as unconstitutional and its authors as a 'gang of criminals', and calling for an immediate general strike. In a direct appeal to the soldiers he said: 'I believe, at this tragic hour, you will take the right decision. The honour of Russian arms will not be covered with the blood of the people.'[63] More tanks joined those already lined up to defend the Russian Parliament. The crowd swelled to 5000.

Protests continued to mount on Monday and Tuesday despite the ban on demonstrations. The plotters, meanwhile, held back from taking the Russian Parliament building by storm, perhaps because it symbolised so concretely the progress towards democratic government over the previous five years. By Tuesday, there were scenes reminiscent of those that had occurred in Prague in 1968, as demonstrators stood in the path of tanks, or clambered onto them to argue with their crews. Newspapers that had been shut down produced samizdat editions. A radio transmitter began broadcasting, albeit weakly, from inside the Russian Parliament building. Short-wave transmissions from the BBC and other foreign stations remained unjammed, and were eagerly listened to by people wanting a more independent view about what was going on.

On Tuesday, the presidents of the two largest republics, the Ukraine and Kazakhstan, denounced the coup; so too did the Patriarch of the Russian Orthodox Church, Alexi. In Leningrad the newly elected liberal mayor, Anatoly Sobchak, told 200,000 demonstrators that he had been promised by the military that no tanks would enter the city. Police both in that city and Moscow remained loyal to the local authorities. In the Baltic republics of Estonia and Latvia, general strikes were called, and the deputies inside the barricaded Estonian Parliament unanimously declared complete independence. As noted above, mines in the Arctic

Vorkuta region and in the West Siberian Kuzbass coalfield, observed Yeltsin's call for a general strike.

Pressure also came from outside. President Bush declared his support for Yeltsin and was able to speak to him directly by phone inside the Russian Parliament building. Both the US and the European Community Foreign Ministers announced the suspension of food and technical aid until legitimate government was restored. The UN Secretary General, Pérez de Cuellar, urged all Soviet leaders to show restraint.

The crunch came on Tuesday night/Wednesday morning. A curfew declared by the Emergency Committee was simply ignored, and several thousand demonstrators set up barricades of buses and concrete blocks around the Russian Parliament building in Moscow. At midnight, columns of tanks started moving towards the Parliament building and demolishing the barricades. The first shots were fired in clashes with demonstrators, four of whom were killed. Several tanks were set ablaze by Molotov cocktails. At 12.45, the former Soviet Foreign Minister, Shevardnadze, joined Yeltsin inside the Parliament building in a public gesture of support. The expected all-out assault on the building did not materialise, and early on Wednesday morning rumours began to circulate that Defence Minister Yazov and KGB chief Kryuchkov had quit. By Wednesday afternoon the coup attempt had collapsed, with several of its leaders flying to the Crimea to try to make their peace with Gorbachev. At 5 p.m. the Soviet news agency Tass announced that the emergency restrictions on the media had been lifted. That evening Gorbachev flew back to Moscow and was formally reinstated by the Soviet Parliament.

The struggle between the pro- and anti-coup parties can be seen as a complex battle of manoeuvre for legitimacy. The coup leaders lost a preliminary round when they failed to coerce Gorbachev into resigning on the eve of the coup. They suffered an even heavier defeat by failing to arrest Yeltsin and thereby to prevent him from establishing a base within the Russian Parliament building. At that point they faced a critical dilemma. The longer Yeltsin remained there and continued to denounce them as a gang of criminals and to call for strikes and passive resistance, the more the coup lost credibility in the eyes of the people and the outside world. Yet to have ordered an all-out attack on the building, with the heavy loss of life this was bound to entail among the elected representatives of the Russian people, and amongst the ordinary citizens manning the barricades around it, would have been to surrender all claims to political legitimacy and advertise a return to the politics of naked violence. There must indeed have been a question in the minds of the coup leaders as to whether the troops would carry out such an order, given the sit-down strike of the units from Odessa. Finally, the widespread strikes, particularly by the coalminers, the denunciation of the coup at an early stage by the presidents of the two largest other republics, the Ukraine and Kazakhstan, and the giant demonstrations in Leningrad and cities in the non-Russian republics, showed the coup leaders the extent of the problem they now faced. They had planned a palace coup. They now faced the prospect of defeat in a bloody civil war.

Civil resistance to invasion: Czechoslovakia 1968

Czechoslovakia in 1968 represents the most dramatic instance in recent history of popular non-violent resistance against foreign invasion and in support of a government that had earned the support of the population through its programme of reforms. For seven days Czechs and Slovaks came out into the streets in their tens of thousands to confront the tanks and their crews and give the lie to the Soviet propaganda that Czechoslovakia was in the throes of a counter-revolution. It was a display of unity rare in the history of any country, and particularly impressive in the case of a state where there were historic tensions and divisions between Czechs and Slovaks. Soviet plans to install a client government which would retrospectively legitimise the invasion were also, in the short term, frustrated.

The facts can be briefly summarised. Following the election of Alexander Dubcek as Communist Party secretary in January 1968, the country embarked on a programme of economic and political reform aimed at building 'socialism with a human face'. The reforms were encapsulated in the Action Programme adopted in April 1968. The two aspects of it that Soviet and some other Warsaw Pact leaders found most threatening were the re-orientation of trade towards the West, and towards West Germany in particular, as part of the package of economic reforms, and the virtual lifting of censorship as part of the political reforms. Alarms and tensions over the summer months were punctuated on the one hand by talks between Dubcek and the Soviet leaders, and on the other by menacing Warsaw Pact manoeuvres on Czechoslovakia's borders. Then, on the night of Tuesday, 20 August, 400,000 troops from the Soviet Union, Poland, Hungary and East Germany invaded the country.[64]

The Soviet hope and expectation was that it could quickly install a client government. Indeed, a group within the Czechoslovak Communist Party (CPC) leadership had promised the Kremlin that they would engineer a domestic political justification for the intervention.[65] However, their attempts to do so at a meeting of the Presidium on the afternoon of 20 August were unsuccessful.[66] Instead, as news of the invasion began to come in, the Presidium issued a statement roundly condemning it. The population were urged to maintain calm and not to offer resistance to the troops on the march, but all leading functionaries of the state, the Communist Party and the National Front were to 'remain in their functions as representatives of the people and organs to which they had been properly elected'.[67] In addition, the Presidium brought forward the date of the 14th Congress of the CPCz from 14 September to 22 August to give it the opportunity to express its opposition to the invasion and forestall any attempt to create a puppet government. The battle for legitimacy had been joined, and the Soviet leaders and the Czechoslovak collaborators had lost the first round.

The latter now tried to mitigate their defeat by preventing the dissemination of the Presidium's resolution. Thus no sooner were the first words of the resolution read out on the national broadcasting system than the transmitters went dead. This was a result of the efforts of the Minister of Post and Communications, Karel

Hoffman, a Soviet agent, in cooperation with the Soviet network in the security forces and the Czechoslovak Press Agency. It was, in fact, part of a wider plan to close down the radio and television networks. Thanks, however, to the decisive intervention of the President of the National Assembly, Smrkovsky, and action by alert radio station operators, the appeal was broadcast, after some delay, on an auxiliary transmitter. The editor of the party newspaper, *Rude Pravo*, another pro-Moscow man, tried to substitute a text of his own for the resolution – but this attempt too was thwarted.[68]

Popular protests began as soon as the people of Czechoslovakia woke to find Soviet and Warsaw Pact tanks in the streets next morning. In addition to standing in the path of tanks, many students and young people who had learned Russian at school and university engaged confused Russian soldiers in debate and argument, challenging them to find any evidence of a counter-revolution. In the afternoon, there was a brief protest strike.[69] The following day, 22 August, the 14th Congress of the Communist Party of Czechoslovakia met in secret session in a works canteen in a Prague suburb, and, as anticipated, added its voice to the condemnation of the invasion, calling concretely for the withdrawal of the troops, the return of all public functionaries to their proper, constitutional positions, and the observance of all international legal norms. In the judgement of Zdenek Mylnar, one of Dubcek's closest associates on the Presidium, this had exceptionally important and positive influences on the course of events.[70] Mylnar also describes the scene in the streets on that day:

> Everywhere, building walls were covered with slogans and hand-painted posters. People were reading the newspapers and leaflets that were being turned out by printing presses everywhere, despite the efforts of the occupying forces to stop it. It was the picture of a city whose inhabitants were absolutely united in unarmed passive resistance against alien interlopers. Flags and the Czechoslovak coat-of-arms in various forms decorated

the streets and shop-windows, and people were wearing them in their lapels as well. Wherever anyone had fallen a victim to Soviet bullets, there were improvised memorials with masses of flowers and state flags. Street signs had either been pulled down or altered (most often being renamed 'Dubcek Street'), and sometimes the signs were simply switched with others.[71]

As the 14th Party Congress went into session, the Soviet authorities made a further attempt to regain the political initiative. Eleven members of the Presidium were invited to meet the Soviet Ambassador whose purpose was to get them to establish a 'revolutionary government of workers and peasants'. This also failed because of stalling tactics by a pro-Dubcek faction of the group (led by Mylnar), and the subsequent point-blank refusal of the President, Ludvik Svoboda, to endorse any such move.[72] Instead, he announced his intention of departing next day for Moscow to negotiate with Brezhnev and the other Soviet leaders.

This decision proved to be a tragic mistake, and the turning point in the political battle of wits. The delegation accompanying Svoboda to Moscow, or who subsequently flew out, included the pro-Moscow conspirators inside the party leadership. At Svoboda's insistence, Dubcek and the other imprisoned leaders (who had been moved first to Poland and then to the Carpathians) were released to join the Czechoslovak side. While this represented a significant climb-down by the Soviet leaders, the latter were now in a position of strength. They knew the Czechoslovak delegation was divided and they hinted strongly that if they refused to comply with Russian demands not only would they be putting their own lives and liberties in jeopardy but risking large-scale bloodshed in Czechoslovakia. The Czechs and Slovaks who had just been released from prison were badly shaken, having been shown – literally – instruments of torture, and having mentally accepted that they would be tortured and killed.[73] Dubcek himself was weak and ill, under heavy sedation, and unable to take part in most of the discussions. What finally convinced him, and the pro-Dubcek group, to sign the Moscow

Protocols on 26 August was the fear that the resistance on the streets of Prague, Bratislava and elsewhere would take a tragic turn and result in massacres, and the hope that by agreeing to sign they could rescue something from the wreckage, prevent the minority of pro-Moscow hacks within the party from taking over, and gradually re-introduce reforms, as Kadar had succeeded in doing in Hungary after 1956. In the end only one man, Frantisek Kriegel, refused to sign them. He escaped being held prisoner in Moscow only at the insistence of his colleagues that he should accompany them back to Prague.

The Protocols represented some concessions on the Soviet side, most notably the agreement to allow Dubcek, Prime Minister Cernik, and President of the National Assembly Smrkovsky to resume their previous offices. But these were temporary concessions which the Soviet side had every intention of circumventing at the earliest possible moment, whilst those on the Czechoslovak side were substantial and damaging. They were forced to repudiate the decisions of the 14th Congress, to agree to the re-imposition of censorship, to accept the 'temporary' presence of Soviet forces in the country during a period of 'normalisation', and to withdraw the Czechoslovak issue from the agenda of the Security Council. Worst of all, the terms of the Protocols enjoined that they should remain secret. So instead of the Czechoslovak people and the world as a whole hearing the details of the Protocols, they had to make do with a bland communiqué stating that an accord had been reached between the two sides.

While the 'negotiations' had been going on, resistance continued and indeed escalated inside Czechoslovakia itself. On 25 August the Slovak Party Congress followed the lead of the Czech Party in holding a special Party Congress, and it too condemned the invasion. (This decision was subsequently reversed.) On 26 August, the day the Protocols were signed in Moscow, there was a countrywide protest strike of twenty-five minutes, and the government, Parliament and Central Trade Union Council issued a joint proclamation on the need for discipline under conditions of unarmed resistance. The confidence and élan of the resistance is captured in an editorial in the journal *Reporter* on 26 August:

> We are morally victors. The staging of the aggression has, in the short term, been blocked. The aggressors have been checked by a united resistance of our two nations, unknown up to now in history . . . The army of occupation is completely isolated, powerless and totally rejected . . . The occupiers have occupied the printing works, but the newspapers have nonetheless been published several times a day; they have occupied the radio, but the radio transmits freely; they have occupied the television without succeeding in silencing it.[74]

With the return of the Czechoslovak delegation, the unity of the resistance was broken. The people were asked to desist from their protests, unaware even of the deal that had been struck. The élan of the previous days was replaced by confusion and bitterness. Yet having placed so much faith in the political leadership, and made Dubcek and Svoboda symbols of national unity, the people could not now go against their decisions. In the succeeding months, further concessions were wrung from the Czechoslovak authorities, particularly on the matter of the Soviet troops that remained there in force. One by one the reformist leaders were squeezed out, and seven months later Dubcek himself was ousted and replaced by Husak. Finally, there was a massive purge of pro-Dubcek, or suspected pro-Dubcek, supporters within the Party, the army and all official bodies. A third of all Party members were expelled.

It is clear, then, that the resistance was not defeated in the streets but in the Kremlin 'negotiations' which indeed hardly merit that term. (Mylnar, who was present in Moscow, states that the position of the Czechoslovak delegation was more like that of hostages held by gangsters than of representatives of an independent state parleying on equal terms with those of another state.) Could it have continued and even succeeded had Dubcek and the others refused to sign the Moscow Protocols? Several of them seriously considered refusing to sign, and wondered if this was the moment when Czechoslovakia should redeem her honour by an heroic stance to the bitter end against the invaders. However, reluctance to take a position that could well lead to massacre deterred them. There is, of course, no way of knowing for sure if continued civil resistance could have forced a Soviet withdrawal. Presumably, if the Soviet leaders were determined and ruthless enough, they could have ended the public resistance in the streets, in the manner of the Chinese authorities in Tiananmen Square in 1989. The probability is that the Czechoslovak resistance would have then had to settle down for a longer-term campaign. One factor, however, that might have changed this would have been if the example of Czechoslovakia at this point had provoked unarmed insurrections across Eastern Europe – such as those that did occur in 1989.

As it was, resistance did continue, much of it in low-key ways. Jan Palach's self-immolation in Wenceslas Square in January 1969 had a dramatic impact, both inside and outside the country. Originally, a number of other students and young people had planned to act in the same way, but he expressed the wish from his hospital bed as he lay dying that they should give up this plan, and work in other ways for Czechoslovakia's liberation.[75] Small groups of courageous individuals continued to resist during the years of repression, some spending lengthy periods in prison, others operating from outside the country acting as channels of communication to the outside world, and providing the opposition within the country with books, periodicals and equipment.

The formation of Charter 77, and the public stance of leading writers and intellectuals against the regime, played a major part in keeping hope, and a form of cultural and intellectual resistance, alive. And although it was, in the main, a new generation who took to the streets again in their hundreds of thousands in 1989 and finally succeeded in overthrowing a corrupt and demoralised Party, the continuities in terms of ideas, methods and personalities with the resistance of 1968 are transparent. On the night after Party Secretary Jakes (one of the anti-Dubcek conspirators in 1968) and the whole Politburo resigned in November 1989,

Dubcek stood with Vaclav Havel on a balcony overlooking Wenceslas Square and opened his arms in a gesture of embrace to the 250,000 unarmed, cheering people below.

Chapter 4

The Dynamics of Non-Violent Action

Introduction

Governments need people more than people need governments. If one wanted a slogan that expressed in a few words the political philosophy underlying the concept of civil resistance, this would do as well as any.

There is, of course, more to it than that. For one thing, it is not only states and governments which derive their power from the cooperation of people, but institutions and groups at all levels within society. Nor do all power struggles where civil resistance is employed necessarily involve the state or government as one of the protagonists. However, since the focus in this study is chiefly on conflicts where the state or government is involved, the slogan provides a convenient point of departure.

In Chapter 1 we considered the links between power, authority and popular cooperation. A brief recap may be helpful here before discussing the social and political mechanisms by which civil resistance can bring about change.

Governments, it was pointed out, require the allegiance of key institutions to operate at all – the armed forces, civil servants, administrators. Beyond that they need the cooperation, or at least the compliance, of the majority of the population they seek to govern. Modern industrial society in particular requires a high degree of cooperation by the workforce to function effectively. This has given organised labour an important leverage which it has used at various times since the early nineteenth century to force economic and political concessions. At the present time, when the mass media play such a major role in people's lives, the cooperation of those who work within them may be hardly less important than that of the armed services. Thus, at the height of the Czechoslovak 'velvet revolution', the workers in the State Television Service voted overwhelmingly in favour of transmitting live coverage of the demonstrations in Wenceslas Square and broadcasting a film showing student demonstrators being attacked by the security forces.[1] Other institutions and groups that make up civil society, such as the Churches and political, environmental and community organisations, can also play a crucial role in shaping opinion and providing potential centres of dissent and opposition.

Dictatorial governments may use force, or outright terror, to secure the compliance of the population and this may succeed, sometimes over prolonged periods. In these circumstances, civil society, in so far as it exists at all, will tend to operate clandestinely, and the media is likely to be under tight government control. Even in such extreme cases, however, governments do not rule by force alone. The willingness of the individual soldier to obey orders may be engendered by fear of the consequences of disobedience, but the collective allegiance of the armed services and security forces is dependent on something more intangible – the *authority* of the government and the acceptance of its claim to *legitimacy*.

Civil resistance seeks to challenge the authority and legitimacy of the government and thereby also to deprive it of its source of power in the cooperation of society and state institutions. Where the goal is to remove a specific injustice – such as race discrimination – the challenge to the government's authority is limited; its legitimacy in general is not in question, simply its right to pass or enforce certain laws, or to tolerate particular practices within society. In a more fundamental struggle, civil resistance challenges the government's right to rule and may also contest the whole political and social system within which it operates.

More often than not, coercion is involved in such struggles, not in the sense that violence is used against the opponents, but that certain options are closed off to them, are rendered literally impossible to pursue. The numbers of protesters or strikers may be too great for the authorities to cope with. Jails may be filled to capacity, the economy halted by strikes, the administration brought to a standstill. Resort by the authorities to naked violence – assuming the political and social environment is such as to make this an option – may prove counter-productive, mobilising further opposition at home and abroad, and in the extreme provoking a refusal to cooperate by the police, the military and public servants. The political allies of the authorities may desert them – as happened for instance in both Poland and East Germany in 1989, where the small, formerly client, political parties moved over to the opposition.

We consider in a later chapter the particular problems associated with civil resistance in democratic, or partially democratic, countries where the government rests its claim to legitimacy on the mandate of the electorate. Meanwhile, we may note that even under dictatorial regimes civil resistance will often be directed against a particular aspect of government policy, rather than against the regime as such. However, because authoritarian governments claim absolute authority, a successful challenge by the population to any major aspect of policy can bring about its downfall, or at any rate start the process of disintegration. Thus in Eastern Europe the demand for basic human rights was in one sense limited, yet it posed a radical challenge to the structure and political philosophy of the Leninist state. In this respect dictatorial rule has frequently proved to be at once more rigid and more brittle than democratic systems.

Moral and political jiu-jitsu

The impact of non-violent action has been compared to jiu-jitsu. This analogy was first suggested by the American author Richard Gregg, in his classic study of Gandhian methods published in the 1930s.[2] In a chapter entitled 'Moral Jiu-Jitsu', Gregg argues that just as in jiu-jitsu the defender utilises the force of the attacker to throw him or her *physically* off balance, so the non-violent resister throws the opponent *morally* off balance by the unexpectedness of his or her response. The aggressor expects a reaction of counter-violence or at least a display of fear or anger. Meeting neither, but instead a calm determination not to give way or to strike back, he (or she) is both surprised and perplexed. 'The non-violence and good will of the victim act like the lack of physical opposition by the user of physical jiu-jitsu to cause the attacker to lose his moral balance.'[3]

Gregg goes on to elaborate a moral and psychological explanation for the workings of non-violence at an interpersonal level, emphasising the impact of suffering borne with patience and fearlessness. Some of his claims rest on a quasi-religious view that 'except for a few congenital mental defectives and incorrigible desperate convicts, every person has in them at least some tiny spark or potentiality of goodness . . .' In subsequent chapters, however, Gregg examines the dynamics of *collective*, as opposed to individual, non-violent action, and here he has insights which were to be taken up by later writers of the more tough-minded and 'pragmatic' school. Nevertheless, he continues to emphasise voluntary self-suffering as the mainspring of *satyagraha*, and conversion of the opponent as the means by which the issue in dispute will be resolved:

> As to the outcome of the struggle waged by non-violence, we must understand one point thoroughly. The aim of the non-violent resister is not to injure, or crush and humiliate his opponent, or to 'break his will', as in a violent fight. The aim is to convert the opponent, to change his understanding and his sense of values so that he will join wholeheartedly with the resister in seeking a settlement truly amicable and truly satisfying to both sides.[4]

It is a classic statement of what Boserup and Mack term the 'positive' view of conflict which is present, if somewhat ambiguously, in Gandhi's own writings, and rather more categorically in those of some of his interpreters. (See the discussion below.)

From a more pragmatic standpoint, Gene Sharp later took up the notion of jiu-jitsu in discussing collective non-violent action.

He refers not to 'moral jiu-jitsu' but 'political jiu-jitsu', and employs the term as a way of examining how the attempt to apply repression against civil resistance can backfire on those who employ it.[5] Repression, Sharp argues, if met with disciplined non-violence, is likely to increase sympathy among the general population for the resisters and antipathy and contempt for the regime. It may alienate sections of the population whose support the regime had earlier enjoyed, and thus narrow its power base. It may even move large numbers to participate actively in the campaign, despite the costs, and in favourable circumstances lead to the opponent's downfall. Thus the violent attack on student demonstrators in Prague on 17 November, 1989 was the spark that ignited mass opposition in Czechoslovakia. Third parties are likely to be similarly affected, and this could lead to sanctions and other forms of pressure applied internationally. Finally, the police, armed forces and functionaries of the regime or occupying power may be sickened and repelled by the repeated use of violence against unarmed and non-violent resisters and turn against their masters.

Among the examples Sharp gives are the massacre of petitioners at the Winter Palace in St Petersburg in January 1905 which ignited a general rebellion, the killings of hundreds of demonstrators in March 1917 which led to mutinies, desertions and further mass protests and the eventual resignation of the Tsar in the 'February Revolution', and the beatings, killings and bombings of civil rights protesters in the US in the 1950s and 1960s which had the effect of winning American and international support for the civil rights cause.

Civil resistance and the sociological mechanisms of change

While conversion of the opponent is emphasised by those who adopt the positive view of conflict, it is seen as only one of several mechanisms of change by those who lean towards the 'negative' view of conflict (see the discussion below). Indeed, for the latter, conversion is regarded as unlikely to play a central role in major collective conflict as far as the principal protagonists are concerned. George Lakey, in a Masters thesis in 1962, proposed three main sociological mechanisms of change which were adopted and slightly modified by Sharp in his presentations. They are (in Sharp's formulation): conversion, accommodation and coercion.[6] In his most recent work on 'civilian-based defence'[7], Sharp postulates a fourth mechanism – disintegration.

Conversion refers to the situation where the opponent has a genuine change of heart, having been won over by the argument, or the willingness of the resisters to suffer hardship, imprisonment and even death for their convictions. Its relevance in major struggles between large groups is problematic, and we consider the matter below.

Accommodation describes the process whereby the opposing group, recognising that the balance of forces is shifting against it, opts for negotiation and compromise. It would be physically possible to continue the struggle, but it is judged opportune to reach a settlement because the political and other costs of persisting with it are too high, and perhaps because there is a clear prospect of ultimate defeat. In Poland in 1988–9, General Jaruzelski sought accommodation with the opposition forces when he agreed to round-table talks with Solidarity. This led over a period of months to a peaceful transfer of power. At a less total level of confrontation, the Conservative government in Britain in 1990 found it necessary to withdraw the poll tax, in part because the campaign of civil disobedience was making it prohibitively difficult and expensive to impose, in part because the political backlash had begun to threaten its chances of re-election.

Coercion was touched upon earlier. It refers to the situation in which the opponent's will is forced or thwarted as a result of civil resistance. This may occur in three sets of circumstances. First, the defiance is too widespread to be repressed and social, political and economic change occurs – or is thwarted, as the case may be – regardless of the will of the opponents. Quisling did not change his mind about introducing Nazi indoctrination in the schools of occupied Norway; the non-cooperation of the entire teaching profession made it impossible for him to carry out the plan. Second, widespread non-cooperation may bring the administration and economy – or crucial parts of it – to a standstill, and it may be impossible to get things moving again without acceding to the demands of the protesters. In this way Czar Nicholas II was coerced by the general strike of 1905 to issue the constitutional manifesto of 7 October granting a *duma* (Parliament). Similarly, employers have been coerced into granting recognition of trade unions and allowing them to operate despite, in many instances, their total opposition to such a move. Third, the opponents may lose the capacity to repress the resistance because of the non-cooperation of the police, the army and the bureaucracy. The Shah of Iran was forced to flee the country in 1979 when the army commanders ordered their troops back to the barracks and refused to take further part in the repression. Ferdinand and Imelda Marcos fled from the Philippines when the army refused to open fire on tens of thousands of demonstrators blocking their path in the streets of Manila. In East Germany and Czechoslovakia, the communist governments were forced out of office by mass demonstrations. Similarly, the coup leaders in the Soviet Union in August 1991 found themselves literally unable to hold on to power.

Disintegration. This refers to the situation where the opponent's power structure collapses altogether under the pressure of civil resistance. Sharp distinguishes it from coercion on the grounds that there is no longer a government or political unit to be coerced. Such a point will not be reached, however, without successful coercive pressure on the government or political unit prior to its disintegration. Sharp cites the Kapp putsch in 1920 and the Algiers generals' coup in 1961 among examples where the power base of the usurpers disintegrated. But clearly that disintegration was the result of a process in which the usurpers found it impossible to impose their will on the situation.

Positive and negative modes of waging conflict

Civil resistance can be seen as primarily either a 'positive' or 'negative' mode of waging conflict.[8] The first approach assumes that persuasion and conversion are the essential mechanisms of change. The second is more in line with the traditional, antagonistic view of conflict, and thus accepts that coercion will often be necessary.[9]

Satyagraha, as defined by most of its exponents – though somewhat more ambivalently by Gandhi himself – belongs to the positive approach. It proceeds in stages from discussion and negotiation at the outset through to voluntary self-suffering by the resister, and finally to non-cooperation and civil disobedience. However, the intention, even in the last phase, is not to coerce the opponent but to arrive at a common understanding of the situation and the demands of truth and justice. The self-imposed suffering of the resisters and the withdrawal of cooperation are seen alike as ways of concentrating the mind of the opponent on the reality and seriousness of the issues involved, and inviting him or her to consider them anew.

Exponents of the negative mode see their approach as more pragmatic, more attuned to the real world. They do not rule out conversion in some instances, or at some levels, in the opposing group, but their theory does not depend on any particular assumption about the psychology or moral sensibility of the opponent. The pragmatists can themselves be divided into those who consider that civil resistance has (or may have) the potential to undermine the power of even the most ruthless of opponents, and those who see its viability as rather more limited by the nature of the opponent and the circumstances of the struggle. Those in the latter category normally argue the need to have other forms of enforcement and defence available, including military force.[10]

In practice, the division between the positive and negative approaches is not always clear-cut, since non-cooperation is a technique central to both. In the positive approach it is seen as functioning as a catalyst of conversion; in the negative or antagonistic approach as an instrument of coercion. From the point of view of the opponent, however, the distinction is likely to be regarded as academic. A campaign of mass civil disobedience will come across as coercive whatever the declared intention of its organisers. It was how the British government saw the non-cooperation and civil disobedience campaigns in India in 1920–2 and 1930–1, and perhaps even more so the Quit India campaign of 1942, whatever the protestations to the contrary by Gandhi and the Congress leaders.

Gandhi had a foot in both camps. He appears to be in the positive camp by the very choice of the term *satyagraha* – 'truth force' or 'soul force' – and his emphasis on voluntary suffering to touch the heart of the opponent. His letters to Smuts during the South African campaigns, and to successive viceroys in India on the eve of non-cooperation and civil disobedience, are in keeping with this emphasis on conversion rather than coercion.

But he also followed La Boëtie and Thoreau in insisting that governments could not operate without the cooperation of the people, thereby acknowledging the potentially coercive power of withdrawing that cooperation. It is evident too that many – perhaps a majority – of those who participated in the campaigns under Gandhi's leadership saw them as a way of applying pressure on India's British rulers, rather than as a means of touching their hearts. Indeed, Gandhi himself was too astute a politician not to appreciate the bind in which his campaigns of mass civil disobedience, or, for instance, his hunger strike in 1932 over the issue of separate representation for the Harijans (Untouchables), placed the British authorities.

This is not to suggest that Gandhi's continuing efforts to exert positive means of influence over both supporters and opponents were without effect. In both South Africa and India, he managed most of the time to keep the lines of communication with the opponent open – with Smuts in South Africa and with successive viceroys in India. His public fasts were mostly aimed at self-purification or directed at his fellow Indians in an effort to prevent or end communal bloodshed. Finally, if the British authorities did not experience a change of heart as a result of the *satyagraha* campaigns, many third parties were deeply affected by the conduct and demeanour of the resisters and the drama of the public demonstrations. Third parties here included the British public, and the public and governments of countries allied to, or on friendly terms with, Britain.

The extent to which the positive mode has the chance to operate will vary, in fact, according to the nature and scale of the conflict. Conversion is more likely to occur in struggles between individuals or small groups than in major political confrontations. There is also greater scope for it, and for a process of mediation and reconciliation, where a conflict arises more out of misperception and misjudgement than out of a genuine divergence of interests. Where there is such a fundamental clash of interests, especially between large collectivities, the issue is likely to be settled by a power struggle, rather than through one side convincing the other of the justice of its cause. Nevertheless, moral and political factors remain decisive. The opponent does not have to be converted, but his or her authority – either in general or in relation to a particular aspect of policy – has to be undermined.

Polarisation

One factor which makes the positive approach difficult to apply in situations of large-scale group conflict is the phenomenon of polarisation.[11] *Polarisation* is a process unique to group conflict. It is characterised by the closing of ranks within each group, and the drawing of a sharper boundary line between them which individuals cross at their peril. Extreme polarisation tends to produce undesirable and ugly symptoms – intolerance of dissent, hostility to 'neutral' parties coupled with intense pressure on them to come into line, stereotyping of the opposing group and its views, a tendency to treat its members as less than human, and so forth. These manifestations are often seen at their worst in wartime, particularly in ethnic conflicts. However, some degree of polarisation seems to be an inevitable, and indeed necessary, concomitant of any group conflict. It can be regarded as a social mechanism for achieving concerted action to complement, or replace, centralised controls and sanctions. Thus in Czechoslovakia in 1968, following the Soviet-led invasion, the united front of Czech and Slovak populations against the occupiers deterred the would-be collaborators within the Central Committee of the Czechoslovak Communist Party from declaring their hand and attempting to form a client government. Another positive feature is the heightening of individual self-esteem and group morale which follows from the close identification of the individual with the group. This effect is evident in both violent and non-violent struggles – in the guerrilla warfare campaigns in Cuba and Vietnam, but no less in the Indian independence struggle and the civil rights campaigns in the United States. Polarisation is likely to be particularly acute in the circumstances of, say, a foreign invasion and occupation, or of a settler population attempting by force to maintain its position of power and privilege. By contrast, in some of the European colonies in Africa and Asia where there was a relatively small settler population and a measure of self-government had gradually been introduced, the situation as the countries moved to independence was much less polarised. This allowed greater scope for the positive mode of exerting influence and waging conflict. Gandhi in India, for instance, was operating in a less polarised situation than, say, the Hungarians in 1956, or the Czechs and Slovaks in 1968. Indeed, one of his tasks, like that of so many of the leaders of liberation movements, was actually to increase polarisation by arousing the population to a sense of the injustice and indignity of continued colonial rule, and consolidating group identity so that people were willing to take collective action. In internal struggles, such as that of the civil rights movement in the US, or the struggle for black majority rule in South Africa, the degree of polarisation will vary. In South Africa, it was less acute during the period of Gandhi's campaigns in the early years of the century on behalf of the Indian population than at the time of the Defiance of Unjust Laws campaign in 1952, a few years after the electoral triumph of the Nationalist party and the introduction of apartheid.

The difficulty about applying the positive approach in a highly polarised situation is that it requires contact and communication between the contending parties, the constant reinforcement of goodwill, a mutual endeavour to find common ground – all of which go against the grain in such conditions, and may indeed confuse and divide the population. Thus a policy of fraternisation with opposing troops and officials where a country is under occupation from foreign forces might be seen as the most desirable strategy from the standpoint of the positive approach – rather than, say, ostracisation and social and economic boycott. But such a policy faces a double difficulty. On the opponent's side it is likely to be regarded as a ploy. On the defending side it may be seen by many as a step in the direction of collaboration. Some proponents of the positive approach have proposed a policy that distinguishes the individual soldier or official from his or her function. Thus there would be fraternisation with individual solders – for instance, by welcoming them into one's home – but refusal to cooperate with them in their role as occupiers. In practice this would be a difficult line to draw, and presupposes a civilian population that is highly trained and disciplined and fully understands the strategy that is being pursued.

Of course, those who take the negative approach will for their own reasons want to communicate with occupying forces and officials. Their explicit purpose, however, will be to open up divisions in the opposing side, while making it clear beyond doubt that the right of the aggressor to station forces in the country is totally rejected. Actions here may be a more effective means of communication than words – i.e. non-cooperation coupled with refraining from violent retaliation. The opportunities for verbal communication with the opposing forces are likely to be limited, especially if the opposing regime is aware of the tactics that are being planned. However, such opportunities will tend to be greater in the case of a coup d'état than in that of an invasion by a foreign power, and greater with a mainly conscript army than with an entirely professional one.

To sum up, we can say that in any conflict situation involving large groups of people a degree of polarisation is inevitable. It is likely to be more acute in some situations than others – more acute, for instance, in the immediate aftermath of invasion and occupation than where a pattern of domination of one group by another has come to be seen as almost inevitable. Resistance, whether violent or non-violent in character, will have the effect of increasing polarisation. This is desirable in so far as it strengthens group cohesion and raises morale. However, civil resistance is somewhat less likely than guerrilla or conventional warfare, or terrorism, to give rise to extremes of hatred and intolerance. Indeed, where civil resistance implies a commitment to promoting non-violent solutions, the resistance leadership may take active steps to inhibit the negative manifestations of polarisation. Gandhi in India, Luther King in the United States, Desmond Tutu and Alan Boesak in South Africa, provide examples where such efforts were made. They will not always be successful, but in general one can say that non-violent civil resistance challenges injustice but seeks to inhibit the undesirable features of group conflict and to keep open channels of communication with the opponent.

Elements of a non-violent strategy

In an earlier chapter we noted one approach to classifying the methods of non-violent resistance based mainly on the work of Gene Sharp. He proposed three main categories: methods of protest and persuasion; non-cooperation at social, economic and political levels; and non-violent intervention.[12] Marches, vigils, pickets and the like come under the first category. Social non-cooperation would include the ostracisation of individuals, boycotts of social, academic, artistic and sporting institutions, and total personal non-cooperation. Economic non-cooperation includes strikes of various kinds, go-slows, economic boycotts and sanctions. Political non-cooperation covers such things as boycotts of legislative assemblies, defiance of particular laws, and the boycott of government-supported organisations. Finally, examples of non-violent intervention would be sit-ins, obstruction, fasts and hunger strikes. Sharp listed ninety-eight methods within these major categories.

Boserup and Mack, by contrast, group the methods of non-violent action according to their strategic function. They propose three main categories: symbolic action; denial action; and undermining action.

Symbolic action. Symbolism plays a crucial role in defining and consolidating a community. Symbolic demonstrations – which can cover a wide spectrum of activities – have a threefold function. They draw public attention to a claim or grievance; they are an expression of the unity and determination of the resistance; and they challenge the uncommitted to take a stand in relation to it. Thus they contribute to the polarising process discussed earlier and, in the words of Boserup and Mack, 'serve to define the resistance as a moral community which may then provide a powerful basis for sanctions such as ostracism or social boycott (isolation) of dissenters, collaborators, etc.'[13]

Actions strongly charged with symbolic significance can energise the participants, and have an emotional and galvanising impact on the wider public. They are a form of 'propaganda by the deed'. They communicate at a level deeper than words the conviction that change is possible, and the determination of the resistance to achieve it. Thus they can contribute to the solution of a problem which any group or movement challenging the status quo has to face: namely, that the existing social and political reality takes on an aura of normality and inevitability. Governments and regimes which enjoy minimal support and legitimacy rely heavily on this disempowering sense of the normalcy of the existing order to maintain their authority.

Denial action aims to deprive the opponent of the fruits of aggression or of an unjust social, political or economic order. Strikes, boycotts, go-slows, non-violent obstruction are means by which material and 'non-material' objectives can be denied to the opponent. (Non-material objectives would include such things as establishing – or maintaining – authority, imposing a political ideology, and – in the aftermath of a coup or occupation – receiving *de facto* or *de jure* recognition by the international community as the government of a territory.) Thus industrial strikes can raise the costs of any attempt to exploit the economic resources of the country. Strikes and obstruction by civil servants and officials can hamper the opponent's attempt to establish an administration, raise taxes, impose new laws and regulations. Opposition and non-cooperation by teachers, academics, religious leaders and so forth can make it much more difficult for the opponent to achieve ideological objectives. Campaigns of civil disobedience can obstruct the administration and present the authorities with a dilemma. If they ignore the defiance, their authority has been successfully challenged. If they use draconian methods to suppress non-violent protest they may lose moral and political standing at home and abroad.

It will be clear from the above discussion that denial actions are most effective when they are simultaneously charged with symbolic significance. Thus, at a physical level, it could be more effective to obstruct the entrance to, say, a military base with barriers such as immobilised lorries than to have people sitting down on the road in front of vehicles trying to go in and out of the base. But the symbolism associated with people putting their own bodies on the line, and perhaps risking injury or death, would be lost. This is not to say that there are no circumstances in which the use of physical barricades would be the appropriate tactic. It is simply to stress again the point that the moral and psychological impact is more important than the obstruction as such.

Undermining actions. Undermining actions are those which seek to open up and exploit divisions within the opponent's camp, and to deny it the cooperation of third parties. Clearly, many of what we have termed symbolic and denial activities serve also to undermine the confidence and unity of the opponent. But campaigning actions can also be directed specifically at opening up and exploiting divisions within the opponent's ranks. In the case of a dictatorial regime, this could mean finding ways of rupturing the links between it and that section of society which has hitherto given it support, exploiting disagreements within the ruling clique, seeking to win over previously neutral or indifferent groups or sections of society. In the case of a foreign occupation it could include encouraging disaffection among occupying forces and officials, splitting the opponent on the home front, and seeking international support and sanctions.

There is an on-going debate as to the best means of encouraging disaffection among occupying forces and officials in the context of a foreign occupation. Fraternisation, even at an individual level, is likely to arouse suspicion within the defender's own ranks that collaboration rather than subversion is taking place. Non-cooperation is less ambiguous and may be more effective – though of course it may be coupled with engaging the opponent's forces in open public discussion as happened on the streets of Prague and other cities in Czechoslovakia in 1968.

The potential for opening up divisions within the home country of an occupying power, and seeking allies among opposition groups and independent social institutions such as Churches, centres of learning, and so on, will be affected by the nature of the opponent's regime. We have noted how Gandhi availed himself of the opportunity provided by the Round Table Conference in London in 1931 to meet individuals who might have an influence on the situation and to address religious bodies, university gatherings and other groups, including some of the cotton workers in Lancashire whose jobs had been jeopardised by the Congress-sponsored boycott of foreign cloth. Similarly, Ho Chi Minh visited France in 1946 and rallied support there for the Vietnamese cause. Clearly, such activities are easier to conduct where the occupying or colonial power has a reasonably open and democratic system. Nevertheless, dictatorial governments too have their critics and opponents at home, and there is usually some scope for an occupied country to secure friends and allies amongst them.

Finally there is the need to seek sympathy and active support in the international community. Enlisting support among the political and religious organisations of countries allied to, or having an influence on, the opponent can be particularly important here. In this case the aim ultimately is to get the governments and populations of these countries to apply coercive pressure on the opponents. Among the other obvious goals in this connection are enlisting the support of international bodies such as the United Nations and the European Community, international peace and human rights organisations like Amnesty International, peace movements, socialist and social democratic internationals, and so forth. Probably the most striking success of efforts to enlist international support at the level of individual countries, and international governmental and non-governmental bodies, is the anti-apartheid and pro-democracy movement in South Africa. The Palestinians in the West Bank and Gaza have had successes in this field, too, especially since the start of the *Intifada* resistance.

In a later chapter on defence by civil resistance we consider how the various means of exerting pressure on an opponent can be marshalled to constitute a coherent strategy. It is in the context of a major national struggle – and preparation for it – that strategy assumes a central importance. Hence the decision to discuss it in detail in that context.

The problem of repression

Repression is potentially the most severe problem for a civil resistance movement. At some level it is inevitable, is invited almost, by the very act of resisting an authoritarian or dictatorial government, or occupation regime, or challenging a well-entrenched system of domination and oppression. Indeed, a willingness to endure such hardship and suffering, and to persevere in the face of it, can have a powerful moral impact. As we noted earlier, repression has frequently proved entirely counter-productive. However, in some instances, it has been severe enough to disrupt the organisation and undermine the morale of the resistance, the Sharpeville massacre in South Africa in 1960 being a case in point.

Repression, however, also carries political costs for the side which perpetrates it. Any rational government, therefore, is obliged to weigh these in the balance when deciding how to respond to the challenge of civil resistance. In Beijing in June 1989, the Chinese authorities decided that the balance of risks and costs favoured military intervention and massacre. In East Germany a few months later, Erich Honecker lacked the support of Gorbachev – his key external ally – and of sufficient members of his own party to take similar action against the mass demonstrations in Leipzig, Dresden and Berlin. We have also noted earlier how the British government felt constrained from acting too harshly against the civil resistance in India in 1920–2 and again in 1930–1, but was much better placed to do so during the Quit India campaign of 1942.

For its part, therefore, the resistance movement has to consider how the government is likely to respond and to shape its plans accordingly. It may have to decide, for example, if it is an appropriate moment for an all-out confrontation, or whether it would be more prudent to concentrate on other forms of opposition. However, the 'prudent' course will not always be the right one. If the morale and authority of the government are clearly tottering, all-out resistance may be the right course of action, despite the near certainty that there will be repression and perhaps a heavy loss of life. Sometimes, of course, events will be out of the control of the resistance leadership, as when the anger and frustration of years of repression express themselves in an explosion of popular anger. The ANC in South Africa in the early 1990s is finding it difficult to channel the pent-up anger of its supporters in the townships.

Steps can often be taken which strengthen the constraints against the use of violence by the opponent. Generally a government is more likely to act circumspectly if it knows that its actions are being observed by the national and international media, and by other governments and organisations. For this reason it is clearly in the interest of a resistance movement to ensure that actions take place under the public gaze. When the Freedom and Peace movement (*Wolnosc i Pokoj* – WiP) in Poland undertook their first public demonstrations in 1985, they made a point of informing their friends in the Western peace movement, Radio Free Europe and other Western media, and the Polish underground press, of their intentions. They made sure also that the Polish authorities knew of these moves so that they would understand that their responses to the demonstration were being closely monitored. This was effective in preventing police assaults, and deterring the courts from handing out punitive sentences.[14] There are countless similar instances of resistance movements using advance publicity and the presence of the international media as a shield against excessive retaliation by the authorities.

The form of demonstrations may also be varied to reduce the risk of repression. In 1970, and again in 1976, the Polish army and security forces used tanks and firearms to break up demonstrations by striking workers. This experience was taken into account when the workers in the Lenin Shipyard in Gdansk in 1980, at the time of the birth of Solidarity, opted for a sit-in strike rather than once again taking to the streets.[15]

Actions in which the resisters voluntarily impose hardship and suffering upon themselves rather than directly confronting the opponent have a tendency (though of course no more than a tendency) to inhibit a violent response. Fasts and hunger strikes are the clearest examples of this. In the earlier historical chapters we noted examples of these in Bolivia in 1978 and in Uruguay in 1983.

There may, however, be periods during which the extremity of the repression makes any open confrontation unwise. In such times, symbolic acts such as the wearing of badges, the singing of national songs, the observance of national traditions, can contribute to keeping alive a culture of resistance. Such activities may be supplemented by go-slows and other forms of economic and administrative obstruction which are difficult if not impossible for the opponent to detect or counter. Even at the height of World War II, resistance along these lines occurred in all the countries of occupied Europe.

Meanwhile, the task of building up base communities and organisational networks can continue in an unobtrusive or clandestine fashion. The work in this respect may include the publication of underground newspapers and magazines, the smuggling in of literature, printing and transmitting equipment, the establishment of lines of communication with foreign media, international organisations, and so on. Churches sometimes occupy a privileged position under repressive regimes of both right and left, and can provide an important locus of dissent. This has been true, for instance, in Poland, East Germany, South Africa, and many countries in Central and South America. In Latin America, in particular, the development of 'liberation theology' has provided a crucial underpinning for emancipatory movements. The pattern in several countries in this region has been that after a more or less prolonged period of clandestine and grass-roots activity, including symbolic and 'micro-resistance', a dictatorial government has found it necessary to make concessions to keep the economy and administration going, and to try to allay international hostility. This in turn has made possible more open, public dissent. Such, as noted earlier, is the way things developed in Chile and Uruguay in the late 1970s and 1980s.

Finally, the weapon of humour should never be overlooked. Its puncturing effect on official propaganda throughout Eastern Europe during the period of communist rule has been well documented. Some opposition groups also managed to incorporate humour and irony into their demonstrations – as for instance when WiP in Poland in the mid-1980s staged a street drama in ironic celebration of the Russian Revolution.[16]

Clearly, then, there are circumstances in which a campaign of *confrontational* civil resistance has little immediate prospects of success, and perhaps should not be attempted. This is not of itself, however, an argument for abandoning civil resistance altogether. What may be called for instead is a longer-term strategy of cultural and 'semi-resistance' which eventually renders the regime vulnerable to open defiance. The successes of 'people power' over the last decade or so – often preceded by such a prolonged, low-key resistance – have shown that even regimes that seemed at one point irremovable except by war may be vulnerable in the end to non-violent power.

Chapter 5

An Alternative Defence? –
the Birth of a Concept

Origins

If civil resistance is capable of undermining an oppressive or alien regime, could it replace military preparations, in whole or in part, for the defence of a country or alliance of countries?

Bertrand Russell raised the idea back in 1915 in an article in the *Atlantic Monthly*, arguing that after a generation of training, the British population could defeat a German occupation by systematic non-cooperation.[1] Even earlier than that, in the mid-nineteenth century, the US pacifist Elihu Burritt argued that a country could defend its freedom through non-violent forms of resistance.[2] However, these were straws in the wind, and serious consideration of the idea did not take place until later in the present century.

Gandhi's campaigns in South Africa and India rekindled interest in the concept. This was encouraged by Gandhi himself, who made many pronouncements on non-violent national defence dating mainly from the 1930s in response to the growing world crisis. In a sense, indeed, his major campaigns in India were an example of non-violent national defence aimed at removing the effects of long-standing occupation.

The 1920s and 1930s saw the publication of some of the early classics on non-violence and civil resistance by pacifist writers: Clarence Marsh Case's *Non-Violent Coercion* (1923)[3], Richard Gregg's *The Power of Non-Violence* (1935)[4], and Bart de Ligt's *The Conquest of Violence* (1937)[5]. Case did not specifically address the

121

question of non-violence as a national defence. Gregg came closer to doing so in so far as he devoted much attention to the parallels between mass non-violent action and war; his contribution, and that of De Ligt, to the development of strategy is considered in the next chapter. In 1939, Krishnalal Shridharani published *War without Violence: A Study of Gandhi's Method and Its Accomplishments*[6], in which he argued that Gandhi's militant non-violence was a way of resisting both aggression and tyranny without war, thus solving the classical dilemma of traditional pacifism. The notion of using non-violent resistance as an alternative to military defence to resist invasion is tentatively advanced in the final pages of the book.

The outbreak of war and the occupation of much of Europe by German forces, and of considerable territory in Asia and the Pacific by the Japanese, refocused attention in pacifist circles on possible non-violent responses to invasion and occupation. Among the essays written during this period was one published by the War Resisters League in the United States by Jessie Wallace Hughan entitled *Pacifism and Invasion*, proposing a national policy of non-cooperation in the event of an invasion of the US – however improbable that eventuality might be.[7]

From a more pragmatic starting point, the military and political commentator Commander Stephen King-Hall urged the Danish government in 1938 to give serious consideration to non-violent resistance as an alternative to military defence in view of its vulnerability if Germany were to attack.[8] Whilst his proposals were not taken up at the time, Denmark did not in the event attempt to resist the German invasion in 1940 by military means, whereas its civilian population did engage in both paramilitary and non-violent resistance. The achievements of civil resistance in Denmark, and throughout occupied Europe, were considerable. Broadly, one can say that civil resistance achieved a political victory in that it contributed significantly to thwarting the Nazi plans to create a New Europe unified by a common ideology and political system, thereby keeping alive human and civilising values. However, it did not even attempt to achieve the strategic task of national liberation. Everywhere it was assumed that that task would have to be accomplished by the Allied armies.

At the end of the war, none of the former occupied countries gave serious consideration to replacing military defence by preparations for civil resistance, or to assigning it a place in the overall defence system. This was true even of those countries like Norway and Denmark where civil resistance had been widespread and scored notable successes. Indeed, they, and two other traditionally neutral European states, Belgium and Holland, opted to join NATO on its formation in 1948, and thus to rely for their defence on the military strength of the alliance, and, in due course, the US 'nuclear umbrella'.

But the wider significance of the civil resistance in occupied Europe had not gone unnoticed. Basil Liddell Hart, the British military historian and strategist, concluded that it had caused the German occupiers more problems than the armed resistance and guerrilla warfare, and that they were baffled as to how to deal with it.[9] Gene Sharp, then a young American graduate who had spent nine months in prison in 1953 as a conscientious objector, came to Britain in 1955 as an assistant editor on the weekly pacifist paper *Peace News*. He took a particular interest in the resistance of the teachers in occupied Norway and took up an academic post in Oslo in 1958 to further his research into this topic. His pamphlet, *Tyranny Could Not Quell Them*[10], published in 1959, considered the significance for unarmed defence of the teachers' victory over the Quisling government.

By this time the first mass movement against nuclear weapons was gaining strength and challenging many of the political and military assumptions that had been predominant in the West since the advent of the Cold War in the late 1940s. 1958 saw the birth of the Campaign for Nuclear Disarmament (CND) in Britain, and the first Aldermaston March. Anti-nuclear campaigns soon spread across Western Europe, the United States, and other countries. (They had been a significant movement in Japan somewhat earlier.) At last the general population in many countries was awakening to the potential catastrophe of nuclear war as East and West stockpiled ever more powerful weapons, and developed new and essentially unstoppable ways of delivering them.

One of those who had perceived the strategic significance of nuclear weapons and the challenge they posed to traditional notions of defence was again Commander Stephen King-Hall. In the autumn of 1957, he delivered a lecture to the Royal United Services Institute in which he argued that nuclear war would represent such a total catastrophe, especially for a small, densely populated country like Britain, that the country should unilaterally dispose of its nuclear weapons and embark on a programme of training the civilian population for non-violent resistance. His speech, and the call he made during it for the establishment of a Royal Commission seriously to examine the proposition, was widely reported in Britain and fed into the debate that was then under way about its defence posture. The following year, King-Hall published *Defence in the Nuclear Age*[11], in which he further developed his ideas. These too are discussed later in the chapter.

King-Hall did not get his Royal Commission, and the main anti-nuclear movement in Britain, CND, did not seriously take up his ideas. The notion of non-violent defence was propagated in a rather general way by the Direct Action Committee and, to a lesser extent, by the Committee of 100. Some of those involved in these last-named organisations, and particularly a group in and around *Peace News*, played an active role in developing and propagating the idea.[12] There was also interest in the US in the concept, mainly in Quaker and pacifist circles. In 1958, a non-violent activist, Brad Lyttle, published a booklet entitled *National Defense through Nonviolent Resistance*[13] which explored the idea in relation to the United States, and in 1962 another US publication, *Preventing World War III: Some Proposals*,[14] included articles on aspects of non-violent defence by the Norwegian philosopher Arne Naess, and an American psychologist, Jerome D. Frank.

Two years later, Adam Roberts , then Assistant Editor of *Peace News*, edited a booklet on *Civilian Defence*, which comprised essays by himself and Gene Sharp, and reprinted those by Frank and Naess. The booklet also contained a foreword by Alastair Buchan, Director of the Institute for Strategic Studies in London. The pragmatic spirit of the booklet is summed up in Roberts' observation: 'All the authors of articles in this booklet consider that non-violent action should be judged, not in terms of a doctrine which one may accept or reject, but as a technique, the potentialities of which in particular situations demand the most rigorous and careful study.'[15] The choice of the title 'civilian defence', rather than 'non-violent defence', was itself indicative of this strategic/pragmatic emphasis.

Nevertheless, this was a shift of emphasis rather than a fundamental change. Firstly, Sharp and Roberts (and many of those who followed them) were clearly *motivated* to explore non-violent defence by personal pacifist – or at least anti-nuclear – convictions. Secondly, the best of the earlier pacifist and Gandhian writers on the subject of non-violent resistance – Case, Gregg, de Ligt, Shridharani – had, from very similar if not identical motives, also attempted to provide as objective an analysis as they could of its workings, and succeeded indeed in providing crucial insights into them. This was true too of some of the subsequent studies conducted by Quaker and other pacifist groups.[16] The important distinction which needs to be drawn is between the moral and strategic arguments surrounding the resort to, or conduct of, war – and the personal decisions individuals reach concerning their participation in it – on the one hand, and judgements about the *efficacy* of non-violent resistance/non-violent defence on the other. Clearly the latter need to be systematically investigated with the utmost dispassion and objectivity, preferably by people from a wide range of political perspectives. Using the term 'civilian defence' in preference, for instance, to 'non-violent defence' was a kind of invitation to people who do not hold pacifist or anti-nuclear convictions to join in the investigation and debate.

It is important to stress the point that a commitment to defence by civil resistance, or to exploring its potential, does not imply pacifist or indeed any particular political or ideological beliefs. It is perfectly possible to believe that military defence is right and necessary in some circumstances and yet to wish to explore the potential of non-violent forms of resistance and defence. Clearly, people who have rejected war altogether, or specifically

125

any reliance on nuclear weapons, on religious or ethical grounds, have a particularly strong motivation for exploring alternative methods of conducting social and international conflicts – unless, that is, they have taken refuge in the comfortable illusion that such conflicts can be wished away or settled in every instance by arbitration or negotiation. Thus it is not surprising that pacifists and 'nuclear pacifists' have played a central role in developing the concept. They have not been alone, however, and since the 1960s in particular, social scientists, military historians and strategists, the defence ministries and research establishments of several countries, have shown an interest in the concept and/or have helped explore its potential.

Some of the pioneer researchers in the field have distanced themselves to a greater or lesser extent from a pacifist, or even from a totally anti-nuclear, stance, either on tactical grounds (Sharp) or through having become convinced that the applicability of civilian defence is limited and therefore military force is required in some situations (Roberts). But the crisis of warfare brought about by the invention of nuclear weapons remains the motivation and starting point of much research. Moreover, the moral and strategic debate on warfare in general, and nuclear war and deterrence in particular, remains crucial in its own right.

In the same year as the publication of *Civilian Defence* (1964), Sharp, Roberts, April Carter (former secretary of the Direct Action Committee and subsequently *Peace News* staff member), and Theodor Ebert (a researcher from Berlin) were all closely involved in organising an international conference on the topic at St Hilda's College, Oxford. This brought together academics and specialists in the field – including military historians such as Liddell Hart and D. J. Goodspeed – and resulted in the publication in 1967 of *The Strategy of Civilian Defence*[17], edited by Roberts, which may be regarded as the first systematic study of the concept. It included historical chapters on the 1924 *Ruhrkampf*, the resistance in occupied Norway and Denmark, the East German uprising in 1953, and theoretical chapters covering such topics as the coup d'état, the problems of transition from military to civilian defence, and the political changes which such a changeover might imply.

One of the key notions promoted by the book was that of *transarmament*. The term was coined by Theodor Ebert some years earlier and was proposed as an alternative to the term and idea of *dis*armament. Whereas disarmament implied getting rid of weapons, and perhaps giving people the impression that they were defenceless, transarmament implied defence by different, non-military, means. The term also carried an implication of gradualism. Whatever individuals might decide about their participation or otherwise in war, military means of defence at the national level would be laid aside only to the extent that alternative non-military means had been developed to take their place. The term is now widely, though not universally, used among writers and researchers in the field.

The term 'civilian defence' is used less frequently today because of the possible confusion with 'civil defence'. Sharp and his colleagues in the US have opted for 'civilian-based defence' or 'CBD', but 'social defence', 'defence by civil resistance', and 'civilian defence' are more widely used in Europe. Nor is this simply a matter of terminology. Civilian-based defence purposely conveys the notion of moral and ideological neutrality, while its abbreviated form, CBD, has a quasi-military ring to it. This corresponds to Sharp's view that one is dealing essentially with a technological change from one system of defence to another and more efficient one. Indeed, Gene Sharp's most recent (1990) book on the subject bears the subtitle 'A Post-Military Weapons System'.[18] Terms such as 'social defence' tend to reflect an emphasis on defending the social institutions of society rather than territory as such, though they do not exclude concern about the latter. Some of the anti-militarist grass-roots movements have adopted the term 'popular non-violent defence' to make explicit the non-violent character and commitment of their approach, and to indicate that this is defence by and for the people rather than being state-controlled and directed. There are also other variants, mostly indicating nuances of political and ideological viewpoint. Here I have settled for 'defence by civil resistance'[19], or 'civilian defence' where that phrase would be too clumsy. 'Defence by civil resistance' has the advantage of indicating the links with civil resistance in other contexts, rather than implying that it is a completely separate phenomenon; at the same time it indicates that civil resistance in this particular context requires special attention.[20]

Studies and research projects continued during the 1970s and 1980s, some under the aegis of the peace movement, some promoted by educational and charitable trusts, some promoted and funded by the state in various countries.[21] Not surprisingly, there was another peak of interest and debate on alternative non-nuclear defence during the political crisis over new nuclear missiles in Europe and the resurgence of a mass peace movement. While the focus of the debate was on non-offensive (military) defence, the notion of civil resistance as a 'fall-back' strategy, or a strategy to be used in particular circumstances, figured in many of the proposals, notably those of the Alternative Defence Commission in Britain whose first report was published in 1983.

Governments in Norway, Sweden, Finland, Denmark and Holland have shown varying degrees of interest in the idea, and all but the first sponsored research into it during the 1970s; France began to do so in the mid-1980s. In Holland the government showed serious interest in exploring the idea during the 1970s and early 1980s. A working group was established in 1976 in which various government ministries were represented, including the Ministries of Foreign Affairs, Defence, and Internal Affairs. Its report recommending the establishment of a university-based research programme was published in 1976 and accepted by the government. A new group with the task of developing the research programme was then established with the participation of four recognised foreign experts – Theodor Ebert, Johan Galtung, Adam Roberts and Gene Sharp.[22] Despite this promising start, and the drawing up of an impressive list of research topics, official interest waned during the 1980s, and in 1985 the government dropped the project altogether.[23] The project produced, however, one important contribution to the field by Alex P. Schmid on the subject of social defence and Soviet military power, which raises

128

some key questions about the conditions affecting the viability of civilian defence.[24] Civil resistance figures as a sub-theme in the Swiss defence system[25] and did so in Yugoslavia's 'General People's Defence' until the break-up of that country.[26]

The Swedish authorities have shown the most serious and consistent interest in the concept and how it could be incorporated into Swedish defence plans. Starting from the early 1970s, the Research Institute of Swedish National Defence sponsored a series of studies by Adam Roberts;[27] it also organised an international conference in Uppsala in 1972 on non-military forms of defence. Swedish Parliamentary Defence Committees produced several reports on the topic, the most recent in 1984. The Defence Committees insisted that 'non-military defence' was to be strictly regarded as a *complement* to military defence, not a substitute for it, or in any sense a measure of disarmament. Moreover, they defined non-military defence as including not only civil resistance but also 'irregular armed resistance by organised civilian groups'.[28] In 1986 the Swedish Parliament unanimously agreed that non-military defence should be adopted as part of Sweden's total defence posture.

Civil resistance played a major part in the struggle of the former Soviet Baltic republics – Estonia, Latvia and Lithuania – to regain, and defend, their independence. For this reason, and also on account of their obvious military vulnerability in the event of an attack by their powerful Russian neighbour, there has been a strong interest in civilian defence at both government and popular level since pro-independence movements first won power in the 1990 elections.

In Latvia, in December 1990, the Popular Front issued an 'Appeal for Hour X' calling for total non-cooperation of the civilian population in the event of a Soviet attack, while the Supreme Council's Commission on Defence and Home Affairs devised plans to use chains of unarmed people to protect public buildings. (The plan was put into effect to protect the Parliament building in January 1991.) In June 1991, the Latvian Supreme Council voted to establish a Centre for Non-Violent Resistance which subsequently published separate pamphlets on non-cooperation for government bodies, social institutions and individuals.[29]

In Lithuania, in February 1991, following the attempted Soviet clamp-down in Vilnius, the Lithuanian Supreme Council declared non-violent resistance to be the primary means of struggle in the event of a Soviet occupation.[30]

In Estonia, in January 1991, government officials and Popular Front members devised a resistance plan entitled 'Civilian Disobedience' urging citizens, amongst other things, 'to treat all commands contradicting Estonian law as illegitimate, and to carry out strict disobedience to and non-cooperation with all Soviet attempts to strengthen control.'[31]

In June 1992, the Ministry of Defence of the Republic of Lithuania co-sponsored with the US Albert Einstein Institute (of which Gene Sharp is President) a conference in Vilnius on civilian-based defence attended by defence ministry representatives from Lithuania, Latvia, Estonia and Sweden – as well as political leaders, defence specialists and civilian defence researchers from a total of nine countries. Among the topics discussed was international assistance to countries using civilian defence. A final resolution proposed the formation of a Baltic Civilian-Based Defence Mutual Aid Treaty.[32]

Development of the concept

Defence by civil resistance, then, is a prepared system of national defence based on non-violent forms of action and/or the actual deployment of such means against foreign invasion or occupation, coups d'état, or other forms of attack on the independence and integrity of a society. Thus, like the term defence in its traditional military sense, it covers both the system of prior planning and preparation for resistance, and resistance itself. It could either complement or replace the traditional military system of deterrence and defence.

Some of the chief exponents of the concept – including Roberts and Sharp – define it still more narrowly, so that it would exclude instances of civil resistance against invasions, occupations or coups which occurred without a pre-arranged national plan.[33] Indeed, on these grounds, Sharp concludes that there has never been an historical instance of 'civilian-based defence', but only improvised prototypes of it. Clearly, advance preparation is desirable, and the deterrent effect will be greatly diminished, if it does not disappear altogether, without it. However, to deny that, for instance, the Czechoslovak resistance to the Soviet invasion in 1968 was an example of defence by civil resistance on the grounds that it had not been planned and organised in advance is to split hairs. It could also lead one to ignore or misread some of the lessons to be learned from this and other historical instances. If one was advocating a system of national defence by guerrilla warfare, it would be fair to point to certain differences in context and situation between, say, the national resistance of the Vietnamese to French and US imperialism and that which might follow an attack on a country with a prepared plan for guerrilla resistance ready to go into operation; it would not be reasonable to claim on these grounds that the Vietnamese case should be discounted as an example of national defence by guerrilla warfare.

There is indeed a case for grouping together under the rubric of defence by civil resistance all the instances where this method is used for defence or liberation at a national level. Sharp himself adopted this approach at one point. Thus, in an essay in 1970 on Gandhi as a national defence strategist, he wrote: 'National defense in this context includes both preparations and resistance for dealing with new attacks on a country's independence and freedom, *as well as efforts to liberate a country already under foreign occupation and rule*' (emphasis added).[34] One is dealing here with what another researcher, Gene Keyes, calls 'strategic nonviolence' – i.e. the use of mass non-violent action for strategic ends: the achievement or preservation of national independence, the defence of constitutional liberty against coups, the overthrow of dictatorial rule.

Within this broad category, it is then helpful to distinguish cases where the struggle was conducted by or in support of an existing legitimate government. The campaigns against the Kapp putsch in 1920, against the Algerian Generals' Revolt in 1961, against the 1991 coup in Russia, and against the Soviet and Warsaw Pact invasion of Czechoslovakia in 1968, fall within this sub-group. They come closest to civilian (or civilian-based) defence as Sharp and Roberts define it, differing from it only in that there was no advance national plan for civil resistance. These cases tell us a great deal about the appropriate tactics and strategy of civilian defence in its initial phase, where the principal aim is to prevent the opponent from establishing control of political and social institutions at all levels.

However, one important reason for grouping together all actual or potential campaigns for national defence and liberation is that they tend if prolonged to take on the same characteristics. Civil resistance against invasion and occupation conducted according to a prepared national plan would have some unique features in the early period; but if it continued for years or decades, the context and dynamics would tend to approximate to those of previous historical campaigns for national liberation, such as those of Gandhi in India, or the 1989 national revolutions in Eastern Europe. Similarly, where civil resistance fails to thwart a coup attempt – as in Haiti in 1992 – it quickly develops into yet another instance of resistance against domestic tyranny. It is important to recognise this if one is to profit from historical experience and not treat civilian defence as a more singular phenomenon than it actually is. The argument, however, for focusing in particular on civilian defence as a *prepared* system of national defence is that this raises questions and provides opportunities that do not apply even to the cases of improvised civil resistance to coups and invasions. Thus it involves decisions about the degree of responsibility to be assigned to civil resistance in the overall strategy, about the process of transition from existing military defence arrangements to ones in which civil resistance plays at least a serious part, about the respective role of governments and voluntary bodies, and so forth. While there is not space here to discuss all these aspects, it is upon defence by civil resistance in this more restricted sense that this chapter focuses.

The debate about how to define and delimit defence by civil resistance has a further dimension: does it necessarily imply adoption at state and government level? If so, should one seek to work from the base upwards in promoting it or concentrate on convincing political and military élites of the viability of the concept?

On the first of these questions, it is clearly desirable that civilian defence should become official policy. However, there are situations where it is quite unrealistic to think of this occurring short of radical social and political upheaval – in a military dictatorship, for instance. In such a situation, an opposition movement might take on the responsibility not only for campaigning for democracy within the country but also for preparing it for civil resistance against foreign aggression. If it was sufficiently strong and united, it might take society a long way down the path of systematic preparation and training for defence by civil resistance, particularly if the opposition to the military regime also involved a sustained campaign of non-cooperation. Had Gandhi in 1940 succeeded in persuading Congress to prepare people to defend the country against possible Japanese aggression, this would have met all the essential criteria of civilian-based defence. Nor would there have been the slightest chance of this approach to defence being adopted, even as a complementary strategy, by the imperial government.

A more recent example is that of Solidarity in Poland in the period between its birth in August 1980 and the imposition of martial law in mid-December 1981. Anticipating just such a development, the Solidarity leadership had made plans and preparations for civil resistance to oppose it, and they subsequently put these into effect when the crackdown came. Hence, although there was no government involvement, both the prior planning and the subsequent resistance qualify it to be considered an example of civilian defence. Jan Zielonka, a Polish academic, implies that it should be seen as such and argues that it shows that advance preparation may not confer quite as big an advantage as Sharp and some others have assumed.[35]

On the second point there is a continuing debate. The strategy of building 'popular non-violent defence' from below is chiefly associated with anti-militarist and other oppositionist groups who are sceptical that the modern bureaucratic state would ever become involved in a non-violent approach to defence, except as a very minor adjunct to military defence and perhaps as an additional means of regimenting and controlling the population. (There are particularly strong grounds for scepticism in the case of a nuclear superpower – the United States today and the Soviet Union until its break-up.) The radical anti-militarist project for non-violent defence is thus part of a broader project for creating a 'non-violent participatory democracy'.

Differences in the conception of how civilian defence could be implemented were reflected in an intellectual debate during the 1970s between those who defined themselves as 'structuralists' and their opponents – Sharp, Roberts, Ebert and others – whom they characterised as 'instrumentalists'. The structuralists argued that it was unrealistic to think that a non-violent form of defence could simply be grafted onto the existing social and political system: its introduction would have to go hand in hand with more profound changes. The 'instrumentalists' – though this was not their choice of term – replied that non-violent resistance had taken place in highly imperfect societies, that the adoption of civilian defence would no doubt bring other changes in its wake but that it was self-defeating to suggest that it would only be relevant in some future, and ill-defined, utopia.[36]

The approaches of working from the top down or from the base up can of course complement each other to some degree. The clash between them is at its most marked over the question of confrontational campaigns to secure changes in defence or other policies, in particular nuclear disarmament. Often such campaigns use methods of non-violent direct action against the existing government while (in some cases) simultaneously advocating an alternative, non-violent approach to defence. The strategy underlying this approach is one of acclimatising the population to civil resistance not only by exposition and argument but by encouraging its use for social and political goals in confrontation with an existing political and military establishment. In this way, spreading the concept of civilian defence and promoting the social and political changes in society regarded as necessary for its adoption (or at least as greatly facilitating it) would progress together. Clearly, such an approach is very different in emphasis from that of pursuing academic research into the potential of civilian defence and seeking to convince the public in general, but more particularly sections of the Establishment, of the viability of the idea and the reasonableness – not to say respectability – of those promoting it.

However, rational arguments alone do not bring about major policy changes. Historical and theoretical studies, and the reports of official commissions, have certainly an important role to play, but, as Roberts himself has observed, 'it may only be in a crisis that civilian defence or any other major change in defence policy may be adopted'.[37] He clearly has in mind a disaster or near-disaster – such as an attempted coup, a war, or a military confrontation – in which the inadequacies of the existing system become apparent. But the crisis could take a quite different form, namely a political crisis brought about by a mass popular movement which challenges the morality and/or rationality of the system. There is, in fact, a clear link between the peaks of the nuclear disarmament campaigns in the late 1950s/early 1960s and the early to mid-1980s and the level of public interest in alternative defence in general and defence by civil resistance in particular.

Given the undoubted successes of civil resistance and the risks and uncertainties of any system of defence, particularly in the nuclear age, it would seem to be a matter of prudence and common sense for almost any country in peacetime to make preparations for civil resistance as part of the overall defence strategy, as Sweden has done – if thus far only in a fairly minor way. Probably the major obstacle, especially for medium and large powers, is a psychological/political one – namely that governments find it difficult to acknowledge the possibility that their armies could be defeated or forced to retreat, and that therefore some if not all of the national territory might be occupied by a foreign power. Indeed, they may fear that to do so would weaken the deterrent aspect of their military preparations and perhaps weaken the morale of their fighting forces. It is no coincidence that the states that have so far shown the greatest interest in defence by civil resistance are some of the smaller countries (in population if not always in size) who can more easily acknowledge their vulnerability in the face of an attack by a major power. Nervousness on the part of governments about 'arming' the civilian population with a means of resistance that might be turned against it may also be a factor in some instances.[38]

There is, however, a particularly strong case for civilian defence as a deterrent to, and means of resisting, coups. Here I refer to coups in the broad sense of the term which covers not only the seizure of power by the military or an armed political faction, but also 'executive usurpations' (i.e. the abolition of civil liberty and democratic rule by a government initially appointed by constitutional means). I also assume a context in which a *legitimate* government is overthrown by one intending to impose a more or less dictatorial regime. (Coups have sometimes, of course, been aimed at or secured the overthrow of dictatorships with the declared intention of introducing a more humane and representative system of government, even if this has rarely been achieved in practice without further struggle from below.) Not only have coups, or attempted coups, been defeated by civil resistance in some notable historical instances, they also represent a form of threat to democratic government in which a strong military is often part of the problem rather than its solution. To the classic question 'Who will guard the guardians themselves?' the advocates of civilian defence reply: the people prepared and trained for civil resistance.[39]

Roberts and Sharp have both strongly urged the relevance of civilian defence as a safeguard against military coups. Indeed, Sharp, in *Making Europe Unconquerable*, speculates that countries which have experienced or been threatened by coups 'might initiate civilian-based defence for the limited purpose of preventing and defeating them'.[40] Later, some countries which had adopted it for this limited purpose might decide to use it as one option for dealing with invasions and occupations.

An Alternative Defence?

In the next chapter, we consider the development of ideas concerning the strategy and organisation of civilian defence.

Chapter 6

The Strategy of Civilian Resistance

Approaches to strategy

Defence by civil resistance has much in common with guerrilla warfare. Each uses an 'indirect strategy' to undermine the opponent. In guerrilla warfare, pitched battles with the enemy forces are avoided in favour of a war of attrition. Territory often has to be ceded, but this is turned to advantage in that it obliges the opponents to overextend their forces and leaves them vulnerable to hit-and-run attacks. Finally, the moral and political battle that accompanies the physical war of attrition is seen as crucial.

With civil resistance, the indirect strategy is taken a step further. Here, there is neither a direct assault on the military forces of the opponent nor an attempt to inflict casualties and sap morale by hit-and-run attacks. Other methods are, however, employed with the aim of undermining the opponent's morale, and indeed the moral and political 'warfare' is central. As in guerrilla warfare, territory has for the most part to be ceded, since it can be defended only in a very restricted sense, but again non-cooperation and non-violent obstruction may stretch the resources of the opponent attempting to administer it.

Because of its limited capacity to defend territory as such, civilian defence is essentially an anti-occupation, rather than an anti-invasion, strategy and has been increasingly recognised as such among researchers. In this respect too it is similar to guerrilla warfare. Only in quite exceptional circumstances could it be expected to halt an invasion in its tracks – for instance where the government of the aggressor state was in a weak and vulnerable

position at home, where the decision to invade was massively unpopular among the troops as well as among the general population of the opponent state, and perhaps where mass protests by an exceptionally well-prepared population in the country under attack were matched by intense international pressure and sanctions. Its capacity to deter attack hinges on its demonstrable effectiveness in defeating aggression, and it is therefore considered later in this chapter.

An extended comparison with guerrilla warfare is one of the central features of the Boserup and Mack study of civilian defence referred to in previous chapters.[1] They take as their starting point von Clausewitz's famous work *On War*[2] and seek to show how its theoretical insights apply to defence by civil resistance. They themselves claim at one point that earlier proponents of civilian defence had produced no strategy as such at all, but simply 'a collection of "tactics", of methods for putting pressure on the opponent'.[3] The normal result of applying such pressures haphazardly, they argue, is that they cancel each other out. To be effective, they 'must be given a common point of application and a common direction'.[4] Before expounding their approach, however, it is helpful to trace the development of ideas on strategy as presented by other writers.

Gandhi's discussion of non-violent national defence dates mainly from the early 1930s. In 1931, in answer to enquiries, he outlined his ideas on the possibilities for non-violent defence by neutral Switzerland, and in the course of the 1930s, as the world crisis deepened, he urged successively Jews, Czechs, Poles, Britons and finally all countries faced with Nazi aggression to resist it by non-violent means.[5] In 1939 and 1940 he attempted – unsuccessfully – to persuade Congress to adopt a policy of non-violent defence against any Japanese invasion, and wrote on a number of occasions about his ideas on this topic.[6] Later, in June 1942, he supported the idea of an independent India agreeing to have Allied troops remain in the country to deter and resist a Japanese attack[7], though this probably represented not so much a change in his personal convictions about what could be achieved by non-violent defence as a recognition that neither

Congress nor the majority of his fellow countrymen and women shared his ultimate faith in the 'non-violence of the brave'.

In so far as Gandhi formulated a strategy of national resistance to invasion, it was in the heroic mould – total non-cooperation and willingness to die if necessary rather than submit. In 1931, discussing what a disarmed neutral Switzerland could do faced with an aggressor wanting to march his army through the country to attack other nations, Gandhi proposed total non-cooperation and presenting 'a living wall of men, women and children' to the aggressor.[8] Again in 1940, he wrote: 'If the worst happens [i.e. invasion], there are two ways open to non-violence. To yield possession, but non-cooperate with the aggressor . . . The second way would be non-violent resistance by the people who have been trained in the non-violent way. They would offer themselves unarmed as fodder to the aggressor's cannons.'[9] In April 1942 he stated that if India were a free country 'things could be done non-violently to prevent the Japanese entering the country'. As things now stood, 'non-violent resistance could commence the moment they effected a landing'. Non-violent resisters would refuse the invaders any help, even water. Even if all the resisters were killed, they 'will have won the day inasmuch as they will have preferred extermination to submission'.[10]

Such proposals do not of course amount to a considered strategy. It was mainly Gandhi's work in the field as an organiser and campaign strategist that inspired others to analyse his approach and seek to elucidate its workings and its possible relevance for national defence. The tradition of looking to military parallels in expounding his strategy began in a serious way with Richard Gregg's *The Power of Non-Violence*, first published in 1935.[11] Like Gene Sharp at a later date, Gregg takes as his starting point that 'conflict is an inevitable part of life' and that 'the world is inherently divisive and changing'[12]; the question is how to conduct this conflict in a creative way.

Gregg cites an article by the famous American columnist, Walter Lippman, entitled 'The Political Equivalent of War', which appeared in the *Atlantic Monthly* of August 1928 (itself a critical commentary on William James's essay 'The Moral

Equivalent of War'): 'It is not sufficient to propose an equivalent
for the military virtues. It is even more important to work out
an equivalent for the military methods and objectives. For the
institution of war is not merely an expression of the military
spirit. . . . It is also – and I think primarily – one of the ways by
which great human decisions are made . . . Any real programme
of peace must rest on the premise that there will be causes of
dispute as long as we can foresee, and that those disputes have
to be decided, and that a way of deciding them must be found
which is not war.'[13] Non-violent resistance, Gregg argues, meets
Lippman's requirements. It not only utilises the military virtues
(of courage, discipline and endurance) but 'uses on a moral plane
many of the military methods and principles', employs many of
the same psychological processes, and 'even retains some of the
military objectives, with moral modifications'.[14]

Following the logic of this argument, Gregg draws upon the
writings of classical and contemporary military strategists –
Napoleon, von Clausewitz, Foch, J. C. Fuller, Liddell Hart and
others – to show that the moral and psychological struggle is
central in warfare. In Liddell Hart's words 'the true aim of war
is the mind of the enemy command and government, not the
bodies of their troops, [and] . . . the balance between victory and
defeat turns on mental impressions and only indirectly on physical blows.'[15] Von Clausewitz's approach to strategy is succinctly
summarised in the words of another military commentator whom
Gregg quotes:

> Retaining the initiative, using the defensive as the decis-
> ive form of action, concentration of force at the decisive
> point [the 'centre of gravity'], the determination of that
> point, the superiority of the moral factor to purely
> material resources, the proper relation between attack
> and defence, and the will to victory.[16]

Gregg does not wholly commit himself to the proposition that
the defensive is the 'decisive form of action' and refers to Marshal
Foch's interpretation of von Clausewitz which places more stress
on the offensive. However, non-violent resistance, Gregg argues,

is strong in both defensive and offensive capabilities, and meets the other strategic criteria identified by von Clausewitz, including the 'concentration of force' on the decisive point, namely the morale of the opponent. He also argues that non-violent resistance not only operates to undermine the morale of the opponent at various levels, but 'does much to enhance the morale and unity of those who use it'.[17] The parallels with the later (and more systematic) exposition of an optimum strategy of non-violent defence by Boserup and Mack are striking – though the latter identify unity, rather than morale, as the 'centre of gravity' of the defence.

Gregg's work was original in the sense that while written from an unambiguously pacifist perspective, it was not anti-militarist in a traditional sense. Rather it accepted that war fulfilled social and political functions and would not disappear until alternative means were developed to replace it. Therefore, instead of turning his back on the writings of military strategists, he delved into them to elucidate the workings of mass non-violent action, particularly as practised by Gandhi in India.

Bart de Ligt, by contrast, belonged squarely to the Western anti-militarist tradition.[18] He shared Gregg's admiration for Gandhi, but did so more critically, and exchanged letters with him in the late 1920s and early 1930s charging him with inconsistencies in his opposition to war.[19] In *The Conquest of Violence*, first published in English in 1937, he also suggested ways in which non-violent action at national and international levels could be used against current and future aggression, including a German invasion of Holland and a Japanese attack on the Dutch East Indies (now Indonesia).

De Ligt approached these problems from a consistently internationalist, anti-imperialist and anti-capitalist standpoint. International action by the working class and anti-militarist movement taking the form of boycotts, strikes (including where possible and appropriate a general strike against war), 'blacking' the handling of war materials and strategic goods to states engaged in aggression, would constitute the principal external pressure. The model here was the concerted action in 1920 by French, English and

Irish dock workers who refused to load arms onto ships bound for Poland or for other states taking part in the interventionist war in Soviet Russia[20], and the proposals put forward by War Resisters International in 1935, on the eve of Mussolini's invasion of Abyssinia, for international working-class action to deprive the Italian government of materials necessary for war production.[21]

Such external pressure was to be accompanied by collective non-cooperation and other forms of non-violent resistance on the part of people who suffered aggression – whether this was the Dutch people facing occupation by Hitler's forces, or the peoples of the Dutch East Indies facing Japanese rather than Dutch imperialism. The moral force exerted by an occupied Netherlands engaged in non-violent resistance was likely, he argued, to attract sympathy even among the German people – indeed, 'it might quite well be that the violent annexation of so free a people might be the right remedy for the Nazi disease!'[22]

De Ligt was not, however, primarily concerned to develop a *national* strategy for non-violent defence. He was above all an internationalist, and had a deeply ingrained distrust of states and governments.[23] Resistance at a national level was rather to be part of a revolutionary movement for the transformation of the international system:

> The fighters for freedom and peace will have nothing to do with 'national defence', whether it be of the Netherlands, of Germany, of the British Empire or of Russia: they will form an International of all who resist horizontal and vertical violence, and who fight for the transformation of the international-imperialist system into an international and truly humane society.[24]

In keeping with this approach, de Ligt's book concludes with a plan of campaign not for national defence against occupation but rather for national and international direct action against war itself and preparations for war.

Jessie Wallace Hughan's 1942 essay on pacifism and invasion was mentioned earlier. She characterises her proposed strategy as 'a general strike raised to the nth power'.[25] In fact, in its specific recommendations it is more nuanced than that. She sets out four principles which should guide the conduct of resistance: no services or supplies to be furnished to the invaders; no orders to be obeyed except those of the constitutional civil authorities; no insult or injury to be offered to the invaders; all public officials to be pledged to die rather than surrender.[26] As part of the preparation for such resistance, the population would have been educated 'by all the resources of school, church and radio' and 'trained in the exercise of individual courage'.[27]

But there is an ambiguity about her recommendations. One line of resistance she recommends follows the principle of continuing work without collaboration, and in order to sustain that she proposes a chain of succession for officials and people in responsible posts so that as soon as one is arrested or killed another is ready to take over. The other line of resistance is a total stoppage of work. It is not clear, however, what criteria are to be used in deciding which option to follow. Thus she discusses what should happen if invading forces enter a city and arrest the mayor:

> The first vice-mayor automatically succeeds, but the invaders exclude him from the City Hall, setting in his place a traitor or an officer of their own. Executives and clerks continue to perform their duties, however, until commands arrive from the enemy usurper, when they either ignore the orders *or cease work altogether* [emphasis added].[28]

There is an identical ambiguity about how other city departments – fire, police, the public utility services of telegraph, telephone and electricity – should respond. They are to continue working until they receive enemy orders, at which point 'they, too, will disregard specific commands or declare an instantaneous strike'. So too with workers in other spheres. Finally, if confronted with an utterly ruthless occupier, prepared to starve the civilian population into surrender, Hughan envisages mass evacuations from cities with people 'destroying crops and stores as they go' to prevent them falling into the opponent's hands.

King-Hall, in his 1958 book – focused specifically on non-violent defence for Britain and Western Europe against a Soviet invasion – criticises Hughan's strategy: it amounts, he suggests, to a 'scorched earth policy and a kind of sit-down strike on a national scale'.[29] This does not do justice to that part of Hughan's proposed strategy which envisages society and its institutions continuing to function without collaboration. It is, however, a fair characterisation of the more extreme scenario she envisages, and King-Hall is understandably sceptical that such out-and-out resistance could be maintained for any length of time. His more central criticism – which again does her less than justice – is that Hughan's strategy is 'entirely negative' in character, concentrating solely on making occupation difficult for the enemy rather than on what should, in his view, be the crucial objective:'*to make the occupation dangerous for the enemy*' (emphasis in original).[30]

King-Hall himself viewed non-violent defence as essentially a form of political and psychological warfare in which victory, if it could be achieved, would be decisive. Conceivably, a Soviet occupation of the United Kingdom could bring about the downfall of communism.[31] (Compare this with de Ligt's view that Nazism might be undermined if an attempted German occupation of Holland was met with non-violent resistance.) Moreover, if plans were sufficiently well known and publicised in advance, the Soviet Union might be deterred from attempting any such occupation. He expressed more faith in such a 'psychological deterrent' than in the 'present H-bomb retaliation deterrent'.[32]

Although he did not present a detailed strategy for non-violent defence, King-Hall, like Hughan, sets out the general principles which should guide it. To a far greater extent than Hughan's, these allow for cooperation with the occupiers in the area of economic life and administration, but involve absolute refusal 'at all costs' to say or write anything 'contrary to the principles of our way of life' or to accept denial of freedom of speech and association. The offensive element of the strategy consists of using every opportunity in personal contact with occupying forces to expose the fallacies of communism and the advantages of democracy, while behaving 'with dignity and moral superiority' towards them.[33] In sum, defensive resistance was to be concentrated on those key areas where the integrity and way of life of the nation were regarded as being at stake, while the major offensive thrust was to be concentrated on the unity and morale of the opponent's forces. (Elsewhere in the book he makes it clear that the moral and psychological warfare will be directed not solely at the occupying forces but in three 'operational theatres': the home fronts – directed at the opponent's soldiers and officials; the uncommitted nations' fronts; and the enemy fronts.)[34]

One highly original idea of King-Hall's was that of a European Treaty Organisation – a defensive alliance of European states which would have disavowed any reliance on nuclear weapons. The strategy of the ETO countries would be switched 'so far as its main foundation is concerned from a basis of armed force to one of political and moral force', and would be organised for use in the three operational theatres mentioned above. However, ETO states would maintain sufficient conventional armed forces not only for internal security purposes but to put up a token resistance to Russian non-nuclear armed aggression across ETO frontiers.[35] Thus the first line of defence would remain a military one, though essentially 'to provide a trip wire and put the Soviet Union psychologically in the wrong if they attempted non-nuclear armed aggression across frontiers'.[36]

The wisdom of this last suggestion was queried by Adam Roberts in a chapter on 'Civilian Defence Strategy' in the book he edited in 1967. A token resistance in which many of the attackers would inevitably be killed or injured was likely to reinforce their unity and resolve, and convince them that the claims of the defenders to be pursuing a peaceful policy were a sham.[37] He was critical too both of Gandhi's proposal for a 'human wall' to confront the invader, and the more extreme proposals of Jessie Wallace Hughan. Non-cooperation, he argued, need not necessarily involve strikes, much less a general strike: it could take the almost diametrically opposite course of working on without collaboration.[38] In the main he concurred with King-Hall's strategy of keeping the economy and society functioning and concentrating opposition at key points.

Theodor Ebert, however, in the same volume, argued that

civilian defence should proceed 'from the basis of the existing legitimate government with a strict refusal at all levels to recognize the usurper's legality and obey his orders'.[39] His approach is much closer to Hughan's than to King-Hall's, and he has subsequently developed his ideas on strategy. In a paper to an international conference on Civilian Defence Strategies in Strasbourg in November 1985 he argued that civilian defence strategists had not paid enough attention to the question of who the enemy might be, and what would be his aims. A coup d'état by the military, or intervention by allied powers to halt the process of transition to civilian defence, was a distinct danger, much as one might hope and work for a transition by consensus. However, in so far as it was useful to make generalisations outside of a specific resistance context, he remained of the view that 'working on without collaboration' should be the basis of strategy. The chief difference between civilian defence and civil resistance in other situations, he pointed out, was precisely that it was conducted in defence of existing legal institutions.

> The usurpers or occupiers should be considered as private persons who have no legitimacy to exercise power, and their orders should be disregarded because illegitimate. Every MP, minister, civil servant or ordinary citizen ought automatically, in case of coup d'état or occupation, without special mobilisation, become a sworn soldier in his place of work. His bureau or his tools are the trench which he must defend with his life. The general rule is: no-one hides, no-one resigns, everyone stays at his normal place and does his duty according to the traditions of the country.[40]

Ebert rejects King-Hall's criticism that such a strategy is 'entirely negative', arguing – as indeed Hughan had done – that nothing could be better calculated to undermine enemy morale than such solid yet peaceful refusal to collaborate. He contrasts his approach based on legality to the 'casuistry' of King-Hall's strategy. The essential difficulty with the latter was that it permitted the usurper to have his say in certain sectors of national and social life, thereby allowing him to construct political bridgeheads. As a result, an enormous burden would be placed on the individual who would have to decide whether he or she should or should not cooperate in any given situation. This was likely to lead to the frittering away of resistance. The policy of total non-cooperation should be introduced from the start and the aim should be for it to continue at least long enough to allow international pressure against the aggressor to build up. He acknowledges the possibility that as a result of intimidation the aggressor might eventually manage to take control of the apparatus of government, as Husak had done in Czechoslovakia and Jaruzelski in Poland. In that case the resistance would enter a second stage of selective resistance – similar to that of the Dutch and Norwegian resistance during World War II. In a third and final stage, there could be a 'non-violent insurrection' of the sort experienced inside countries with authoritarian regimes.

Sharp, Roberts and Ebert collaborated closely in the 1960s and established themselves among the leading exponents of civilian defence. But the first two are less totally committed to the 'work on without collaboration' approach advocated by Ebert, seeing it as one of several possibilities. Both have attempted to order the various means of applying pressure into a coherent phased strategy.[41] In *Making Europe Unconquerable*, published in 1985, Sharp envisages resistance in two main phases, followed possibly by a third to drive home success. In phase one there would either be a 'non-violent blitzkrieg'[42] or a policy of 'communication and warning'. The blitzkrieg involves all-out non-cooperation, coupled with mass protests and demonstrations, including possibly such tactics as a general strike, non-violent intervention and obstruction. It would be employed, however, only where it was judged that there was a reasonable chance of striking a decisive blow against the opponent at this early stage, and where the resistance itself was united and well prepared. Moreover, the intention from the outset would be to maintain the blitzkrieg for a limited duration only. Either it would succeed in defeating invasion or coup, or the resistance would move to the second phase of sustained struggle. The alternative to the 'blitzkrieg' in

148

the initial phase – that of 'communication and warning' – would involve a more measured degree of protest and resistance, coupled with public denunciations and calls for international sanctions in order to signal to the opponent and to the world in general that here was an act of blatant aggression which would be opposed by sustained civil resistance.

The resistance to the attempted Kapp putsch in Berlin clearly qualifies as an example of a successful blitzkrieg. 'Invading' Freikorps and regular army units entering Berlin were faced with a general strike and non-cooperation by the state bureaucracy and at every level of society, while the elected government denounced the coup leaders. The coup attempt in the Soviet Union in August 1991 was defeated in very similar style. The Czechoslovak resistance in 1968 to the Soviet invasion also had many of the characteristics of the blitzkrieg. Wisely, however, there was a decision not to attempt more than a symbolic general strike because it was clear that an indefinite strike would mainly hurt the civilian population rather than the invading armies. Instead, the Czechs and Slovaks adopted what amounted to a policy of 'working on without collaboration'.

Vigorous international protest and action could prove immensely important at this early stage, possibly even tilting the balance between success and failure. In the attempted coup against Gorbachev in August 1991, for instance, the United States and the European Community not only condemned the coup but announced the immediate imposition of sanctions against the usurper regime, thus signalling that the growing cooperation between the Soviet Union and the West would be abruptly terminated if the usurpers retained power. International action, even in the minimal form of publicising what is going on, can act as an important constraint on dictatorships and occupation regimes, thereby opening up space for protest and non-violent action by the people in the countries concerned.

Assuming, however, that there is no quick victory, the next phase of 'sustained struggle' would begin. While warning against trying to create a single blueprint to meet all situations, and insisting on the need to vary tactics and strategy according to the demands of the situation, Sharp emphasises selective resistance at key points during the period of sustained struggle, possibly interspersed with all-out resistance at critical junctures. An important strategic advantage of selective resistance is that it will usually result in the main burden of struggle shifting from one group or section of society to another. In choosing the key points for selective resistance, Sharp suggests six questions to be considered:

1. What are the attackers' main objectives?
2. What will prevent the attackers from gaining or maintaining control of the state apparatus or key parts of it?
3. What will prevent the attackers from weakening or destroying the society's independent institutions and their capacity to resist?
4. What are the specific issues which typify the general principles and objectives of the struggle?
5. What will enable the defenders to act in ways in which they can use their strongest issues, resources and sections of the population (and avoid relying on their weakest ones) to advance the defence?
6. What will concentrate defence strength on the especially vulnerable points in the attackers' system, regime or policies, which, if broken, will imperil the attackers' ability to achieve their objectives and continue the venture?[43]

Sharp does not discuss the difficulty that some of these criteria could conflict with others in some circumstances. For instance, giving priority, as Sharp does, to denying the opponent the objective of his attack could conflict with the advice to the defenders to act 'in ways in which they can use their strongest issues, resources and sections of the population'; nor would it necessarily be compatible with the advice to 'concentrate the defence strength on the especially vulnerable points in the attackers' system'. He acknowledges, however, that it is more difficult for civilian-based defence effectively to oppose aggression undertaken for some objectives than others – a point discussed later.

Selective resistance may sometimes be interspersed, in Sharp's presentation, by episodes of general open defiance, amounting even to a return to 'blitzkrieg' tactics. This would be aimed at expressing opposition to, or obstructing, a particularly objectionable facet of the opponent's policy, for instance the use of terror or massacre, or an attempt to eliminate crucial features of a free society such as an independent press and trade unions, or freely elected local government. Sharp warns against precipitate mass action as an emotional response to events and insists that decisions must be made rationally and in accordance with a strategic plan. In an ideal sense, he is no doubt correct. But leaders have to work with the grain of public sentiment and in practice mass action is likely to be possible only when large numbers of people are deeply stirred by some particular event or have reached the end of their patience. Moreover, this point will often be reached precisely when the opponent takes some action that threatens the way of life of the community or outrages its moral sensibility. Thus the passionate impulse and the strategic calculation need not necessarily be in conflict.

In addition to the selective resistance envisaged by Sharp, one can anticipate a more general policy of semi-resistance or 'micro-resistance' by the majority, taking the form of go-slows, working to rule, 'Schweikism'[44], obstructionism of various kinds, certain forms of sabotage, and so forth. These tactics have in common the fact that they seek to avoid open confrontation with the opponent yet hamper his ability to impose his will on the population and achieve his objectives. This kind of resistance was common in occupied Europe and is likely to occur spontaneously to some degree even without centralised coordination or an advance plan. Its main drawback, as Roberts has observed, is that it blurs the distinction between resistance and collaboration. Such forms of resistance, he comments, 'may be based on the belief that over a period of time – perhaps even generations – civilised values are bound to survive, or the values of the conquered will impose themselves on the conquerors: "Genghis Khan was a barbarian but his grandson Kublai Khan was a gentleman." '[45]

During a prolonged struggle, there are also likely to be dedicated individuals and small groups who are willing to take more high-risk actions. These will sometimes be open – the signing of public protests, participation in demonstrations, and so on, which are certain to lead to imprisonment or worse. (One thinks of Havel and many of the Charter 77 supporters in Czechoslovakia in the 1970s and 1980s, and of similar courageous individuals and groups in other East European countries.) At other times they will be clandestine – setting up escape lines, hiding wanted individuals, smuggling information in and out of the country, and so forth. Such individuals and groups can help to keep alive the spirit of resistance and may take on a key leadership role when the moment comes for renewed mass protest. Again, Havel's role in the events of November 1989 in Czechoslovakia is an obvious example.

When the period of sustained resistance succeeds in loosening the stranglehold of the occupying power or dictatorial regime, and in opening up new possibilities for dissent and open resistance, a final phase of mass action may be necessary to achieve victory. The duration and intensity of this phase will depend in large degree on the way in which the power of the opponent crumbles. Where power and authority have slowly withered away, a final push of mass protest may not even be necessary – though open expressions of dissent will almost certainly become more common and play their part in the undermining process. Poland towards the end of 1988 and the beginning of 1989 springs to mind in this connection. By contrast, in East Germany and Czechoslovakia a weakened communist regime collapsed in the face of a virtual civilian insurrection.[46]

These, then, are the phases as envisaged by Sharp and others. Often, however, there is a coda. This occurs where a repressive regime or the representatives of an occupying state have entered into negotiations for a transfer of power but then prevaricate and seek ways of retaining much of the real power in their hands. Thus, in the case of an occupation, the opponent state may seek to circumscribe the independence of the occupied country in unacceptable ways. Similarly, where the opponent is a dictatorial regime, its leaders may try to prevent the introduction of a fully democratic constitution. Manoeuvres of this kind on the part of the authorities, countered by shows of strength by the opposition, frequently mark also the end of a successful military confrontation such as a guerrilla war.

The strategy outlined here broadly corresponds to the pattern and rhythm of resistance, whether violent or non-violent, that tends to occur naturally following a military takeover or foreign occupation. There is the initial shock and anger which are likely to be expressed in open protest. (Not necessarily so, of course: prudence or trauma may lead to a more muted response, or even to paralysis if the population is completely unprepared and untrained.) These are followed by a more or less prolonged period of semi-collaboration, semi-resistance by the majority of the population, interspersed with selective resistance to particularly intolerable measures, and sometimes more widespread protest. Meanwhile committed individuals and groups help to maintain morale and provide a focus of intellectual and cultural dissent. Finally, if and when the authority of the opponent weakens, mass protests may again become both possible and necessary to win final success. Education, training, efficient organisation and methods of communication, a well-publicised plan of campaign, could all be expected to make the resistance more effective and – ideally – prevent an opponent from ever establishing solid control of the country.

The approach of Boserup and Mack to the discussion of strategy is very different from those discussed so far. They categorically reject an approach which takes as its point of departure a decision as to 'what is really worth defending and what is not, what the enemy might want to conquer and how . . . he is likely to go about it,' and then proceeds to build successive defensive scenarios, each in turn designed to overcome perceived weaknesses in the earlier model and anticipated counter moves by the opponent. Although this ' "stop-gap" procedure,' they say, 'is the one by which military planners normally proceed, this approach to the problem is a complete mistake and the surest path to disaster.'[47] By implication, at least, they make the same criticism of strategists of civilian defence who go about their work in a similar fashion.

As noted above, Boserup and Mack base their approach on von Clausewitz and present a summary of his strategic theory. First the *aim* of war is distinguished from the broader political or other *purpose*. In warfare the purpose is displaced by the aim, and that aim is always the same: 'the overthrow of the enemy'. It is this that gives unity to wars waged for very varied (political and economic) purposes, and makes possible the construction of a unified strategic theory.

Second, the defence, according to von Clausewitz, enjoys an inherent superiority over the offence – at a strategic rather than tactical level (i.e., for 'the offence', read the aggressor or invader; for 'the defence', read the invaded country). Resources, knowledge of terrain, popular hostility to the aggressor, the jealousy of other states towards the aggressor, all work to the advantage of the defence and mean the aggressor must seek a rapid victory.

Thirdly, and crucially, von Clausewitz proposes the notion of the 'centre of gravity' for both defence and offence. He defines this as 'the centre of power and movement' whose destruction would mark a decisive defeat for the one side and a victory for the other. Against the centre of gravity of the opponent 'the concentrated blow of all the forces must be directed'.[48] This centre of gravity will depend on the means each has chosen in pursuing his ends. For Alexander the Great, Gustavus Adolphus, Charles XII and Frederick the Great, according to von Clausewitz, it lay in their armies; in small states dependent on greater ones, it lies in the armies of its allies; in states torn by internal disorder, it generally lies in the capital city.

For civilian defence, Boserup and Mack assert, the centre of gravity is the unity of the population. It is this that must be protected and maintained at all costs as far as the defensive strategy of the resistance is concerned. The centre of gravity of the *counter-offensive* will, they argue, depend on the details of each particular confrontation, and they consider particularly the case in which repression is being used in the form of physical violence against the resistance. But in general the counter-offensive must concentrate on exploiting 'those strains and contradictions which the act of occupation and the struggle themselves generate within an enemy camp for it is these which are most readily manipulable by the resistance'.[49] In Mao Tse-Tung's famous phrase, the aim is to exploit and deepen 'the internal contradictions in the enemy camp'. In sum, 'non-violence seeks to do two things: on the one hand it so organises the defence as to leave as little scope as possible for the use of the enemy's military force; on the other hand it seeks to achieve the attrition of these forces at the ideological level'.[50]

The Canadian researcher Gene Keyes, in an important contribution, argues that 'morale' rather than unity should be considered the centre of gravity of both offence and defence in a non-violent struggle.[51] Roberts too warns against making a fetish of unity and points out that nationwide non-violent struggle has been successfully maintained in spite of deep divisions.[52] (India is a case in point.) He concludes that civil resistance 'would not be equally suitable in all situations, and that the strategies employed in civil resistance should not be confined to those which require total national unity'.[53] Perhaps, then, the double notion of 'coherence and morale' comes close to describing the concept one is looking for here.

Despite their different starting points, the two schools of thought concur about the counter-offensive strategy of the country that has suffered aggression. There is nothing in the general description of its task by Boserup and Mack cited above that conflicts with the writings of King-Hall, Sharp or Roberts. Moreover, the two approaches are at one in identifying three areas in which the counter-offensive operates. In Boserup and Mack's words these are 'the local executioners of repression (troops), the domestic political base of the enemy leaders, and the international alignments on which they may depend'.[54] These are the same 'three fronts' which King-Hall specified as the area of moral and psychological warfare for his projected European Treaty Organisation.

On the defensive strategy of the civilian resistance, the

155

differences in approach result in some instances in substantive disagreement. Sharp argues that 'denial of the attackers' main objectives is obviously crucial and the defence must focus on means to achieve that'.[55] Not so, say Boserup and Mack. Defending the 'centre of gravity' of the defence, i.e. unity, in their analysis, is what is crucial, and it is a complete mistake to believe that this 'must somehow be the ability to perpetuate denial' of the opponent's *purpose*.

> . . . it is not necessarily so that one must seek to bar access to the purpose, and therefore there need not exist any simple relationship of 'protection' between centre of gravity and purpose. The above view would be as false as the idea than in military strategy the defence must somehow be situated 'in front of' purpose, constituting a kind of physical obstruction. This is obviously false and completely ignores the possibility of a strategic withdrawal, pending counter-attack (strategic withdrawal of Russian forces before Napoleon in 1812, guerrilla strategy of withdrawal, etc.). What really matters is that the centre of gravity should be so chosen that as long as it is preserved, counter-offensive and reconquest are possible.[56]

To illustrate the point with a concrete example, the political/economic purpose of the Franco-Belgian occupation of the Ruhr in 1923 was to mine and requisition coal supplies as a means of enforcing the sanctions against Germany. The civil resistance focused on denying the occupiers this purpose chiefly through strikes by the miners and the railway personnel. This was only partially successful because France and Belgium were able to bring in their own labour force, and for this and other reasons the resistance eventually became demoralised and capitulated. In fact the main achievement of the resistance lay not in denying the occupiers their immediate purpose, but in causing divisions within French and Belgian society, and gaining sympathy worldwide, and it was these successes that enabled the German authorities to snatch some concrete gains from the jaws of defeat. As

Wolfgang Sternstein comments, the resistance would have been better advised to have made more use of other forms of non-violent action such as demonstrations, propaganda, protests and complaints, and sought to rouse public opinion in the occupier's countries and internationally[57] rather than concentrating so much on the physical denial of the invaders' purpose and turning this into the barometer of success or failure.

However, where the purpose of the opponent strikes at the very heart of national culture and identity, the distinction between aim and purpose may become wholly artificial. For the aggressor to achieve the purpose is, in these circumstances, to destroy the unity (and morale) of the defence. Unity after all has to be constructed around aspects of the political culture which people prize most highly. The people in Norway could unite behind the teachers precisely because the attempt to introduce Nazi indoctrination in the schools was regarded with total repugnance by most people; had Quisling succeeded here, the Nazis would have achieved both their political *purpose* (or an important element of it) and advanced towards their *aim* of undermining the continued resistance. Indeed, Boserup and Mack themselves cite von Clausewitz to the effect that 'Without a "grand and powerful purpose" the full mobilisation of the forces of the defence is not possible'.[58] Elsewhere they note that non-cooperation and denial in general may be important not in denying the enemy his purpose as such but the means to the aim.[59] Clearly, however, if the opponent can achieve his aim of dividing and demoralising the resistance through achieving one or several of his political goals – e.g. taking over the government and administration of the country, introducing a new ideology into schools and universities – then thwarting these purposes is a crucial aspect of the struggle to defeat his war aim. Success in thwarting his more immediate purposes may also, as Hughan and Ebert noted, serve to demoralise the opponent's forces and administrators and thus contribute simultaneously to the counter-offensive.

Despite the disputes and differences of emphasis, there is in fact a considerable measure of agreement about what the aims of a civil resistance strategy should be, and, to a lesser extent, how to go about achieving them. The grand purpose must be to deter or dissuade attack on the country as much as to defend it. This involves advance preparation and planning, well publicised to ensure that potential aggressors are aware of the problems they will encounter. In an actual struggle, there must be an initial strong response to signal the determination to resist. It will be vital to build up and sustain cohesion and morale, and to defend those key aspects of the national political culture around which the cohesion of the resistance is built. It will be necessary to devise a short- and longer-term plan of campaign and to construct strategies appropriate to different phases of the struggle. These must take into account the nature of the attacking and defending societies and their relative strengths and weaknesses. The aim must be not only to defend the society under attack but to undermine the power and authority of the opponent. This may be possible through contact with the occupying forces and functionaries on the spot; through elements within the opponent's society; and through the other states, or the international community as represented by the UN or regional organisations.

Problems and limitations

Greater attention has been devoted in recent years to the possible limits of defence by civil resistance. Roberts, in his studies for the Research Institute of Swedish National Defence, argued that it was unlikely to prove effective in replacing some of the functions of the Swedish armed forces, including notably the defence of sparsely populated areas in the north of the country. He has moved away from any inclination to see civilian defence 'as a total and self-contained alternative to all aspects of military defence'.[60] Boserup and Mack take it for granted that it has no relevance to an attack aimed at genocide. Sharp and some other researchers are not prepared to concede this point, at least in the absence of further research. Indeed, though Sharp generally couches his claims for civilian defence in cautiously academic language, it is apparent from some of his statements that he sees civilian defence as having the potential to replace completely military forms of defence.

The Dutch researcher Alex Schmid is representative of a generation of researchers who have cast a rather colder eye on some of the claims made for civilian defence. In a study of civil resistance against communist regimes published in 1985,[61] he argues that the research had previously paid insufficient attention to the nature of the aggressor regime. This does less than justice to Gene Sharp's work, much of which has focused on the nature of state power in general, and dictatorial state power in particular, with the aim of demonstrating the fallacy of assuming that civil resistance can be effective only against 'liberal' democratic opponents, such as the British in India, and showing how even the most brutal dictatorships can be – and have been – undermined by non-violent forms of action. Schmid, however, has done valuable work in identifying those conditions that facilitate the success of civilian defence, some of which are indeed, in his view, necessary for it to be viable.[62] These are, in summary form:

1. The presence of a well-trained non-violent core group to act as the social carrier.
2. A degree of independence on the part of the defending society in terms of the skills and resources necessary for a defence effort.
3. The capacity to communicate a) within its own ranks, b) with third parties, c) with the aggressor's social base.
4. A tradition of free democratic activity where there is widespread capacity to take initiatives.
5. A social system which is perceived as more legitimate than that imported by the attacker.
6. An ability on the part of defenders to maintain social cohesion.
7. Great dependence of the aggressor on the defender's (or an ally's) economic, social or administrative system.
8. Human contact between resisters and aggressors.

9. Widespread acceptance by public opinion, foreign governments or the attacker of the legitimate status of the defenders.

10. The absence of total irrationality and permanent fanaticism on the part of the chief adversary or at least on the part of those who can influence him.[63]

While all conditions will be present only under optimum circumstances, some, Schmid argues, are necessary for civil resistance to come into existence (conditions 1, 2, 3a), some are important to make it viable (notably conditions 9 and 10), while two of them (conditions 3 and 7) are crucial 'since they indicate susceptibility to the persuasion and noncooperation instruments of nonviolence'.[64] On the basis of past failures of civil resistance against communist regimes – in postwar Lithuania, East Germany (1953), Hungary (1956), Czechoslovakia (1968), Schmid rules out the idea that 'social defence' (civilian defence) could replace military defence as the chief instrument of national security. He concludes, however, that there is much to be said for it as a *supplement* to military defence.[65]

Sharp, by contrast, is unwilling to accord it simply a subordinate and supportive role. He points to the strategic risks and dilemmas of continuing to rely on nuclear weapons, to the limitations of non-nuclear (military) defence proposals such as 'defensive defence', and to the likelihood that further research will uncover the full potential of civilian-based defence, leading to the elimination of war. Sharp, as we noted, accepts that aggression for some objectives is harder to counter by civil resistance than others. If the aims of the aggression are ideological (e.g. spreading the doctrines of communism), the kind of moral and psychological warfare as recommended by King-Hall and others, coupled with non-cooperation and (ideally) international pressure, has a reasonable chance of being effective. If the aggression has been undertaken for economic objectives, it can often be countered by mass non-cooperation – though, as the *Ruhrkampf* showed, non-cooperation alone will not suffice where the aggressor can function quite adequately without indigenous support. (See condition 7 of Schmid's list.)

More difficult are the cases where the objective is simply to occupy territory. If, for instance, the opponent's aim is to establish a strategic outpost in a remote area, there may be little or no face-to-face contact with the indigenous population. Obviously any dependence on local supplies offers a possible point of leverage, but, as Sharp suggests, it may be more appropriate in such cases to concentrate on mustering international pressure, for instance by third-party countries and by the UN. Some of his suggestions for meeting this kind of situation have a flavour of de Ligt – 'organised action by dock workers, pilots, airport workers and others to halt travel, transportation, and shipping of needed materials'. In exceptional circumstances, he suggests, a 'non-violent invasion', along the lines of the attempted invasion of the Portuguese enclave of Goa in 1955 by Indian *satyagrahis*, might be attempted.

Most difficult of all is where – as in the case of Serb aggression against Bosnia – the object is forcibly to remove the population, or even to carry out a policy of genocide, in order to colonise the territory. But mass non-cooperation can sometimes prove effective even here, Sharp argues, since it is physically difficult to remove tens or perhaps hundreds of thousands of people who refuse to cooperate, while the attempt to do so could have an insidiously undermining effect on the morale of troops psychologically prepared for combat against an armed opponent rather than the deportation or massacre of an unarmed yet defiant population. War, he states, has not proved effective in preventing genocide and on occasions has provided the conditions for it to take place. Thus the context of global war facilitated – and was perhaps necessary to – the introduction of the Nazis' 'final solution' of the so-called 'Jewish problem'. Even then, the success or otherwise of Hitler's genocidal policies against the Jews in occupied Europe depended greatly on the extent to which there was already widespread anti-Semitic prejudice, and to which the Nazis could count on local cooperation.[66]

This does not demonstrate that non-violent forms of resistance to invasion by an opponent bent on genocide would succeed, only that they would not necessarily fail. But sustained civil resistance of an open confrontational kind seems highly improbable in the foreseeable future in circumstances of such extreme repression, unless one is thinking of a trained 'non-violent army' (as envisaged by Gandhi) taking a stand to protect the civilian population. Certainly persistence in the face of repeated massacre, coupled with the maintenance of a strictly non-violent discipline, would require a dedication that is far removed from the spirit of Sharp's approach in recent decades, which has sought to distance civilian-based defence from non-violence as an ethical or ideological commitment.[67]

An heroic non-violent defence in such a situation, if it were to become a genuine political possibility at some future date, could cause grave and perhaps insurmountable problems for the opponents because of its impact on their troops, on the population at home, and on the international community. The latter could be expected to react vigorously, perhaps even to the extent of authorising military intervention. However, if the response was to be confined to non-military sanctions (as advocates of civilian defence as a total substitute for war would want) this would be unlikely to save the lives of those at immediate risk. The Bosnian situation at the time of writing underlines the difficulty and provides little comfort. Nevertheless, one may reasonably wonder if mass civil resistance, had it been possible, would not have served the Bosnian defenders better than territorial defence with inferior weapons which provided the attackers with the excuse for shelling Sarajevo and other cities, and contributing to the hatred and extremism in which atrocities and massacres have become commonplace.[68]

One weakness of civil resistance, at least as it has so far been developed, is that in the situation where the attackers are prepared to resort to repeated massacre, and even genocide, it has to rely maximally on its moral and psychological impact and minimally on 'non-violent coercion' – when one would want things to be the other way round. Of course, if the opponents' forces can be induced to rebel, or if their authority at home can be undermined, non-violent coercion can come into play. But in that case the power to coerce rests in the hands of others who must first be won over and perhaps be prepared to put their own lives on the line to bring the aggression to an end. This is a different situation from that, say, in Berlin in 1920, when the leaders of the Kapp putsch found themselves paralysed by the non-cooperation of the population. International sanctions, rigorously applied, can be coercive, but again this requires the preliminary mobilisation of third parties. Moreover, as noted earlier, sanctions tend to take effect only gradually, and their political – as opposed to their economic – impact is often unpredictable and may even at times be counter-productive.[69]

Clearly, whatever the strategy adopted, and however careful the advance preparation, there will be some situations in which the balance of forces is such that civilian defence will not succeed within any kind of time-span that politicians have to reckon with. (The same is often true, of course, of military defence.) It may contribute, as argued in an earlier chapter, to a long-term shift in the balance of power so that a point is reached, perhaps after several years or decades, at which non-violent struggle can succeed. The long struggle against Soviet hegemony in Eastern Europe is a case in point; another is that against dictatorship and exploitation in much of Latin America.

Finally, however, a judgement that civil resistance is unlikely to succeed in the short to medium term is not necessarily a sufficient argument for embarking on war – even a war of self-defence. Civil resistance may be seen as a more effective way of contributing to eventual liberation than engaging in a desperate military struggle. The argument against a military response is particularly strong where there is a serious risk of nuclear escalation. A war to 'roll back the curtain' and liberate Eastern Europe or the Baltic republics in the 1950s and 1960s – favoured by some US politicians and military strategists – would have been disastrous, even though there was no foreseeable possibility of successful liberation by civil resistance at that point. In the long term, in quite different international circumstances, liberation proved possible without the ultimate disaster of unleashing a third, and in all probability nuclear, world war.

Deterrence and dissuasion

Given the strategic strengths and limitations of defence by civil resistance, what potential does it have to deter attack? It is useful, in considering this, to distinguish between deterrence and the broader concept of dissuasion. Dissuasion covers all the pressures and calculations which might convince a rational government that it is more to their advantage to maintain peace than to seek advantage by an aggressive war. Deterrence refers more narrowly to the fear of the consequences of embarking on war. In a sense there is a level of background dissuasion and deterrence built into the international system – leaving aside for a moment the threat of provoking military retaliation and more general war – as a result of the interdependence of national economies, the reluctance of states to be cast in the role of international pariahs, and the possibility of facing international economic and political sanctions. It breaks down in extreme circumstances but it contributes to keeping the peace between most states most of the time.

A system of civilian defence could certainly increase the stakes, and it thus has some dissuasive and deterrent force. King-Hall, as we noted, thought it rather more convincing a deterrent to Soviet aggression than the threat of all-out nuclear war, which would have led to total devastation on both sides. As he pointed out, to invade a country prepared and trained to offer mass civil resistance involves considerable risks. The economic and political goals that prompted the attack may be thwarted, leading to humiliation and loss of face. Troops and civil servants may prove unreliable, and disaffection may spread to the home country. Other states which the potential aggressor already rules or dominates may take advantage of the situation to stage violent or non-violent insurrections. Allied states may desert one's cause and international sanctions may well be invoked, especially as it will be self-evident which side is the aggressor.

Applying this concretely to the East–West situation during at least the final phases of the East–West confrontation during the 1970s and 1980s, the Soviet Union stood to lose far more than it was likely to gain by invading Western Europe, quite aside from the fact that this would have triggered a global, and probably nuclear, war. For even if the threat of war had been completely absent, the occupation of Western Europe would have represented a massive overextension of Soviet power. The probable disruption of the Western economy alone would have had dire consequences for the whole of Eastern Europe and the Soviet Union, to say nothing of the risk that the Warsaw Pact countries would have seized the opportunity to mount a concerted insurrection. Had there been, in addition, a well-publicised plan for mass non-cooperation and non-violent action of various kinds, this would certainly have made the prospect even less attractive. Liddell Hart has suggested that at a much earlier point, during the 1940s, the Soviet leaders hesitated to attack Western Europe because they feared the effects on Soviet forces of contact with the West.[70]

There are positive and negative facets to dissuasion and deterrence. The benefits other countries enjoy from maintaining peaceful relations are the positive facet. The losses they will incur if they break the peace are the negative facet.[71] Thus Switzerland as a world financial centre has made it self-evidently disadvantageous for neighbouring countries to attack it. During World War II, it threatened, in the event of a German attack, to blow up the St Gotthard and Simplon tunnels which were a vital supply route between Germany and Italy.[72] (However, it did also mobilise its defences to resist any incursion by military means.) In 1940, Britain and France cancelled a plan to send troops across northern Norway and Sweden to assist Finland in its war against the Soviet Union, in part because of a Swedish threat to cut off the electricity supply to the railways in that part of the country.[73] Some commentators have also suggested that the Soviet Union's unwillingness to intervene during the 1970–1 crisis in Poland's Baltic ports was the result of the difficulties it experienced in Czechoslovakia in 1968.

One of the limitations, however, of civilian defence as a deterrent is that many of the sanctions it threatens are slow-acting. Thus a government that saw some immediate advantage in invading another state might be tempted to take the risk of doing so in the hope and expectation that it could deal with the longer-term problems as they arose. Another is that in those situations where civil resistance itself is a relatively weak sanction with respect to the aggressor's purpose – for instance, where the intention is to seize a limited tract of territory for strategic advantage – its deterrence value is correspondingly reduced.

The relative weakness of civilian defence as a deterrent in the face of certain kinds of threat is one of the arguments put forward for maintaining a mixed system of defence, i.e. one in which there is preparation for both military and civil resistance. This is considered below. Clearly, however, if civilian defence were adopted as the major – or sole – element in the defence system, it would be necessary to strengthen its deterrent capability to the greatest possible extent. Adequate preparation and training would be the key element here. In addition, international support could be made more tangible by the formation of a regional civilian defence organisation on the lines of the European Treaty Organisation proposed by King-Hall, and more recently, the proposed Baltic Civilian-Based Defence Mutual Aid Treaty. The members of such an organisation could proffer help in the event of an attack on any member by, for instance, offering to provide sanctuary to a government in exile, printing material for distribution to the country under attack and the aggressor state, broadcasting information that the aggressor is trying to conceal, establishing contact with potential opponents within the aggressor state, and so forth. This would be in addition to the imposition of sanctions preferably in concert with all UN member states.

The effectiveness of a deterrent is related not merely to the direness of the threatened retaliation but to its credibility. Nuclear weapons may appear at first glance to represent the ultimate in deterrence. In practice the nuclear planners themselves realised that the threat to use them was not wholly credible in a number of circumstances. This applied, for instance, to the threat during the 1950s and early 1960s to respond to a conventional Soviet attack with all-out nuclear war, since such a response would have been suicidal for the countries of Western Europe once the Soviet Union possessed a large stockpile of nuclear weapons of its own. Some strategists have argued that the threat need only be credible enough to create a doubt in the opponent's mind for it to work. But this is to gamble with a weak hand for very high stakes. Clearly, it was not acceptable to NATO's planners, since the organisation modified its doctrine of Mutual Assured Destruction (MAD) in 1967 to one of flexible response. This allowed for retaliation in stages of increasing severity, starting with conventional warfare and escalating to the use of tactical and 'theatre' nuclear weapons, and finally to all-out strategic nuclear attack. The US, Britain and France also developed and deployed a whole range of weapons to correspond to this new doctrine. Even so it rested on extremely shaky foundations, since the use of nuclear weapons at any level was likely to lead rapidly to full-scale nuclear war. It was in part the realisation of this that created the huge upsurge of protest against the deployment of a new generation of 'theatre' nuclear weapons in Europe in the early 1980s. France's threat to use its nuclear *force de frappe* against the Soviet Union in the event of a conventional attack – 'the deterrence of the strong by the weak' – is even less credible.

No defence policy, in fact, guarantees security, or is without its drawbacks and limitations. The nuclear deterrent strategy of the superpowers and their allies during the period of the Cold War put all the eggs in a rather rickety deterrent basket and severed the age-old link between deterrence and defence. Either deterrence worked – or there was a disaster without parallel. The Western European countries that opted to join NATO associated themselves with the nuclear deterrent strategy. The countries that remained outside it, like Sweden and Switzerland, had to accept that they were ultimately vulnerable to an attack from a major power, or to nuclear blackmail, but decided on balance that their best interest lay in remaining neutral. In both these countries there was also a national debate in the 1960s about the wisdom or otherwise of manufacturing and deploying tactical nuclear weapons, and in both cases the decision went against doing so.[74] Those decisions involved taking a certain kind of risk but made an important contribution to preventing the spread of nuclear weapons.

Opting for civilian defence would be no different in principle. It would bring benefits and it would entail risks. The benefits – especially if a number of countries adopted it – would include enormous savings on military expenditure, and perhaps moving humankind a step closer to the abolition of war. The risks would include, in some situations, an increased likelihood of invasion and occupation, and perhaps other forms of attack. But the traditional link between deterrence and defence would be reinstated. If deterrence broke down, civilian defence would – at least in most instances – offer some reasonable prospect of successfully resisting domination and ensuring the survival of the society and its values.

A mixed strategy?

The obvious problem about employing a mixed strategy *in the course of an actual struggle* is that the dynamics of military and civil resistance are at some levels diametrically opposed to each other. The problem is likely to be particularly severe where civilians are conducting 'irregular armed resistance' as envisaged in Sweden's plans.[75] Thus actions aimed specifically at undermining the allegiance of troops and officials through moral and psychological pressure depend crucially on the opponents not feeling physically threatened. This is no less important for the resisters, whose very lives may depend on their armed opponents keeping their heads and acting with restraint. The students and young people in the streets of Prague in 1968 were able to engage the Russian soldiers in heated debates and to block the passage of tanks with their bodies precisely because there were no snipers firing at the invaders from behind barricades, much less regular forces pounding them with artillery and mortar fire.

However, certain forms of civil resistance can and have taken place alongside armed resistance in situations of occupation or struggle against dictatorship. Strikes, boycotts and non-cooperation accompanied some of the anti-colonial and anti-occupation struggles in the present century from the Irish War of Independence of 1919–21 to the Algerian War, and the war in Vietnam. In occupied Europe, too, civil and military resistance occurred side by side, sometimes coordinated, especially in the latter part of the war. In Norway there were separate organisations for military resistance (Milorg) and civil resistance (Silorg). In Denmark, following the general strike of 1943 which brought direct German rule to the country, civil and military resistance (mainly sabotage) were coordinated through the Freedom Council.

There is disagreement amongst analysts as to how far the guerrilla warfare in occupied Europe encouraged or restricted civil resistance. Certainly there were instances in which acts of sabotage – plus the German retaliation it provoked – aroused the population to mass civil resistance. Thus sabotage, and German reprisals, sparked off the 1943 strikes and demonstrations in Denmark that brought the period of indirect German rule to an end. Writing of these events, the British historian Jeremy Bennett has stated that they 'showed that both violent and non-violent resistance could work effectively together, and that an activist policy did not necessarily bring reprisals on those who resisted by non-violent means'.[76] He also argues that in general it was sabotage that sparked off strikes and other forms of civil resistance, not the other way round. Here, however, military resistance took the form mainly of acts of sabotage, not assassinations of military personnel or full-scale guerrilla warfare. In occupied Norway, too, sabotage was the chief form of military resistance.

Liddell Hart, following discussions with German officers at the end of World War II, came to the conclusion that non-violent resistance was far more baffling to the occupation forces than guerrilla warfare, and on the whole more effective.[77] In general, violent forms of resistance, he argued, tended to handicap the non-violent forms. Sabotage was a borderline case.[78] Where it involved loss of life, as for instance where one blew up a bridge which a troop train was about to cross, it would be 'asking for trouble and reaction'. But more non-violent forms of sabotage, or even destroying bridges and so forth where there was no danger to life, might possibly be combined with non-violent resistance. In the *Ruhrkampf* campaign of 1923, acts of sabotage in which French and Belgian soldiers lost their lives provoked savage retaliation and, in the view of some commentators at least, fatally undermined the civil resistance.[79] In Northern Ireland, the Civil Rights campaign of 1968–9 was upstaged and eventually eclipsed by urban guerrilla warfare and outright terrorism.

What of the relationship between civil resistance and conventional military defence? Obviously, if civilian defence has completely replaced a military system that question no longer arises. But that could only happen, if at all, over a more or less prolonged period during which time military and civilian defence systems would have to co-exist, however uneasily. This does not however imply that they need be deployed simultaneously – or even in succession to each other – if an invasion or occupation occurred. Military defence might be chosen in one situation, civil resistance in another. The Czechoslovaks in 1968 had armed forces, but deliberately chose in the circumstances of an attack by overwhelmingly stronger forces not to offer military resistance but to rely instead on civil resistance.

In its 1983 report, the British Alternative Defence Commission[80] suggested there were four principal ways in which civil resistance could contribute to national defence. It could replace military preparations altogether; it could become the major element in the defence strategy but with some military forces being maintained for essentially 'policing' functions; it could be an option for use in particular circumstances – for instance against the threat of overwhelming force, against nuclear blackmail, or against some peripheral threats; and finally it could be regarded as a fall-back strategy to be used against the occupying power if the military defence was unsuccessful.[81]

Sweden, as we noted earlier, has adopted it essentially as a fall-back strategy to complement military defence in the event of part of the national territory being occupied for a period of time. But, as the summary of the report of the Swedish Defence Commission in 1984 on *Complementary Forms of Resistance* states:

Since Swedish security policy presupposes that every part of the country will be militarily defended, any military occupation by the enemy would be preceded by intensive military struggle. If some part of Swedish territory should have to be temporarily abandoned, considerable destruction of communications, landscape, industry, housing areas, etc., must be reckoned with. Inhabitants may have been evacuated and the number of dead and wounded persons may be very large. Medical resources will be extremely strained, and probably even limited due to actions of war.[82]

It would be difficult to imagine a less propitious starting point for a major campaign of civil resistance, and the Commission itself goes on to observe that 'there may well, therefore, be varying time-lags before anything resembling non-military resistance may come about'. There is every reason, indeed, to doubt if it would take place at all in such a situation, at any rate in accordance with a pre-arranged national plan coordinated by government and having its own command system and infrastructure. Boserup and Mack state the problem in strategic terms. To choose military defence as the first line of resistance is, they argue, to place the centre of gravity of the defence in the military forces rather than in the unity of the civilian population. It is highly questionable whether it could be changed round in mid-stream.

In time, of course, however demoralised the population after the defeat of the military resistance, there would almost certainly be a resurgence of resistance, as in occupied Europe during World War II, in communist Eastern Europe, and even in the Soviet Baltic republics after fifty years of Soviet rule. But that would essentially be a new resistance, improvised at first and then built up from below. Such long-term cultural and political resistance probably should be distinguished from specific, government-coordinated plans for civil resistance with a quasi-military structure and organisation. Nevertheless, civil resistance would be likely to emerge, and to do so within a shorter period of time, if the general public had become fully alive to its possibilities through

171

education and preparation, whether propagated by government or by mass opposition movements like the peace movements of the early 1960s and 1980s.

Lithuania's defence plans, at least as they were developing in 1991–2 prior to the change of government in October 1992, also envisaged a 'mix' of military and civilian forms of defence. But the role assigned to the military was relatively limited. It would a) counter terrorist attacks; b) engage an enemy to signal to the international community that it had been attacked (compare King-Hall's notion of a 'tripwire' military defence by his projected European Treaty Organisation); and c) perform an unspecified role in some future European collective security system. However, in the event of an attack by a well-armed, clearly superior force, the country would rely on some form of civilian-based defence.[83] In Latvia, too, discussions in 1992 centred on the idea of preparations for both military and civil resistance. Its Minister of Defence, Talavs Jundzis, and other members of the Supreme Council's Commission on Defence and Home Affairs, affirmed that it was Latvia's intention to employ civil resistance in the event of a large-scale attack.[84]

It remains to be seen whether such plans will be put into effect and backed with an adequate programme of organisation and training. If it were to be so, it would not be the fully non-violent defence which Gandhi and many pacifists have dreamed of. But it would be a radical departure from traditional military defence and probably represents the closest approximation to a non-violent defence that any state is likely to consider as official policy in the foreseeable future.

Organisation

The question of organisation arises in relation to the peacetime preparations for civilian defence, and civil resistance itself during an occupation, coup or other emergency. We noted earlier that there is a general consensus that it must be based essentially on the independent organisations of civil society – trade unions, professional associations, political movements, Churches, and so forth. This follows logically from the fact that civilians are expected to play the central role in this form of resistance. At the same time there clearly is a need for coordination, and probably also for a specially trained body of men and women with experience in the skills of both mediation and non-violent intervention.

The role of central and local government in the earliest phase of introducing civilian defence would primarily be an educational one – to provide funding for research, to promote public discussion, to establish commissions of inquiry and the like. As we noted earlier, a number of European countries have sponsored studies since the 1960s. Apart from the intrinsic value of the research, one advantage of state sponsorship or involvement is that it gives the ideas greater currency and credibility.

Theodor Ebert is among those who have stressed the importance of sound organisation. He attributes the relative success of the 1930–1 civil disobedience campaign in India as compared with the earlier campaign in 1920–2 largely to organisational factors. In the latter campaign, Congress had strength in depth, with a chain of substitute leaders to step into the breach as soon as one lot of leaders was arrested. As a result, the repressive measures introduced by Britain failed to disrupt the campaign as they had done to a considerable extent in 1922.[85] Civilian defence too, he argues, will be strong in proportion largely to the effectiveness of advance organisation, planning and training. The government of any country adopting civilian defence would need to establish a special ministry of civilian defence which would be responsible for drawing up and publishing a resistance plan, coordinating the preparations of trade unions and professional groups, and 'organising widespread training and education in civilian defence'.[86] He proposes that the education and training should be compulsory. Any tendency for such a ministry to become too powerful and intrusive would, in his view, be offset by the nature of the resistance methods it would be set up to inculcate.

Ebert's organisational proposals are linked to his proposed strategy in the event of a coup or invasion – of working on without collaboration and refusing to cooperate with, or in any way grant legitimacy to, a usurper regime. A chain of substitutes would seek to maintain the governmental system, probably underpinned by a government in exile. To avoid estrangement between such a government and resistance leaders, continuing contact between the two would be necessary, with exchanges of personnel from time to time. Local and regional administration would have a similar prepared chain of substitutes, and there would be provision under the defence laws of the country for the establishment of citizens' councils within offices, factories, associations or areas, perhaps with their work coordinated by a body similar to the general staff of an army. These citizens' councils would take over administrative duties only if and when the legitimate officials and functionaries had been removed by the usurpers, or had begun to collaborate. At the base of the organisation, he suggests, a cell structure would probably be suitable, comprising people with a particular commitment to the notion of civilian defence – an idea also favoured by King-Hall. Thus, at places of work, groups of people would form themselves into cells to draft and expound resistance plans and exert pressure where necessary on the executives and rank and file regarding defence issues.

Boserup and Mack argue that during a resistance struggle there are three functions of leadership which should be divided between different groups of people. First, there is the constitutional role as a source of legitimacy which is often best guaranteed by a government in exile. Secondly, there is the legislative and executive role and the day-to-day strategic and tactical planning and guidance. The part of the leadership fulfilling this function should operate underground within the country. Finally, there is the purely symbolic role – whose importance should not be underestimated. This is often best fulfilled by people who are not part of the political or administrative leadership. They should operate openly but should not be irreplaceable because of their vulnerability. The world-famous long-distance runner, Emil Zatopek, was able to perform such a role in the resistance to the Soviet-led invasion of Czechoslovakia in 1968.[87]

The peacetime training programme envisaged by Ebert would be extensive, focused particularly on three groups: executives at various levels in government and society; leaders of resistance cells; and defence ministry personnel. War games and socio-drama would be used to accustom people to the problems they might have to face, and would train them for the strategy of continuing work without collaboration. There could also be larger-scale 'manoeuvres' where the scene of action 'could be a railway station, a newspaper office, a residential area comprising perhaps twenty cells or a barracks occupied by enemy troops'. Such manoeuvres might eventually be extended to cover whole cities, provinces, or the whole country. This preparation and training would have the additional virtue of signalling to any likely aggressor that the country was well prepared for resistance, and could therefore have also an important deterrent effect.

Ebert's organisational proposals reveal some of the potential social and political dangers of civilian defence. April Carter has noted that it could, paradoxically, lead both to greater freedom and popular participation in politics, and to greater social regimentation:

> . . . civilian defence could also lead to the government making considerable demands on people and to some regimentation. It might for example involve conscription for special training, compulsory training of all citizens, and emergency laws. Civilian defence organisation could also be secret and hierarchical. How far non-violent defence would require regimentation would depend a good deal on the kind of non-violent campaign planned, and how far it was conducted by existing groups and initiated from below.[88]

On the whole, in this essay Carter stresses the tendency of civilian defence to encourage a democratic polity, and points out that 'the propagation of non-violent action, and the radical tendencies inherent in an actual resistance movement, would certainly tend to increase the importance of popular pressure against a government denuded of military power'.[89] However, Carter was looking at the theoretical instance where civilian defence had been adopted as the *total* defence system of the country. Where it was adopted as a complementary strategy to military strategy – as would almost certainly be the case in the early stages and perhaps for an indefinite period – the government would not be denuded of military power and the danger of regimentation would need to be taken very seriously.

There is indeed something of a parallel between this discussion and that relating to the effects of having a system of territorial defence in which the total adult population (or the male section of it) receives military training, and weapons are dispersed throughout the country. This is sometimes seen as an ultimate guarantee against the abuse of power by the central government and a stimulus to political decentralisation. However, where the arms, and the military organisation and training, are all under the control and direction of the state, the effect can be to strengthen rather than weaken state power and even to produce new social mechanisms for ensuring conformity. Adam Roberts points out that Yugoslavia's institution of a decentralised defence policy, which was brought into effect between 1967 and 1969, placed equal reliance on the Yugoslav People's Army and Territorial Defence Units with a largely guerrilla purpose. Far from leading to political decentralisation, however, it contributed to a general tightening up of Yugoslav society, including the introduction of new laws on defence, military service, and a new constitution of a more centralist character. One important reason for this was that it was felt that a decentralised defence system, where guerrilla units were assigned an important role, called for a 'fairly rigid system of command and control and also for a unifying ideology, in order to prevent the decentralised system from degenerating into one where arms might get taken up for local causes'.[90] One hopes, Roberts adds, 'that any introduction of whatever form of civilian defence will not actually lead to some increased centralisation of societies, but it is not impossible'.

One of the leading French researchers in the field of non-violent action and civilian defence, Jean-Marie Muller, though no less insistent than Ebert on the importance of organisation, argues that it must be based on 'the voluntary commitment of each person, not on the forced obedience of all'. The organisation, he envisages, is solidly grounded in civil society, and allows for the maximum democratic participation and self-management. A single decision-making centre would, he concedes, be necessary to ensure cohesion and the effectiveness of an action. But the organisation should consist of a decentralised network with local groups being encouraged to take it in turns to organise nationwide actions.[91]

In some of the more anarchist-oriented anti-militarist groups and organisations, the notion of the government playing any role in organising civil resistance is viewed with suspicion, if not rejected outright. Muller's position is different. 'To defend society,' he says, 'is also to defend the democratic state, i.e. to defend the institutions which permit the free exercise of executive, legislative and judicial powers.' The responsibility of government in the process of constructing civilian defence is 'to envisage concretely in each sector of the administration and the public services what could be the modalities of non-collaboration with an illegitimate power'. However, resistance can only be organised effectively if it is the result of the conjunction of two movements – 'the one being impelled from above by the public authorities and the other from below by citizens aware of their proper responsibilities and determined to assume them'.[92]

For Muller, civilian defence and democracy are inextricably linked. At present, all preparation of civilians for defence takes place within the framework of the military institution, and it is precisely this that hampers the development of a spirit of defence among the population, for it is a framework outside their daily life and experience. By contrast, the preparation and organisation of civilian defence takes place within the framework of the same structures of civil society where citizens 'daily exercise their civic responsibilities and social activities'. It is essential, he argues, to think of mobilising citizens for defence in the framework of the same institutions that guarantee democracy. In order for the spirit of defence effectively to spread throughout society 'it is necessary to *civilise defence*, not to *militarise civil society*'. Finally, he maintains that one of the postulates of civilian defence is that 'the best means of preparing for the defence of democracy at a time of crisis is to strengthen it and make it more effective in time of peace. The more the citizens of a country, men and women, have the feeling of living in a society which gives them justice, the more they will be motivated to defend that society against the threats it could encounter.'[93]

This touches upon the wider point of the relationship between civil resistance and popular empowerment.

Chapter 7

Popular Empowerment and Democratic Values

Civil resistance played a central role in the creation of representative democracy. We noted in Chapter 2 the role of the Corresponding Societies in Britain from the late eighteenth century onwards, the establishment of press freedom in the post-Napoleonic period through the defiance of publishers of stamp duties and other restrictions, the central importance of the Peterloo Massacre in establishing the right of assembly and the use made of that right by the Political Union which spearheaded the campaign for the first Reform Bill in 1832. Subsequently the Chartist movement, with its mass marches, petitions and public demonstrations, and its threat of a general strike, popularised the notion of universal suffrage and democratic representation as it is understood today, even if the political establishment was able to resist the demands at the time. The right to strike, and to form trade unions, was established through similar grass-roots organisation and agitation, often in open defiance of the laws of the day. And, of course, in the present century, the women's suffrage movement used both constitutional agitation and direct action in their campaign for women to be given the vote.

This story of pressure from below, and the open defiance of unjust or restrictive laws, is repeated in many other European countries which today have a system of representative – if still far from fully participatory – democracy.[1] In the European colonies, starting with Britain's colonies in America and Ireland in the late eighteenth century, agitation for independence and a more representative political system went hand in hand. The American

179

Declaration of Independence encapsulated the ideals and democratic stirrings of the time, and its influence down to the present time is well documented. In the present century, as we have seen, civil resistance was the key element in the Indian independence struggle, which had a profound influence on all post-World War II anti-colonial struggles. Independence has not always brought democracy, but it opened the way to democratic rule, and, where it was preceded by mass non-violent agitation, put a tool in the hands of the ordinary people which they could later use to assert their rights. Finally, civil resistance has been at the heart of the campaigns for civil rights and democracy that have so dramatically changed the world over the last decade or so – in Europe, Latin America, parts of Asia, South Africa.

But if civil resistance has played an undeniable role in establishing democratic self-government, does it continue to have a role once a representative system has been installed? Is it a mode of acting that can deepen and enhance grass-roots participation in government, or might it, on the contrary, constitute a threat to democracy?[2]

The latter question does not, of course, arise in respect of purely persuasive forms of civil resistance such as marches, demonstrations, vigils, symbolic actions, and so forth. The right of assembly and peaceful demonstration is indeed one of the touchstones of a democratic system. The question arises only where civil disobedience or other more or less coercive forms of resistance are involved. Since a democratically elected government and legislature has passed or endorsed the laws, so the argument runs, it is incumbent upon every citizen to obey them. The proper course of action where a law is considered objectionable is to use the constitutional channels to have it rescinded. Similarly, political strikes, and other forms of direct action intended to obstruct the carrying out of government policy in domestic or foreign affairs, are undemocratic and unconstitutional.

Let us acknowledge that civil disobedience, normally in conjunction with the threat or use of military force, can pose a threat to a democratically elected government. Nor is this simply a theoretical possibility. In Czechoslovakia in 1948, mass demonstrations of factory workers under communist direction precipitated the overthrow of a democratic coalition government and the start of over forty years of dictatorial one-party rule. The coup in Chile in 1973 was preceded by a strike of transport and other workers. The Ulster workers' strike in Northern Ireland in 1974 which overturned the power-sharing executive might be cited as another example. However, the fact that civil disobedience is capable in some circumstances of undermining democratic government does not mean that it has no place at all in a democratic state. Two factors are central in unscrambling the issue. First, the type of civil disobedience. Second, the circumstances in which it is being used.

It is important, firstly, to distinguish between 'defensive' and 'offensive' civil disobedience. The most clear-cut form of defensive disobedience is conscientious objection, where individuals disobey the law at the point at which it makes demands on them which they cannot in good conscience comply with. Conscientious objection to military service is the best-known example of this type of civil disobedience, but not the only one. War-tax refusal is another which has been undertaken by both men and women at various times and places. Many people in Britain in 1990–1 refused to pay the new poll tax because they considered it fundamentally unjust.

The civil disobedience of tens of thousands of conscientious objectors during the First World War led to modifications in the law in many countries, most notably Britain. Exemptions were made easier, punishment for disobedience reduced. This reflected a belated acknowledgement that the conscientious objector was entitled to act as he did, and in a sense could do no other, even though this meant disobeying the law. Where exemption was ruled out, for whatever reason, there occurred a clash of conflicting obligations. The objector, if he was sincere, could not abandon his principles by agreeing to be conscripted. Indeed, democracy itself would have been the poorer had he done so. The state, on the other hand, felt obliged to prosecute in order to uphold the law.

Over time, the strength of the objector's case was implicitly acknowledged, at least in most Western democratic countries, by broadening the provision for conscientious objection within the law and by the imposition of more lenient sentences on those who nevertheless fell foul of it. In the best cases the object of the sentence was not so much to punish the genuine objector as to deter the bogus one.

The more tolerant latter-day treatment of conscientious objectors in some countries reflected an acknowledgement within liberal democracies of the individual right of conscience. The individual had a duty to break the law where it made unacceptable demands on him or her personally. In doing so, however, the objector had to be prepared to accept any reasonable penalty which the law prescribed. The state for its part had to see that the law was upheld, but also had an obligation to do so in a way that took account of the validity and social contribution of conscientious disobedience.

A second type of defensive disobedience occurs where the state, instead of making unacceptable demands on the individual, imposes unreasonable restrictions on individual or collective freedom of action – for instance, by introducing laws or injunctions which limit traditional rights of assembly. Defying such restrictions is a more assertive kind of civil disobedience than conscientious objection. The conscientious objector is forced to make a choice at the point at which the state demands his cooperation. But the person who decides, say, to join in a public protest in defiance of restrictions imposed by the authorities has greater freedom of action. He or she can simply ignore the problem or postpone challenging it until another occasion. But though more assertive, this form of civil resistance remains essentially defensive in character.

Gandhi, as we noted earlier, distinguished between defensive and offensive civil disobedience in his campaigns in India. During the 1920–2 campaign of non-cooperation, he had planned 'offensive' civil disobedience to take place in its final stage when he was sure the people who would be involved were fully versed in the discipline of non-violence. However, when the British authorities passed emergency measures banning meetings, demonstrations and the distribution of 'subversive' literature, he authorised the defiance of those particular injunctions. Not to have done so would, of course, have risked seeing the whole Congress organisation paralysed.

The case for defensive civil resistance of this second type in a democracy is self-evident when the laws or injunctions themselves represent a denial of basic human rights. The respect of those rights is even more fundamental to the notion of democracy than majority rule. No majority, however large, no government, however strong its mandate from the electorate, is entitled to disregard them. To the degree that it does so, it is acting undemocratically. If the violations are sufficiently serious and widespread, the government in question forfeits altogether its right to be considered democratic. In short, there are two principles embodied in a democratic system: rule by the majority is one; but respect for certain individual and collective rights and freedoms is the other and more fundamental one. Should the two principles collide, it is the second that must at all costs be defended. Thus to resist the encroachment of basic rights by a duly elected government is not to deny democracy but to uphold it.

This dual nature of democratic self-government is in fact embodied in the Bill of Rights in the US and some other constitutions, which define limits within which every government is obliged to act in relation to its own citizens. The civil rights movement in the United States in the 1950s and 1960s made use of this fact and had recourse both to civil disobedience (against discriminatory states' laws) and the Federal courts in pursuit of its cause.

The central point here hardly needs to be laboured. Hitler came to power constitutionally in Germany in 1933. It is a moot point how far his persecution of the Jews accorded with the wishes of the majority of the German people at that time. But it makes no difference to the point of principle. The policy would have been not only heinous but fundamentally undemocratic, however many people supported it, and civil disobedience of the most assertive and obstructive kind would have been justified in resisting it. The tragedy is that whereas the Kapp putsch in Berlin in 1920 was defeated by a general strike and non-cooperation, the constitutionalism of Hitler's accession to power left the social democrats, the trade unions and other opponents of Nazism unsure of how to react.[3] (The relative weakness of the trade union movement after years of depression was, of course, another important factor.)

Hitler represents the extreme case, though one that clarifies the basic argument. A less obvious case is that of indigenous peoples in many parts of the world, from Guatemala and Brazil in the 'Third World' to the US, Canada and the Scandinavian countries, who have found their rights ignored and their culture threatened with destruction. In the 1970s and 1980s many indigenous peoples began to use civil disobedience and non-violent direct action in defence of their rights. They were clearly entitled to do so even in the face of governments duly chosen by a majority of the electorate. The justification, in morality and even in law, for the use of non-violent direct action and civil disobedience by the civil rights movement in the US led by Martin Luther King is now hardly a matter of dispute. It was those Southern states which continued to practise discrimination that were acting against the whole spirit of democracy and in fact violating Federal law and the US constitution. Rosa Parks defied Alabama State law when she refused to move from the front of a bus in Montgomery in 1955. But she was asserting her basic right as a human being, and as a US citizen, and in due course the Supreme Court found in her favour.

The debate about civil disobedience and democracy has perhaps focused most intensely in the postwar years on the strategy and tactics of part of the nuclear disarmament movement in the late 1950s/early 1960s and again in the 1980s.[4] The debate is worth recapitulating since it touches upon all the central issues we are considering. I look here at the debate in Britain, though there were parallel debates in every country where the policy of relying on nuclear weapons was seriously challenged.

The accusation made against the non-violent direct actionists by their critics was that they were acting undemocratically. In

Britain, a duly elected government had decided upon a defence policy that involved both the manufacture of Britain's own Bomb and the deployment of British and US nuclear weapons in Britain. The opponents of this policy had the right to campaign against it and to persuade their fellow citizens to elect a government in the future which would pursue a different one. They had no right, said their critics, to obstruct the implementation of the existing policy through sit-downs, occupations, the fomenting of political strikes and other obstructive tactics. It was an objection raised not only by people outside the anti-nuclear movement, but by some within it, including the leadership of CND, who regarded civil disobedience in these circumstances as mistaken and wrong.

The reply focused on two points. First, the disarmers challenged the democratic credentials of the British decision to manufacture nuclear weapons. The Attlee government had taken it in secret in 1947 at a meeting of an inner core of Cabinet members, and Parliament had not even been informed until some years later – not, indeed, until after the election of a Conservative government! This was an important point, but not decisive. Parliament could, after all, have challenged the policy once they were aware of it. Labour, in opposition, could have taken up the anti-nuclear cause. It did in fact adopt an anti-Bomb resolution at its conference in the autumn of 1960 only to reverse the decision the following year after a vigorous campaign by Gaitskell and others. It took up the anti-nuclear cause in earnest in the 1980s, and fought (and lost) the 1983 and 1987 elections with nuclear disarmament by Britain as the central focus of its defence policy. Thus, despite the wholly unsatisfactory way in which the crucial decision was taken to manufacture and deploy British nuclear weapons, the disarmers could not claim that the policy represented a denial of democracy in the sense of going against the express wishes of the majority of the population. The evidence, down the years, has rather pointed the other way. Labour eventually abandoned its anti-nuclear stance in the 1992 election precisely because it had become, in their judgement, an electoral embarrassment.

The crux of the direct actionist case, however, related to the issue of human rights. Nuclear weapons, proponents argued, represented a denial of the most fundamental of all human rights, the right to live. While their deployment alone was clearly not comparable in moral or legal terms to the actual extermination in the Nazi death camps, their use would be a crime against humanity of exactly the same order and would be likely to have even more catastrophic consequences. And since their manufacture and deployment involved a conditional intent to use them, this justified, in principle at least, resorting to civil disobedience and direct action in opposing them.

In addition to the fact that nuclear deployment represented potential rather than actual genocide, there was another difference between it and the persecution of Jews in Nazi Germany: the citizens whose lives were threatened lived outside the jurisdiction of the state deploying the weapons. In other words, the state was not threatening its own citizens with mass extermination but those of another country. However, the mass killing of citizens of a foreign country is no less heinous a crime than the slaughter of one's fellow citizens. (We can ignore at this point in the argument the fact that the latter would almost certainly have been massacred anyhow in an East–West war by the weapons of the other side.)

The legality, as well as the morality, of nuclear weapons is also questionable under international law. Just as the Bill of Rights in a written constitution sets the limits on acceptable behaviour inside the state, so an accumulating corpus of international law is doing so with regard to the way states may act in relation to other states and their citizens. Nuclear disarmers facing prosecution for their acts of civil disobedience have from time to time claimed that they were upholding the international law that prohibits genocide, and that it was governments which were acting illegally in manufacturing and deploying nuclear weapons. There is an analogy here with the way the civil rights movement in the US sought and obtained Supreme Court rulings in their favour against the laws of individual states. The main difference is that the powers of bodies like the International Court of Justice are strictly limited, being dependent on the willingness of individual states to respect their rulings. Moreover, a definitive ruling on whether or not nuclear weapons constitute a breach of the law against genocide has yet to be given. However, there is currently an international campaign – the World Court Project – to have nuclear weapons declared illegal by the ICJ.[5]

The other point, namely that genocide and mass destruction were only a *potential* consequence of deploying nuclear weapons, not something that was actually happening, is a secondary one. Clearly, there is a greater sense of urgency when massacres are taking place, and it is right that priority should be given to halting them. It is not surprising, for instance, that the Vietnam War replaced nuclear weapons as a worldwide campaigning issue by the mid to late 1960s. However, as nuclear campaigners pointed out, there is an obligation to prevent a crime at the point at which this can be done. Trying to stop the bombers taking off, or the missiles being fired, when war had started would – in most instances – be too late. If effective action was to be taken, it had to be taken in peacetime before the holocaust had begun.

The counter-argument from the supporters of a nuclear-based defence policy was that the weapons were intended for deterrence not use. For one side to renounce nuclear weapons unconditionally would leave it vulnerable to attack or blackmail, and could prove dangerously destabilising. Some defenders of the policy argued that not only was nuclear deterrence compatible with just war principles, but, provided certain conditions were met, actually waging nuclear war could also be so.[6] The more common response, even at government level, was to refuse to face the moral and strategic problem by asserting that the whole point of nuclear deterrence was to ensure that the weapons themselves would never be used.

This is an evasion. Deterrence itself cannot work unless there is a clear intention, a determination even, to use nuclear weapons in given circumstances. This implies the preparation and training of military personnel, and a command structure designed and tested to ensure that if the order to use them is given, it will be promptly and efficiently obeyed.

The unwillingness on the part of many advocates of a nuclear strategy to face up to the possibility that nuclear deterrence might fail was an implicit acknowledgement of the irrationality at the heart of the strategy. The failure of nuclear deterrence and its consequences was almost literally unthinkable to many of those who put their faith in this approach. Not that the notion of deterrence as such was anything new. 'If you want peace, prepare for war' was a dictum from classical Roman times. However, if armed deterrence broke down in the pre-nuclear age, military means might still afford genuine protection. In the confrontation between superpowers armed with nuclear weapons, this no longer applied; deterrence was now based on a threat which it would be suicidal and irrational ever to carry out. To strike first would be to condemn one's own society to destruction, as well as being morally indefensible. To strike second would be an act simply of retaliation, without strategic or political purpose.

Here, then, was an irreconcilable clash of beliefs and values. On the one hand, the disarmers for whom preparations for nuclear war were comparable to the building of death camps in Nazi Germany, and no less incompatible with democratic values; on the other, the government and (for most of the time) the major political parties, who were equally adamant that a principled renunciation of nuclear weapons would be a recipe for disaster. Such fundamental divisions cannot easily be accommodated within any kind of political system, including a democratic one. Frequently they lead to violent confrontation. Non-violent civil resistance provides a possible alternative way forward in such circumstances, and it is in this light that the campaigns of the direct action wing of the peace movement need to be viewed.

Accepting, then, that there are occasions on which it is right in principle to obstruct the implementation of a policy decided upon by a democratically elected government, the question remains as to whether this has any hope of succeeding, and in what way it could be expected to achieve success. On the issue of nuclear weapons, for instance, was the government to be coerced, literally, into abandoning its nuclear strategy?

If there were people who believed that a duly elected government could be coerced into changing the whole basis of its military policy by mass civil disobedience, they were deluded. There was no such possibility and most nuclear disarmers knew it. Even if it had been possible, it is hard to see how a new non-nuclear policy could have been made to stick if the government, Parliament and the majority of the population remained opposed to it.

Probably most protesters who took part in civil disobedience and non-violent direct action saw these as a means of expressing and communicating their abhorrence of nuclear weapons at a level deeper than simply making public speeches and taking part in conventional demonstrations. Some hoped that the movement might herald a new era of more direct democracy, without imagining, however, that the government was about to be toppled. Civil disobedience was theatre, was 'propaganda by the deed'. For many the non-violent discipline, the cheerful acceptance of hardship, the willingness to face fines and imprisonment, were seen as ways of communicating a sense of the seriousness and urgency of the issues at stake. When successful, non-violent direct action could highlight the issues, touch people's imagination and perhaps persuade them to reconsider their position; it could lead some to take part in the civil disobedience, others to join the larger movement. Thus, although there was a coercive – or at least an obstructive – element in civil disobedience, its success depended ultimately upon winning over the population, not forcing views upon it or making it physically impossible for the government to continue its policies by sheer weight of numbers. If the latter should ever be possible, it was assumed that the protesters would have won over the vast majority of the population and the government itself would be fighting a last-ditch battle to maintain its authority. Essentially, even the largest civil disobedience demonstrations against nuclear weapons, and later against the Vietnam War, operated at the level of symbolism not coercion.

This is not to say that numbers were unimportant. Protests by small numbers of people could be effective, as some of the actions of the Direct Action Committee Against Nuclear War in Britain in the late 1950s showed. But large demonstrations pose a more

189

serious dilemma for governments and authorities. They have to make difficult judgements about what level of force they can use without seeming to be heavy-handed and making martyrs of their opponents. If they ignore the breaches of the law, their authority suffers. If they come down too heavily, the publicity can be equally damaging.

The point is well illustrated by the reaction of the authorities to the successive demonstrations of the Committee of 100 in Britain in 1961. Despite prohibitions and warnings, no action was taken against 5000 people who sat down outside the Ministry of Defence in Whitehall in February of that year. Consequently the demonstration was hailed as a triumph for the Committee, which went on to organise further actions along the same lines. In April, police arrested 1000 people making their way down Whitehall to a 'Public Assembly' in Parliament Square. However, those arrested were charged simply with obstruction and received small fines or nominal prison sentences. In both these instances the authorities under-reacted, and the Committee and its supporters were encouraged rather than deterred. The following September, faced with yet another sit-down demonstration in the centre of London, the authorities went too far the other way. Bertrand Russell and about half the Committee were arrested and imprisoned or bound over prior to the demonstration, while the Public Order Act was invoked to ban a meeting in Trafalgar Square. The arrests provided invaluable advance publicity for the demonstration. And as a result of the banning order, thousands of people, who might otherwise have stayed away, flocked to the Square to assert the traditional right of protest.

Governments in countries where there is a long-established democratic tradition are not likely to be overthrown or to abandon a central tenet of their foreign or domestic policy as a result of civil resistance, unless the latter enjoys overwhelming support. However, on a less central issue where the government and its supporters in the country lack the courage of their proclaimed convictions, a campaign might succeed in forcing change without necessarily convincing the majority. One could, for instance, imagine a government abandoning capital punishment in the face of mass protests and civil disobedience, even if it, and the majority of the people in the country, still believed in it but in a rather tepid and half-hearted way, and perhaps with something of a guilty conscience. Even then, in a parliamentary democracy, the policy would have to be ratified by Parliament so that ultimately, unless the resisters managed to convince at least the country's elected representatives, the change of policy would be short-lived.

Non-violent forms of obstruction and intervention may temporarily halt the implementation of a particular aspect of government policy – say the building of a missile base, or the dispatch of troops to a war abroad. But so long as the army, police and military forces remain loyal to the state, the latter ultimately has the physical power to remove the resisters and to maintain the policy. In doing so, however, it has to take account, as we suggested earlier, of public reaction. If it employs excessive force, public sympathy and support may swing against it.

For the protesters, too, winning and maintaining public sympathy and understanding – if not active support – is crucial. If they come across as fanatical and unreasonable, they will lose this and with it the protection it affords against harsh measures by the authorities. If, however, they maintain a non-violent discipline, if they put their case with reason and good humour, and if the symbolism of the action is fresh and imaginative, they may reach out to people in a way that is not possible in more conventional types of public meeting and demonstration. Thus it is ultimately the battle for public opinion which is crucial, not the physical obstruction of a ministry of defence or even of a lorry delivering missiles to a base.

In a situation of immediate crisis, where, for instance, lives are at stake, coercive civil resistance would be both justified and more readily understood. During the Algerian war of independence, demonstrators in France blocked railway tracks to impede trains carrying conscripts to Marseilles for embarkation to Algeria. Since trains were held up for no more than a few hours, this had no operational significance for the conduct of the war. But it is possible to imagine situations where an obstruction of this kind would frustrate a government's intention; mass obstruction at an airbase, for example, might prevent planes taking off for a bombing mission for long enough to cause the mission to be aborted. The judgement as to whether the action was justified would have to take into account the objective circumstances. In retrospect, for example, many British people, perhaps a majority, would feel that if action of this kind had managed to prevent British planes from taking off from Cyprus to bomb Port Said during the Suez War in 1956, hence saving the lives of the hundreds of civilians maimed and killed in the raids, this would have been entirely justified and in no sense undemocratic. Nor is this an entirely fanciful speculation. The well-known Methodist preacher and pacifist, the Reverend Donald Soper, was one of several people who called for civil disobedience to halt the British government's aggression. And although mass civil disobedience at airbases was not a practical possibility, there were reported instances of airmen causing minor damage to aircraft in order to prevent them from taking off.

The problem about granting civil disobedience a recognised place within the democratic process is that if one group can take advantage of it, so can another – racist and extreme right-wing groups, for instance, who have no commitment to democracy either in so far as it implies respect for fundamental human rights, or for majority rule. There will also be many in-between cases where the merits of conflicting claims are extremely difficult to decide. If one allows the possibility of all such groups furthering their claims by non-violent direct action and civil disobedience, is this not a recipe for administrative chaos and making democracy unworkable?

Yes, there is that danger. But there are no sets of rules and procedures for democratic self-government that are free of risk. However, we are talking here not of making civil disobedience *lawful* – that is a contradiction in terms – but rather of fostering a culture in which it has a recognised place but where its validity in any given instance is a matter for public debate and judgement. One safeguard against civil disobedience leading to a kind of non-military coup is precisely that the groups involved in civil disobedience have to face the penalties the law prescribes.

Another is that the effectiveness of civil disobedience and any form of civil resistance depends crucially on public reaction. If the cause is anti-human or irrational, it is less likely to attract the kind of public sympathy and understanding that give civil disobedience its social and political leverage.

Yet there are situations in which it might do so. There clearly is considerable support for racism in much of Europe at the present time, and it is not difficult to imagine a situation in which, for instance, demands for forcible repatriation of people of a different national or racial origin – demands supported by mass demonstrations and civil disobedience – might have the backing of a very large proportion of the population. The chief danger here, however, would not arise from civil resistance but from violent attacks on 'immigrant' communities, as some current experiences in Europe tragically demonstrate – and of course from an eventual election victory of a political party prepared to put such policies into effect. In so far as the culture tolerates non-violent civil resistance as the method of last resort, but firmly rules out organised violence, this would provide a safeguard against threats from extremist groups rather than an opportunity for them to undermine democratic government. Demonstrations of solidarity with ethnic or national minorities, and other forms of non-violent action such as forming human barriers around houses, estates and so on under threat, can also play a positive role in undermining political support for racism, defusing tensions, and preventing the outbreak of violence. One hopeful development in Germany at the time of writing is that millions of people have taken part in demonstrations denouncing racism and racist violence. However, this in itself will not be sufficient unless the social and economic causes of unrest are seriously tackled.

It is sometimes claimed that civil resistance is self-regulating as a democratic tool in the sense that the people willing to take to the streets and risk arrest and imprisonment always represent only a small proportion of those who support the cause in the country. Thus, by the time civil resistance demonstrations reached a size where they threatened the government's ability to rule, the cause in question would inevitably enjoy massive

193

support in the country. There is an element of truth in this argument, but it claims too much. A cause might have the enthusiastic support of a very large section of the population, and its activists be in a position to cause massive disruption, and yet be far from enjoying majority support.

In the 1960s and 1970s a similar argument was often advanced for revolutionary guerrilla warfare. It could only succeed, so the argument ran, where it enjoyed the sympathy and active support of the civilian population. In Mao's phrase, the latter were the sea in which guerrilla fighters swam like fish. This, however, was in the days before the victory of the Khmer Rouge in Cambodia, and the terror and massacre wrought by the Renamo guerrillas in Mozambique, and the Shining Path in Peru.

The problems to which extensive and habitual resort to civil disobedience could give rise are an argument for those committed to democratic self-rule to resort to it with care and discrimination. This in any case is the prudent course if one wants to retain public sympathy. The public are likely to react in one way if they perceive the protesters as people who are driven by deep conviction openly to break particular laws, and to suffer the consequences of doing so, and quite another if they think they are people out to make a nuisance of themselves on every possible occasion. (That a hostile press will do their utmost to present the second image even where it does not apply is another problem.)

Openness in organising and staging demonstrations can also be beneficial in establishing public confidence in the integrity of the protest movement and minimising the risk of violence. Some writers on civil resistance insist on complete openness, virtually ruling out any kind of clandestine activity. In the first period of postwar peace movement activity, beginning in the late 1950s, organisations – in Britain at least – scrupulously adhered to this principle. Thus the Direct Action Committee Against Nuclear War and the Committee of 100 regularly informed the police of their intentions, sending them copies of press releases and plans. However, even they did not publicise every discussion and planning meeting, and there clearly is a degree of privacy which every organisation needs to preserve in the interest of uninhibited discussion. Moreover, total openness about every detail of an action could be very restricting and would rule out some kinds of action altogether. Thus the networks established by Church organisations in the US in the 1980s to support and shelter refugees from dictatorships in Central America would not have been possible without secrecy about the actual operations. In the 1970s and 1980s, Western peace activists (among others) assisted emigré organisations to smuggle literature and equipment to peace and human rights groups in Eastern Europe; this too, obviously, required secrecy. And of course secrecy is crucial for successfully carrying out a whole range of activities under dictatorships. Thus the rescue of ninety-five per cent of Danish Jews in 1943 had perforce to be a clandestine operation.

Although the debate about coercive civil resistance in a democratic context has focused chiefly on public demonstrations, it is in fact extensive non-cooperation which is more likely to render a policy impossible to implement. This is the lesson of the anti-poll tax campaign in Britain in 1990–1. If enough people decided to declare themselves conscientious objectors, or refused to co-operate with the conscription laws, these too would be impossible to implement. Yet conscientious objection or refusal on principle to cooperate is probably the least contentious form of civil resistance, the one most readily accepted as justified within democratic systems. The safeguard here for the democratic process is that non-cooperation does not begin to be coercive unless it is taken up by very large numbers of people (though, again, not necessarily, of course, by the majority).

Political strikes represent another and more controversial form of non-cooperation. Modern industrial society is vulnerable to shut-downs in a few key industries, the electricity-generating industry being an obvious example. It was the backing of the power workers that probably tipped the balance in the Ulster workers' strike in Northern Ireland in 1974. Political strikes can occasionally bring society to a standstill without involving more than a minority of the workforce, provided they are part of a strategically placed industry.

Even so the point should not be overstated. Prolonged strikes impose extraordinary hardships on those involved, and it is highly improbable in any stable industrial democracy that a union could actually dictate political terms to a government under threat of strike action. Even the Ulster workers' strike owed its success as much to the support it enjoyed among the Protestant/Unionist population in Northern Ireland, and the uncertainty and lack of resolve of the government in London, as to the leverage of the strike itself. It is difficult to imagine the exercise being repeated in mainland Britain. True, the miners' strike was the undoing of the Heath government in 1974. But Heath was not forced to go to the country; he did so to strengthen his hand in dealing with the miners and found instead that he did not have the necessary support in the population to do so. He was defeated finally at the polls, not by a kind of non-violent coup d'état.

There are occasions when political strikes, like other forms of civil resistance, are fully justified, even against the policies of elected governments. Strikes would certainly have been justified against the increasingly repressive anti-Jewish measures introduced by the Nazis after their election victory in Germany in 1933. In 1920, dockworkers in Britain refused to load the *Jolly George* with weapons bound for Poland during the war of intervention against Soviet Russia; that too was both justified and effective.

While it is possible to imagine strikes and demonstrations bringing down a weak government in a newly emerging democracy, this is much less likely in the more stable industrialised democracies of the West. In the latter, the reality is that the power of the unions has universally declined due to high unemployment, the introduction of new technology, and legislation restricting union powers and limiting the right to strike. Indeed, the problem at the present time is not whether the unions are so powerful as to pose a threat to the democratic process through politically motivated strikes, but whether they are powerful enough to protect their members' legitimate interests.

Governments, including elected governments enjoying strong public support, do not in practice have complete freedom of action. Vested interests of various kinds within a country, and often outside it, constrain them. The power exercised by organised labour will often be a rather poor counterweight to the subtle and pervasive power exercised by industrial and financial interests. In fact, the real obstacle to the full functioning of the democratic process is not excessive power in the hands of organised labour but the inequalities of wealth and power created by the free-market system − inequalities, indeed, which made trade union organisation a necessity in the first place. This is not to brush aside the problems which politically motivated strikes could cause; as we noted earlier, they have sometimes been used in conjunction with military and political moves to overturn democratic government. It is simply to put them in context.

As long as it remains non-violent, civil resistance cannot directly threaten the democratic system. It may make certain policies − like the poll tax − difficult if not impossible to implement, and it can undermine the authority and credibility of a government, as the de Gaulle government was undermined by the student/worker revolt of 1968, and as the Heath government was undermined by the miners' strike of 1974. It can obstruct government but it cannot impose one on a country against the wishes of the majority. That would require the repressive use of the state's military and security forces, which is the very antithesis of the non-violent ethic. The danger that those who organise civil resistance have to be aware of is that if civil resistance causes a sufficient degree of disruption, it could provide an opportunity for unscrupulous forces to seize power and overturn democracy. This is hardly a danger in the long-established democracies. It could be so in some of the more recently created and fragile ones in Africa, Asia and Latin America, and in parts of Eastern Europe and the successor states of the Soviet Union.

On the positive side, civil resistance can protect and enhance democracy. It can protect it not only against military coups but against more subtle processes of creeping authoritarianism, or an outright bid by an elected government to make its power absolute. It can enhance it by the empowerment of ordinary people. The upsurge of civil disobedience in the US, Britain, Western Europe and other countries in the mid to late 1950s, associated initially with civil rights and peace movements, led to its extensive use throughout society in the 1960s by all sorts of groups and communities, as we noted in a previous chapter. Far from democracy being endangered by this development, all the evidence suggests that it was strengthened and enriched. Indeed, something approaching a consensus emerged in the culture of Western societies concerning the place of civil disobedience in the democratic process. The clearest evidence of this is the relative ease with which even mainstream peace organisations were able to organise civil disobedience on a large scale when they experienced a revival in the 1980s.

Civil resistance is frequently closely associated with a groundswell of support for more direct and participatory democracy, and tends to evolve embryonic institutions which give expression to this tendency. One thinks of the civic forums in Eastern Europe in 1989, the open debates and participatory decision-making in the student revolts across Europe, North America and elsewhere in 1968, the close association with 'base communities' in Latin America and with Gandhi's constructive programme in India. Going back still further to the early years of the century, the aborted 1905 revolution across the Russian empire saw the emergence of the local soviet as a unit of self-government. The fact that the Soviets were taken over by the Bolsheviks after the October Revolution (or more accurately coup) should not blind us to their genuinely innovative and revolutionary potential. As Hannah Arendt has noted, they represent one of the major contributions to the ideal of self-government in the twentieth century.

Civil resistance on the one hand and community-building on the other hold the promise of creating new institutions of self-government and breathing new life into those that already exist. Indeed, if this promise is not fulfilled, there is a danger that the democratic impulse will be frustrated by the huge disparities of wealth and power created by the prevailing economic system, and suffocated by the alienating and disempowering force of the modern bureaucratic state.

Chapter 8

Civil Resistance in the 1990s

What contribution are civil resistance and/or civilian defence likely to make firstly to internal and international security and secondly to social and political struggles in the 1990s? In raising these questions at the beginning of 1993, it is easy to be overwhelmed by the magnitude of the new problems and dangers, particularly the war in former Yugoslavia, the ethnic and nationalist conflict in some of the successor states of the Soviet Union, and the resurgence of racist and even fascist groups in Germany, France, and other parts of Europe. It is as well therefore to remind ourselves again of the positive achievements of the last three to four years and of the central contribution to them of civil resistance.

The overthrow of authoritarian communist rule and Soviet hegemony in the former Warsaw Pact countries of Eastern Europe virtually without bloodshed (except in Romania) was a stunning achievement. In the mid-1980s, such a development seemed almost unthinkable. The few who did suggest that Eastern Europe might rid itself of Soviet domination within a decade or so mostly anticipated that liberation would be preceded by a bloody confrontation with the Soviet Union. Even at the beginning of 1989, when the Gorbachev reforms in the Soviet Union had opened up the situation, a radical transformation in Eastern Europe still seemed a distant dream. The democratisation of the Soviet Union, and its subsequent dissolution as a single state, has been no less remarkable. If the latter has led to instability and bloodshed in some areas, we have to remind ourselves that this is a tragically frequent occurrence when established empires collapse, and that, so far at least, it has not reached the proportions of, say, the communal bloodshed in India and Pakistan following British withdrawal from the sub-continent. The truly extraordinary thing is that the dissolution of the Soviet Union was achieved without major colonialist wars between the centre in Moscow and the constituent republics.

Russia's withdrawal from empire was smoother and more peaceful than many of the withdrawals of the European powers from Africa and Asia in the postwar years. It was far from clear in the late 1980s and early 1990s that it could be so. As many commentators pointed out, there were much closer political links and a stronger sense of common nationality between Russia and the Ukraine, or Russia and Byelorussia, than there had ever been between Britain and India, or France and Algeria, in part because the territories constituting the Soviet Union were contiguous. It therefore seemed likely that any secession would be a particularly painful and probably bloody affair. Indeed, Moscow's military interventions and crackdown on nationalists in Baku (Azerbaijan) in December 1988, in Tbilisi (Georgia) in 1989, and in Lithuania and Latvia in January 1991 augured ill for a peaceful transition, even with Gorbachev at the helm in Moscow. The break-up finally occurred in, again, the most extraordinary circumstances. The attempted coup by hardline communists with the backing of senior Party and army leaders and the KGB was timed to prevent the signing of a new Union Treaty, but was defeated by demonstrations, strikes and other forms of defiance and civil resistance. Had that coup succeeded, there is every likelihood that there would have been not just a return to the Cold War, but the beginning of a very hot war across the length and breadth of the Soviet Union, mirroring the war in former Yugoslavia but on a vast scale and with the very real threat of nuclear weapons being used at some stage.

The developments in Eastern Europe and the Soviet Union have gone hand in hand with the running down, and eventual demise, of the Cold War. This too has brought dangers as well as opportunities. It opens up the prospect of radical nuclear and conventional disarmament, a process that has already begun in a modest way. It removes the strategic rationale for East or West to prop up corrupt dictatorships in the Third World. It gives the United Nations a new opportunity to become an effective force in international affairs. On the negative side, the collapse of the Soviet Union means that the United States is now the sole super-power in the world, with all the temptation that entails to pursue its self-interest at the expense of other states and the international community as a whole.

Elsewhere in the world, as we have noted at several points, civil resistance has contributed during the 1980s and early 1990s to the overthrow of dictatorships, and the process of democratis-ation, from Chile to the Philippines, and from Thailand to South Africa. At the time of writing there is a campaign of civil resist-ance taking place in Burma, where the military have refused to accept the outcome of democratic elections. Cultural resistance also continues in Tibet against Chinese domination. And in China itself, there is unfinished business after the bloody suppression of the democracy movement in 1989.

Given this general setting, then, how are we to assess the likely contribution of civil resistance/civilian defence in the closing years of the century?

Defence by civil resistance

In the restricted sense of governments adopting defence by civil resistance as a major element of security policy *against the threat of foreign invasion and occupation*, the prospects are limited, at least as far as Europe (including Russia) and North America are con-cerned. The exception here could be the Baltic states, whose experience in gaining and protecting their independence through non-violent action has given them a particular interest in the policy. And perhaps if they took it up in a serious way, and the proposed Baltic Civilian-Based Defence Treaty Organisation came into existence, this could have a snowball effect within Europe. The Czech and Slovak republics would seem to be poss-ible candidates, since civil resistance played so central a part in the overthrow of the old regime; however, there was little or no official interest prior to the break-up of the federal state. Sweden since 1986 officially supports 'non-military' defence as a complementary strategy which would come into effect, in the event of war, in areas from which the Swedish military had had to withdraw. It is thus part of the 'total defence' strategy, though still at present a fairly minor part. Moreover, as we noted, 'non-military defence' is defined so as to cover not only civil resistance but 'irregular armed resistance by organised civilian groups'. Other small European states, such as Holland, Denmark and Finland, who have shown an interest in the idea in the past, might reconsider it if circumstances changed. Some of the smaller countries in other parts of the world with an extremely limited capacity for military self-defence – such as Costa Rica – might also consider the option. In the longer term, the requirement for demilitarisation if the threat of nuclear war is to be permanently removed could lead to its adoption on a broader scale.

The reasons for modesty in one's expectations with regard to the remaining years of this decade, however, are that the circumstances seem to be changing in a way that is reducing rather than augmenting interest in the notion of civilian defence against occupation. First, for the countries of northern and Western Europe, invasion and occupation seem an even more remote contingency today than in the final phases of the Cold War. It is almost unthinkable that they should go to war with one another, and the danger of attack from outside has diminished almost to vanishing point – at least in people's consciousness – since the demise of the Soviet Union. Similarly, the threat of nuclear war has receded. Both these facts make it difficult in the short to medium term to generate the degree of interest in civilian defence which is required for it to be seriously entertained as state policy. The point probably applies to a greater or lesser extent to a number of other states – the US, Canada, Japan, New Zealand, Australia.

Second, the trend during the 1990s has been in the direction of relying on collective *military* security at both regional and UN level. Within Europe, this trend is likely to be strengthened if the process of European integration, including the integration of security arrangements, continues. East European countries and the Baltic states seem likely, too, to be included in this process through association with the European Community, or through the Conference on Security and Cooperation in Europe (CSCE), of which they are already members, taking on a military role.

Third, in those parts of Europe (and in the successor states of the Soviet Union outside Europe) where there is the threat or reality of conflict with neighbouring states, it is of a kind which civilian defence is not well equipped to deter or deal with – namely ethnic conflict linked to rival territorial claims. This has so far arisen chiefly in the context of the break-up of former multi-ethnic and multi-nation states such as the Soviet Union and Yugoslavia (though the fighting between Armenia and Azerbaijan broke out some years before the final dissolution of the Soviet Union).

It is likely to prove difficult to persuade states threatened by such conflict to adopt civilian defence – and for those in the thick of it, it is too late to do so. Outside states, and regional and international organisations, wishing to prevent or halt such conflicts, are likely to see military intervention as a necessary ultimate threat and remedy. This means having the military personnel and equipment to carry out intervention. Peacekeeping measures will no doubt continue to play a role, both to prevent conflict and police agreements. This normally takes the form of deploying UN troops who – though lightly armed for self-defence – rely chiefly for their protection upon the authority they derive from the UN mandate. There is scope here for unarmed peacekeepers drawn from people committed to promoting international non-violent action, such as the group that worked alongside UN forces in Cyprus in 1972–4, or the Shanti Sena teams which intervened to halt riots in Ahmadabad and other Indian cities in the 1970s.[1]

Economic and political sanctions may be imposed on offenders to try to bring them to heel, constituting a form of non-cooperation and non-military pressure at the international level. Their limitations were discussed in an earlier chapter. Even when rigorously enforced (which usually entails some military deployment), they tend to be slow-acting. Thus they are not usually capable of bringing an on-going conflict to an immediate halt. (In an exceptional configuration of circumstances, they may do so. Thus US fiscal pressures on Britain, coupled with UN condemnation and the undertaking to deploy peacekeeping forces, brought the Anglo-French-Israeli attack on Egypt to a halt within a few days in 1956.)

The ultimate sanction available to outside states and to the international community as a whole is military intervention, such as that taken against Iraq in January 1991 and as is being called for in some quarters against Serbia at the time of writing. While there is considerable scope for non-violent initiatives, both national and international, as a means of defusing tensions and preventing bloodshed, there is no obvious non-violent alternative currently available, at least at government and inter-governmental level, once serious fighting has broken out. At the level of civil society, there have been pioneering efforts in the shape of teams going into areas of war or conflict, in some cases with the aim of interposing themselves as a kind of human barrier in order to exert pressure on one or both parties. The example of the intervention by Peace Brigades International and US Christian pacifists in the early 1980s on the border between Nicaragua and Honduras was mentioned in an earlier chapter; so too was the expedition by a team of seventy-three British pacifists who travelled to Cambodia in 1968 to try to shame the US into halting its bombing campaign there. Pacifist groups have also attempted interventions along these lines in the Gulf War and the war in Bosnia-Hercegovina. In a sense, President Mitterrand's visit to Sarajevo in the autumn of 1992 can be seen as an act of this character – and proposals have at times been put forward for well-known political, religious and artistic personalities to undertake this kind of intervention. Such actions can be effective, and there would be greater scope for them in the context of a country or community under attack choosing non-violent forms of resistance. But while unarmed intervention and peacekeeping may be able to play a more central role at some future date, it clearly is not at this point an option available to individual states or to the international community.[2]

Nevertheless, the wisdom of the switch towards more direct military intervention by the UN and other bodies, and the willingness to take on a major war-fighting role in disputes and crises around the world, is questionable. It may be that, despite its limitations, an appropriate combination of diplomacy, peacekeeping and sanctions – coupled where possible with imaginative non-violent interventions – will be more conducive to lasting peace than a switch by international bodies towards sanctioning major military interventions. One serious problem with active military interventionism by the UN is that US participation is likely to be required against relatively minor powers if the opponent has acquired modern weapons and built up a strong defensive position. This could lead to the UN itself being seen as – or indeed becoming – a tool of US policy, and eventually to a new split within the organisation, perhaps on North–South lines. (The situation would, of course, be no different – or might be rather worse – if some other state had evolved as the unique world superpower.) The UN will not be able to intervene in all the disputes for which, in a moral sense, there is a strong argument for it to do so, and it would require almost saintly forbearance on the part of the US for it not to give priority to those cases where its own vital interests were judged to be at issue. Already its reluctance to intervene in Bosnia-Hercegovina to rescue a Muslim population under attack from Christian Serbs and Croats is being compared unfavourably with its willingness to intervene against Iraq, its decision to follow up the 1991 war with further missile and bombing raids in January 1993, and its unwillingness to enforce UN resolutions relating to Israel.

Another drawback to the move in this direction is that it requires the United States, and other powers wishing to play a leading role in interventions, to deploy forces strongly geared to the offensive. They need to have the capability to project forces at great distance against opponents liable to be armed with sophisticated defensive weaponry. Thus they would require tanks, bombers, ground-to-ground missiles and in general highly mobile forces, rather than (chiefly) fighter aircraft, surface-to-air missiles and anti-tank weapons deployed defensively. This reverses the moves, or proposed moves, to postures of non-offensive defence which were seriously debated in many countries in the 1980s as a means of confidence-building and reducing the likelihood of aggressive war. The dangers are multiplied when the countries playing a lead role in UN interventions, such as the US and Britain, are competing with one another to supply offensive weapons to oil-rich Middle Eastern countries including Saudi Arabia and Oman.

UN intervention could lead to the forces concerned becoming bogged down in a protracted war – as in the case of the US in Vietnam and the Soviet Union in Afghanistan. This is the nightmare which in part explains the reluctance of the US, Britain and others to intervene more actively against Serbia. But there is an even more terrible nightmare which might indeed have occurred in Iraq if Saddam Hussein had stayed his hand for a few more years: confronting an opponent with nuclear weapons. Sooner or later, if the US/UN takes on an actively interventionist role, this scenario is likely to be realised.

Rather more countries might be prepared to consider introducing an element of defence by civil resistance into their security arrangements as a precaution not against invasion but against coups (including 'executive usurpations' and other forms of internal aggression). Currently there is interest in this in Russia at various levels. In general it is more likely to be taken seriously by countries which have been the victims of coups and attempted coups or who might have reasonable grounds for fearing they could occur than those who have no such imminent fears or historical memories. Among NATO countries, this would apply to Turkey, Greece and Spain, and possibly France. It may apply still more strongly to former communist countries of Eastern Europe and to the Soviet successor states where democracy is still fragile. The more established democracies of Western Europe and North America may feel they are immune to such dangers. But economic and environmental breakdown could change the situation in these countries. They have no more reason than France in the 1960s to be complacent.

The danger is still more tangible in many countries in Latin America, Africa and Asia. There too systematic preparations for civil resistance against military coups would be an eminently sensible precaution. However, in those cases where the government is already closely aligned with the military and has authoritarian leanings, the preparations for civil resistance may well have to be initiated by the organisations and institutions of civil society. Moreover, even where the government is prepared to take a lead in planning and coordination, the active participation of civil society is a *sine qua non* for building an effective system.

Civil resistance at the grass roots

At the grass-roots level, civil resistance will undoubtedly continue during the 1990s and beyond to be a crucial weapon in the hands of those campaigning for civil rights, social and economic justice and democratic self-government – as well as for those struggling to preserve hard-won rights.

In many parts of the Third World, non-violent struggles against dictatorships, and against abuses of human rights, are currently taking place. Probably the best known of these at the time of writing is that against the military dictatorship in Burma led by the human rights activist and Nobel Peace Prize-winner, Aung San Suu Kyi. She has maintained her opposition and leadership role despite being under house arrest since July 1989. In December 1992, in a move clearly influenced by the Gandhian tradition, she embarked on a public fast in support of her demand that the military open talks with the opposition.[3] There are many other lesser-known struggles taking place: struggles by exploited and marginalised people, by indigenous populations threatened with extinction, by communities whose environment and way of life are being destroyed by the actions of central government or international conglomerates.

The defeat of military coups or dictatorships of long standing often contributes simultaneously to international security. This was true in a special sense of the defeat of the August 1991 coup in the Soviet Union because of the country's status as a major power, and because a return to neo-Stalinist rule could have had such dire repercussions. But it is true also in the more general sense that the establishment of stable democratic government is a necessary – though far from sufficient – condition for the establishment of a stable peace.

Some caveats are necessary when making that claim. The collapse of rigid dictatorships may bring long-buried problems to the surface and actually give rise to wars and conflicts – as we see in the states of former Yugoslavia and some of the former states of the Soviet Union. Yet it is evident that there are now groups of states in various regions of the world who are not preparing to attack each other and who do not expect or fear to be attacked by each other. This is true of the states of northern and Western Europe, of the United States and Canada, of Australia and New Zealand. To say that war between such states is impossible would be to offer a hostage to fortune, but it is clearly unlikely short of radical internal changes in one or more of them. As Bruce Russett has expressed it: 'In a real if still partial sense, peace is already among us. We need only to recognize it and try to learn from it.'[4] Democratic government is one common feature of these states. Another is a modicum of prosperity and economic stability. If either of these features disappeared, war between them might again become thinkable. The crucial point, however, is that the struggles against dictatorship, against economic exploitation and impoverishment and against environmental devastation, are at the same time a struggle to establish some of the necessary conditions for a stable peace.

But if these states, mostly in the Northern Hemisphere, are unlikely under present conditions to go to war against each other, they bear in many cases a heavy responsibility for creating and maintaining the structural conditions for dictatorship and instability in the South. Susan George and her associates have demonstrated the economic and social consequences of the debt burden of the Third World brought about by the unequal trading relations and division of labour between the prosperous North and the impoverished South. The problems are moreover now being visited on the North. Deforestation, for instance, with its potentially devastating global consequences, is spurred by the desperate efforts of Third World countries to service their mounting indebtedness. Other problems in the North attributable in part to the same cause include the massive influx of cocaine, the burden on the taxpayer as governments cushion the heavy losses incurred by banks, the loss of jobs in the North as the South attempts to repay debt by reducing imports and expanding exports, and terrorism and war.[5]

The campaigns of environmental movements like Greenpeace and Friends of the Earth, and of organisations such as Oxfam, who are drawing attention to the inequalities of North–South economic relationships, are also making a potentially crucial contribution to security. While most such organisations tend – for good reasons – to concentrate on orthodox campaigning methods, Greenpeace in particular frequently resorts to the methods of non-violent intervention and obstruction pioneered by the Gandhian wing of the peace movement in the 1950s and 1960s. Amnesty International's media campaigns on behalf of political prisoners have also provided a lifeline for civil rights activists in countries under dictatorships, and other countries where human rights are being violated. The attention they have been able to draw to particular cases has not only saved individuals from torture, imprisonment and death, but has thereby, in many instances, won space for civil rights campaigners and community workers building democracy at the grass roots to continue their work. In a rather similar fashion, the Western peace movements of the 1980s were particularly well placed to put pressure on governments in the Soviet Union and Eastern Europe not to harass and imprison human rights and peace activists – and to release individuals who had been arrested.

With the end of the Cold War, and the removal of an immediate threat of global conflict, the peace movement has ceased to be a mass movement. Yet peace and radical movements continue to have a vital role to play. Firstly, there is a continuing need to press for nuclear disarmament. At the Reykjavik summit between Reagan and Gorbachev in 1986, the latter enunciated the goal of achieving global nuclear disarmament by the end of the century. With only one superpower left in the world, and with Russia seeking the cooperation of the West in economic and security issues, there is now a unique opportunity to realise that vision. The START 2 Treaty signed by Presidents Bush and Yeltsin in January 1993 represents a significant step in the right direction. But even when fully implemented it will still leave the US and Russia with enough strategic weapons to destroy each other and much of the rest of the world several times over. Now, therefore, is the time to make plans for global nuclear disarmament and strengthening the provision for inspection and control. If this opportunity is not seized, nuclear proliferation may become inevitable and unstoppable. The declarations by the newly independent states of the Ukraine, Kazakhstan and Belarus that they intend to join the ranks of non-nuclear states represent a bold and welcome initiative to maintain nuclear non-proliferation. Pressure must now be put on other nuclear powers, especially those that make no claim to superpower status – Britain, France, Israel and South Africa – to follow suit.

Secondly, peace and other grass-roots movements have new responsibility in a world in which there is only one superpower. The problems this raises have been touched upon in the discussion of UN intervention. In the bi-polar world of the Cold War period, each side had to take into account the reaction of the other in deciding whether or not to intervene militarily in any part of the world. This provided a measure of constraint on superpower ambitions, and gave Third World governments some room to manoeuvre in playing one side off against the other. That has now gone. Different kinds of institutional and popular barriers must now therefore be constructed or strengthened to prevent the 'New World Order' becoming a euphemism for US (and Western) interventionism and domination. This is not a point against the US in particular. The dictum that power corrupts applies as much in international as in national politics.

Peace and related movements have an important role to play in applying pressure on rich and powerful governments in the North not to arm, support and prop up brutal dictatorships in the South. Obvious examples are the US support in the past for dictatorships in Central and South America, and Soviet support for pseudo-Marxist dictatorships in Somalia and, subsequently, Ethiopia. As we noted, the strategic rationale for so doing has largely disappeared. Often, however, this was simply a camouflage for the pursuit of narrow self-interest, and that motivation could continue to dictate policy. Indeed, as the consequences of environmental destruction and global economic dislocation begin to bite more deeply in the North, the temptation to prop up pro-Western élites in the South, regardless of their democratic credentials or human rights records, may well increase.

Finally, the movements and organisations of civil society, both North and South, can pioneer imaginative forms of non-violent action, including international intervention to prevent, or halt, conflicts. Similarly, they can take the initiative in preparing society for civil resistance against coups or invasions. We noted in an earlier chapter how the Centre for Non-Violent Resistance in Latvia published a series of pamphlets prior to the August 1991 coup in Moscow instructing government bodies, social institutions and individuals on how to respond in the event of an attempted Soviet takeover. In Moscow, following the August coup, a group calling itself the Living Ring was set up to develop plans to thwart any future coup attempts.[6] Peace groups in Sweden, Belgium, Australia and elsewhere have undertaken similar work to promote civilian defence against invasions or coups.

Civil resistance is not only about defence and security but also about empowerment. As such it can add an important dimension to the democratic process. Clearly there are dangers here which were considered in the previous chapter. Nevertheless, even in a democracy, civil disobedience and other forms of interventionist non-violent action may sometimes be both right and necessary to prevent the denial of fundamental human rights to individuals or groups whether inside or outside the state, and preparations for aggressive or genocidal warfare.

Civil resistance, in whatever part of the world, provides people with a means of intervening directly on issues that affect their daily lives. It is clearly empowering when the struggle achieves its objective. But even where it does not, or succeeds only partially, the cohesion generated within the group taking collective action can enhance individual and group self-confidence and self-respect, and open up new possibilities for democratic participation at the grass roots. It thus operates as an antidote to apathy, and to the sense of powerlessness that is often mistaken for apathy. And, in the older-established democracies in particular, these two things represent perhaps as serious threat as any other to civil liberties and to genuine participation in government. They can lead to a situation where the democratic form remains but is largely denuded of substance. Electorates become clay to be kneaded and manipulated by governments and mass parties, rather than active participants in the process of *self*-government. The state too, in the absence of active participation by a vigilant civil society, is tempted to over-reach itself, to pass laws which progressively curtail traditional liberties and extend executive power.

Civil resistance has helped create democracies by overthrowing dictatorships. It has defended them by thwarting attempted coups and usurpations. It has consolidated and enriched democratic life, taking its place alongside the institutional structures designed to provide checks and balances to the exercise of state power. It cannot of and by itself solve the deep-seated inequalities of power and wealth which are a feature of the modern world or the ever more menacing environmental crisis. For that, new cooperative economic and political structures are needed at the base of societies, and cooperation between countries and regions. This is the equivalent in present-day circumstances of Gandhi's constructive programme which he insisted must accompany any campaign of non-violent resistance. However, civil resistance can inform and strengthen the struggle and in doing so reveal the potential of alternative, less hierarchical modes of organisation. It is vital to peace-building. It also holds out the promise of providing a means of waging conflict without violence in a variety of contexts and thus, in the longer term, contributing to the removal of the threat of international war and nuclear devastation.

Appendix

Selection of publications in English related to defence by civil resistance

Elihu Burritt, 'Passive Resistance', first published 1854, reprinted in Staughton Lynd (ed.), *Nonviolence in America: A Documentary History*, Bobbs-Merrill, Indianapolis, 1966, pp. 93–108.

Bertrand Russell, 'War and Non-Resistance', in *Atlantic Monthly*, August 1915, pp. 266–74. Reprinted in Russell, *Justice in War Time*, Open Court, Chicago and London, 1916, pp. 38–57.

Clarence Marsh Case, *Non-Violent Coercion*, first published 1923; reprinted by Garland, New York and London, 1972.

Richard B. Gregg, *The Power of Non-Violence*, George Routledge & Sons, London, 1935.

Bart de Ligt, *The Conquest of Violence*, George Routledge & Sons, London, 1937; Pluto Press, London, 1989, with an introduction by Peter van den Dungen.

Krishnalal Shridharani, *War without Violence: A Study of Gandhi's Method and its Accomplishments*, Harcourt, Brace & Co., New York, 1939; reprinted by Garland, New York and London, 1972, with an introduction by Gene Sharp.

Jessie Wallace Hughan, *Pacifism and Invasion*, War Resisters League, New York, 1942; republished in edited form in Mulford Q. Sibley, *The Quiet Battle*, Anchor Books, New York, 1963.

American Friends Service Committee, *Speak Truth to Power: A Quaker Search for an Alternative to Violence*, AFSC, Philadelphia, 1955. (Includes a discussion of non-violent defence against invasion.)

'Is there another way?' – a debate on 'Speak Truth to Power', with articles by Robert Pickus, Dwight McDonald, Norman Thomas,

Reinhold Niebuhr, Karl Menninger and George Kennan, in *The Progressive*, 19/20 October 1955.

Cecil Hinshaw, *Nonviolent Resistance: A Nation's Way to Peace*, Pendle Hill Pamphlet No. 88, 1956; republished in an abridged version in Mulford Q. Sibley (ed.), *The Quiet Battle*, *op. cit.*

Stephen King-Hall, *Defence in the Nuclear Age*, Victor Gollancz, London, 1958.

Bradford Lyttle, *National Defense through Nonviolent Resistance*, Shann-ti Sena, Chicago, 1958.

Gene Sharp, *Tyranny Could Not Quell Them*, Peace News, London, 1959.

Ralph Bell, *Alternative to War*, James Clarke, London, 1959.

Adam Roberts (ed.), *Civilian Defence*, Peace News, London, 1964.

Theodor Ebert, 'The Reunification of Germany through Non-Violent Resistance', in *Peace News*, 13 September 1963, p. 3.

Adam Roberts (ed.), *The Strategy of Civilian Defence: Non-Violent Resistance to Aggression*, Faber & Faber, London, 1967.

American Friends Service Committee, *In Place of War: An Inquiry into Nonviolent National Defense*, Grossman, New York, 1967.

Adam Roberts, *Total Defence and Civil Resistance: Problems of Sweden's Security Policy*, Research Institute of Danish National Defence, 1972 (mimeo only in English).

Gene Sharp, *The Politics of Nonviolent Action*, Porter Sargent, Boston, 1973.

George Lakey, *Strategy for a Living Revolution*, Freeman, San Francisco, 1973.

Anders Boserup and Andrew Mack, *War without Weapons*, Frances Pinter, London, 1974.

Johan Galtung, *Peace, War and Defence*, Vol. 2, Christian Eijlers, Copenhagen, 1976 (includes essays on 'non-military defence').

Adam Roberts, *The Technique of Civil Resistance*, Research Institute of Swedish National Defence, 1976 (mimeo only in English).

Gustaaf Geeraerts (ed.), *Possibilities of Civilian Defence in Western Europe*, Swets & Zeitlinger, Amsterdam, 1977.

Bulletin of Peace Proposals, Vol. 9, No. 4, 1978 (an issue mainly devoted to a discussion of civilian defence).

Gene Keyes, 'Strategic Non-Violent Defense: The Construct of an Option', in Journal of Strategic Studies, Vol. 4, No. 2, June 1981, pp. 125–51.

Adam Roberts, *Occupation, Resistance and Law: International Law on Military Occupations and on Resistance*, Institute of Swedish National Defence, 1980 (mimeo only in English).

Appendix

Alternative Defence Commission, *Defence without the Bomb*, Taylor & Francis, 1983 (has a chapter on 'Defence by Civil Resistance').

Alex P. Schmid in collaboration with Ellen Berends and Luuk Zonneveld, *Social Defence and Soviet Military Power: an inquiry into the relevance of an alternative defence concept*, University of Leiden, 1985.

Gene Sharp, *Making Europe Unconquerable*, Taylor & Francis, London, and Ballinger, Cambridge, Mass., 1985.

Jan Zielonka, 'Strengths and Weaknesses of Nonviolent Defence' in *Orbis*, Spring 1986, pp. 91–110.

Dietrich Fischer, Wilhelm Nolte, *Winning Peace*, Taylor & Francis, London and New York, 1989.

Gene Sharp (with the assistance of Bruce Jenkins), *Civilian-Based Defence: A Post-Military Weapons System*, Princeton University Press, New Jersey, 1990.

Steven Duncan Huxley, *Constitutionalist Insurgency in Finland*, SHS Helsinki, 1990.

Shelley Anderson and Janet Larmore (eds), *Nonviolent Struggle and Social Defence*, War Resisters International, London, 1991.

An important conference which brought together many of the researchers in the field, organised by the Institut pour la Résolution Nonviolente des Conflits, was held in Strasbourg in 1985 and its proceedings were published under the title 'Les Stratégies Civiles de Défense' by the journal *Alternatives Non Violentes*, 1987. This journal has also devoted several issues to discussion of the topic.

Among French-language publications, I would single out *La Dissuasion Civile* by three people closely associated with *ANV* – Christian Mellon, Jean-Marie Muller and Jacques Semelin – published by the Fondation pour les Etudes de Défense Nationale, Paris, 1985; and Jacques Semelin, *Sans Armes face à Hitler: La Résistance Civile en Europe 1939–1943*, Editions Payot, Paris, 1989 (published in an English translation as *Unarmed Against Hitler: Civilian Resistance in Europe 1939–1943*, Praeger, Westport, Connecticut, 1993).

Since the 1970s, the Mouvement de la Réconciliation–War Resisters International (MIR–IRG) in Belgium has produced a steady stream of materials in French on civilian defence, many translated from English, in their project 'Fiches Documentaires pour une Autre Défense'.

Theodor Ebert's major contributions have been published in German. They include *Gewaltfreir Aufstand: Alternative zum Bürgerkrieg* (*Non-Violent Revolution: Alternative to People's War*), first published by Rombach, Freiburg, 1967, republished in a new edition in

217

paperback by Waldkircher Verlagsgesellschaft, 1980; and *Sociale Verteidigung* (*Social Defence*), Waldkircher Verlagsgesellschaft, 1981. Readers of German may also be interested to obtain a book which advocated a mixed strategy of civil resistance and military defence for NATO in the 1980s: Hans-Heinrich Nolte and Wilhelm Nolte, *Ziviler Widerstand und Autonome Abwehr* (*Civil Resistance and Autonomous Defence*), Nomos Verlagsgesellschaft, Baden-Baden, 1984.

The Program on Nonviolent Sanctions (director Gene Sharp) and the Albert Einstein Institute, both at Cambridge, Mass., promote research in the area. The Civilian-Based Defence Association, also at Cambridge, Mass., produces a regular bulletin containing information and debate on the topic.

Many of the publications mentioned in this book are available at the Commonweal Library, University of Bradford, Bradford, West Yorks. BD7 1DP.

Reference Notes

Chapter 1

1 A point well made by Hannah
  Arendt. See *On Violence*, Allen
  Lane, 1970 edition, pp. 47–50.
2 Arendt, *op. cit.*, p. 44.
3 See, for instance, Michael
  Taylor, *Community, Anarchy and
  Liberty*, Cambridge University
  Press, 1982: the chapter headed
  'Social Order without the State',
  and especially pp. 80–90.
4 Gene Sharp, 'Popular
  Empowerment', in *Social Power
  and Political Freedom*, Porter
  Sargent, Boston, 1980, pp. 331–
  3.
5 The categorisation is Sharp's.
  See his *Politics of Nonviolent Action*,
  Porter Sargent, Boston, 1973.
6 *Guardian*, 15 June 1992.
7 Sulak Sivaraska interviewed in
  ACTivist (Toronto) in May/June
  1992. Reproduced in *Peace News*,
  July 1992.
8 Again a point emphasised by
  Sulak in his interview with
  ACTivist.
9 Arendt, *op. cit.*, p. 53.

Chapter 2

1 Sharp, *The Politics of Nonviolent
  Action, op. cit.*, p. 76. Sharp's
  source is F. R. Cowell, *The
  Revolutions of Ancient Rome*,
  Frederick A. Praeger, New
  York, 1962 and Thames &
  Hudson, London, 1962, pp. 42–
  3. Cowell's account is based on
  the Roman historian Livy.
2 Stan Steiner, *The New Indians*,
  Harper & Row, New York,
  1968, p. 220. Cited in Sharp, *op.
  cit.*, p. 191.
3 The sanctions and inducements
  which societies without states
  rely upon to strengthen social
  cohesion and enforce mores are
  discussed in Taylor, *op. cit.*,
  especially in Ch. 2, 'Social Order
  without the State', pp. 39–94.
4 Taylor, *op. cit.*, especially pp.
  82–6.
5 See Steven Duncan Huxley,
  *Constitutional Insurgency in
  Finland: Finnish 'Passive
  Resistance' against Russification as
  a Case of Nonmilitary Struggle in
  European Resistance Tradition*,
  Finnish Historical Society
  (SHS), Finland, 1990, pp. 52–4.

6 See Charles Tilly, Louise Tilly, and Richard Tilly, *The Rebellious Century: 1830–1930*, J. M. Dent & Sons, London, 1975, especially pp. 276–7.

7 A point noted by Richard Davis in *Arthur Griffith and Non-Violent Sinn Fein*, Anvil Books, Dublin, 1974, p. 92.

8 The account by Flavius Josephus is reproduced in Mulford Q. Sibley, *The Quiet Battle*, Anchor Books, New York, 1963, pp. 111–15.

9 Anthony Black, 'St Thomas Aquinas: the State and Morality', in Brian Redhead (ed.), *Plato to Nato*, BBC Books, London, 1990 edition, p. 71.

10 Clarence Marsh Case, *Non-Violent Coercion: A Study in Methods of Social Pressure*, first published by The Century Co., New York and London, 1923; reprinted by the Garland Publishing Co., New York and London, 1972, p. 64.

11 Sabine and Thorson, *A History of Political Theory*, Holt, Rinehart & Winston, Fort Worth, 1973, p. 338.

12 Cited in Sabine and Thorson, *op. cit.*, p. 345.

13 Huxley, *op. cit.*, discusses this on pp. 69–72. See also the more extended discussion of it in Sabine and Thorson, *op. cit.*, p. 352.

14 Sabine and Thorson, *op. cit.*, p. 352.

15 Christopher Hill, *The World Turned Upside Down: Radical Ideas during the English Revolution*, Penguin, Harmondsworth, 1991 edition, especially pp. 118–23.

16 John Locke, 'The True End of Government', in *Two Treatises of Government*, Everyman (J. M. Dent), London and Melbourne, 1990 edition, p. 233.

17 *Ibid*, p. 237. Cited Huxley, *op. cit.*, p. 73.

18 See Steven Huxley, *op. cit.*, pp. 73–4.

19 Clarence Marsh Case, *op. cit.*, pp. 97–8.

20 As cited by Lord Denning in 'From Precedent to Precedent', The Romanes Lecture, 21 May 1959, Clarendon Press, Oxford, p. 5.

21 Niccolò Machiavelli, *The Prince*, translated with an introduction by George Bull, Penguin Classics, Harmondsworth, 1986 edition, p. 70.

22 Niccolò Machiavelli, *The Discourses*, Penguin Classics, Harmondsworth, 1983 edition, p. 155.

23 See *Anarchy*, Vol. 6, No. 5, May 1966, pp. 129–52, which contains an English translation of the essay with an introduction by Nicolas Walter. The passage quoted appears on p. 142.

24 See *Anarchy*, *op. cit.*, p. 138. Steven Huxley, *op. cit.*, criticises La Boëtie's tract at greater length, pp. 67–9.

25 A point strongly argued by Steven Huxley, *op. cit.*, pp. 67–9.

26 For the history of the essay and its influence on pacifist and anarchist thought, see the introduction to it by Nicolas

Walter in *Anarchy*, *op. cit.*, pp. 129–37.

27 Cited in Huxley, *op. cit.*, p. 26.
28 Cited in George Woodcock, *Anarchism*, Pelican, Harmondsworth, 1963, p. 74.
29 Cited in Huxley, *op. cit.*, p. 27.
30 Woodcock, *op. cit.*, p. 84.
31 Edward Thompson, *The Making of the English Working Class*, Penguin, Harmondsworth, 1968, p. 107n. The book was first published in 1963 by Victor Gollancz, London.
32 Viscount Robert Stewart Castlereagh, Foreign Secretary at that time but widely held to be responsible for the passing of the Five Acts and the Peterloo Massacre.
33 On the reaction to Peterloo, see Thompson, *op. cit.*, pp. 756–7 and 791.
34 *Ibid*, pp. 791–2.
35 Huxley, *op. cit.*, discusses the etymology of passive resistance, pp. 52–3.
36 *Ibid*, p. 53.
37 Cited in Huxley, *op. cit.*, p. 54.
38 *Ibid*, p. 54.
39 See Walter H. Conser, Jnr, Ronald M. McCarthy, David J. Toscano and Gene Sharp (eds), *Resistance, Politics, and the American Struggle for Independence, 1765–1775*, Lynne Rienner Publishers, Boulder, Colorado, 1986. The account here is based on essays in this book.
40 John Adams to Dr Jedediah Morse, 29 November 1815, in *The Works of John Adams*, Charles Francs Adams (ed.), Little Brown, Boston, 1850–6, Vol. 10,
p. 182. Cited by Conser *et al.*, *op. cit.*, p. 3.
41 C. A. Macartney, *Hungary: A Short History*, Edinburgh University Press, 1962, especially Ch. 7, 'Revolution and Reaction', pp. 155–70; and A. J. P. Taylor, *The Habsburg Monarchy*, Macmillan, New York, 1949, Chs V to IX.
42 For details see Huxley, *op. cit.*, especially Ch. IV, 'Constitutionalist Insurgency', pp. 143–252. See also David Thomson, *Europe Since Napoleon*, Penguin, Harmondsworth, 1981 edition, pp. 480–1.
43 Arthur Griffith, *The Resurrection of Hungary: A Parallel for Ireland*, James Duffy & Co., M. H. Gill & Son, and Sealy, Bryers & Walker, Dublin, 1904.
44 T. M. Kettle, 'Would the Hungarian Policy Work?', in *New Ireland Review*, February 1905. Cited in Davis, *op. cit.*, p. 115.
45 See Davis, *op. cit.*, p. 93.
46 See Huxley, *op. cit.*, p. 51, citing Gandhi, *Collected Works of Mohandas K. Gandhi* (Ministry of Information and Broadcasting, Government of India, Delhi, 1958–70), Vol. 7, pp. 213–14.
47 Derek Fraser, 'The Agitation for Parliamentary Reform', in J. T. Ward (ed.), *Popular Movements, c. 1830–1850*, Macmillan, London, 1970, pp. 34–5. Cited in Tilly, *op. cit.*, p. 276.
48 Davis, *op. cit.*, p. 92.
49 See F. S. Lyons, *Ireland Since the Famine*, Weidenfeld and Nicolson, London, 1971; Fontana, London, 1973. See

especially pp. 164–74 in the 1990 Fontana edition.

50 Davis, *op. cit.*, p. 93.

51 See Lyons, *op. cit.*, pp. 407–8.

52 Davis, *op. cit.*, pp. 92–3.

53 Huxley, *op. cit.*, p. 58.

54 Tilly, *op. cit.*, pp. 120–1.

55 Henry David Thoreau, *On the Duty of Civil Disobedience*, Peace News, London, 1963, with an introduction by Gene Sharp, p. 13.

56 See his 'Letter to Dr Eugen Heinrich Schmitt', reprinted in Leo Tolstoy, *Writings on Civil Disobedience and Nonviolence*, New Society Publishers, Philadelphia, 1987, p. 169.

57 Tolstoy, *op. cit.*, p. 210.

58 *Ibid*, p. 213.

59 *Ibid*, p. 183.

60 *Ibid.*, pp. 287–93.

61 Huxley, *op. cit.*, p. 59. I question, however, whether there was a single 'articulated doctrine' since, as we have seen, individuals and groups adopted the method of passive resistance from a variety of motives and ideological perspectives.

62 Tilly, *op. cit.*, especially pp. 48–55.

63 *Ibid*, p. 51.

64 *Ibid*, p. 282.

65 *Ibid*, p. 282.

66 *Ibid*, p. 249.

67 *Ibid*, p. 249.

68 *Ibid*, p. 282.

69 *Ibid*, p. 23.

70 *Ibid*, p. 248.

71 G. D. H. Cole and Raymond Postgate, *The Common People: 1746–1946*, Methuen, London, 1946, p. 223.

72 Tilly, *op. cit.*, p. 288.

Chapter 3

1 See Wolfgang Sternstein, '*The Ruhrkampf* of 1923: Economic Problems of Civilian Defence', in Adam Roberts (ed.), *The Strategy of Civilian Defence*, Faber & Faber, London, 1967, pp. 106–35.

2 A good general account of the non-violent resistance in occupied Europe is to be found in Jorgen Haestrup's *Europe Ablaze: An Analysis of the History of the European Resistance Movement 1939–45*, Odense University Press, 1978. See especially Ch. 3, 'Forms of Civil Disobedience'. For readers of French, I would strongly recommend Jacques Semelin, *Sans Armes face à Hitler: La Résistance Civile en Europe 1939–1943*, Editions Payot, Paris, 1989 (now available in an English translation as *Unarmed Against Hitler: Civilian Resistance in Europe 1939–1943*, Praeger, Westport, Connecticut, 1993). There are also chapters on the resistance in Norway by Magne Skodvin and in Denmark by Jeremy Bennett in Roberts, *op. cit*, pp. 136–53 and 154–72.

3 Gandhi's son, Manilal Gandhi, was among those arrested during the 1952 campaign.

4 See Albert Bigelow, *The Voyage of the Golden Rule*, Doubleday, New York, 1959.

5 The development and

achievements of the civil rights movement in Northern Ireland are succinctly described in Lyons, *op. cit.*, the chapter headed 'The Continuing Crisis', especially pp. 762–5. For a fuller account by one of its leading initiators and organisers, see Conn McCluskey, *Up off Their Knees*, Conn McCluskey & Associates, 1989.

6 See April Carter, *Peace Movements: International Protest and World Politics since 1945*, Longman, London and New York, 1992, esp pp. 158–182.

7 See Vanessa Griffin, 'Social Defence against Coups: the Case of Fiji', in Shelley Anderson and Janet Larmore (eds), *Nonviolent Struggle and Social Defence*, War Resisters International, London, 1991, pp. 59–66.

8 Jan Zielonka, 'Strengths and Weaknesses of Nonviolent Defence', in *Orbis*, spring 1986, p. 93.

9 *Ibid*, p. 93.

10 In the summer of 1992 the then Lithuanian Defence Minister, Audrius Butkevicius, stated that Gene Sharp's book, *Civilian-Based Defence: A Post-Military Weapons System*, Princeton University Press, New Jersey, 1990, had served as a basis for much of his planning for non-violent resistance over the previous year and a half, and that he had had an early draft of the book translated into Lithuanian for use by government officials. The book was also translated into Latvian and had an influence on the civil resistance plans of both Latvia and Estonia. See Bruce Jenkins, 'Civilian-Based Defence Discussed in Moscow and the Baltics', in *Civilian-Based Defence: News and Opinion*, Vol. 7, No. 6, August 1992, pp. 2–3 and 18.

11 Judith M. Brown, *Gandhi: Prisoner of Hope*, Yale University Press, New Haven and London, 1989, pp. 103–4.

12 *Ibid*, p. 104.

13 On this point, see Robert Overy, *Gandhi as an Organiser: An Analysis of Local and National Campaigns in India, 1915–1922*, PhD thesis, School of Peace Studies, University of Bradford, 1982. Overy argues that the programme of constructive work constitutes 'the underlying bedrock of preparation for civil resistance' in Gandhi's campaigns (p. 357). See especially Ch. 4, 'The Place of the Constructive Programme in Local and National Satyagraha Campaigns', pp. 109–29. His thesis also includes a descriptive analysis of the 1920–1 campaign of non-cooperation. See also the chapter entitled 'Non-cooperation: the road to swaraj?' in Brown, *op. cit.*, pp. 139–75.

14 Brown, *op. cit.*, p. 233.

15 *Ibid*, p. 242.

16 *Ibid*, pp. 256–60.

17 *Ibid*, p. 282.

18 *Ibid*, p. 295.

19 *Ibid*, p. 331.

20 *Ibid*, p. 331.

21 *Ibid*, pp. 338–9.

22 See *The Collected Works of M. K. Gandhi (CWMK)*, The Publication Division, Ministry of Information and Broadcasting, Government of India, 1958–70, Vol. 7, p. 455. In *Satyagraha in South Africa*, first published in 1928, more than twenty years after the commencement of the campaign, Gandhi claimed that the new term was coined 'to prevent [the movement] *being confused with* passive resistance generally so called' (emphasis added). See the Navajivan Publishing House 1972 edition, p. 107. While Gandhi is evidently mistaken on this point, it is also clear that he was never happy about the term 'passive resistance' because of the confusions to which it gave rise. On this question see also Huxley, *op. cit.*, p. 43, and also pp. 42–7 in which he makes a critical assessment of what he terms 'Gandhian folklore'.

23 See for instance his letter to the Rand *Daily Mail*, 2 July 1907, in which he described the campaign as 'not resistance but a policy of communal suffering'. *CWMK*, Vol. 7, p. 67.

24 M. K. Gandhi, *Satyagraha*, Navajivan Publishing House, Ahmadabad, 1958 edition, p. 6.

25 *Indian Opinion*, 11 November 1905. See *CWMK*, Vol. 5, pp. 131–2. See also the important essay by Gene Sharp, 'Origins of Gandhi's Use of Nonviolent Struggle', in Sharp, *Gandhi as a Political Strategist*, Porter Sargent, Boston, 1979, pp. 23–41.

26 Brown, *op. cit.*, p. 55.

27 Gandhi spoke enthusiastically about Thoreau's essay, though it did not influence him in launching civil resistance in South Africa as he first read it during a spell in prison. See Judith M. Brown, *Gandhi's Rise to Power: Indian Politics 1915–1922*, Cambridge University Press, 1972, p. 7.

28 See Gandhi's response to a question on this point published in *Harijan*, 12 April 1942: 'Yes, I adhere to my opinion that I did well to present to the Congress non-violence as an expedient. I could not have done otherwise if I was to introduce it into politics. In South Africa, too, I introduced it as an expedient.' The article in which this quote appears is reprinted in M. K. Gandhi, *Non-Violence in Peace and War*, Vol. 1, Navajivan Publishing House, Ahmadabad, 1948 edition, pp. 394–6. The quotation in question appears on p. 396.

29 See Sharp, *Gandhi as a Political Strategist, op. cit.*, p. 26.

30 *Harijan*, 23 August 1939. Reprinted in M. K. Gandhi, *Non-Violence in Peace and War, op. cit.*, p. 226.

31 Strictly speaking, this was the sixth Congress, the first having taken place in London in 1900 under the leadership of a West Indian barrister, Sylvester Williams. But it has become traditional to date the

Congresses from the one convened by DuBois in Paris in 1919, which brought together African and Afro-American leaders to lobby the delegates to the Versailles Conference. DuBois convened subsequent congresses in London (1921), London and Lisbon (1923) and New York (1927). He was also present at the founding Congress in 1900. The Pan-African Congress is not to be confused with the Pan-Africanist Congress (PAC), a breakaway movement from the African National Congress (ANC), founded in South Africa in 1959 by Robert Sobuqwe.

32 Mary Benson, *South Africa: The Struggle for a Birthright*, Penguin, Harmondsworth, 1966 edition, p. 90.

33 In November 1949 Michael Scott addressed the UN Fourth Committee on the situation of the Herero tribe in South-West Africa – Namibia – to the fury of the South African government. See Michael Scott, *A Time to Speak*, Faber & Faber, London, 1958, Ch. 14, 'The General Assembly Decides', pp. 242–68. In 1951, he was declared a prohibited immigrant and had to continue his work from outside the country. Among other Anglican clergymen who played an active role in the opposition to apartheid were Father Trevor Huddleston of the Community of the Resurrection, now (1992) Chair of the Anti-Apartheid Movement in Britain, and the late Rt Rev. Ambrose Reeves, Bishop of Johannesburg.

34 Benson, *op. cit.*, p. 90.

35 The Suppression of Communism Act (1950) prohibited not only any doctrine or scheme which aimed at the dictatorship of the proletariat but also any 'which aims to bring about any political, industrial, social, or economic change within the Union by the promotion of disturbance or disorder, by unlawful acts or omissions or by the threat of such acts or omissions or by means which include the promotion of disturbance or disorder, or such acts or omissions or threats'. See Leo Kuper, *Passive Resistance in South Africa*, Yale University Press, 1960 edition, p. 61.

36 The military wing of the PAC, Poqo, did not officially halt its military activities at that point, though its activities by 1991 were sporadic.

37 See Gene Sharp, *The Politics of Nonviolent Action, op. cit.*, p. 293.

38 Robert Cooney and Helen Michalowski (eds), *The Power of the People*, Peace Press, California, 1977, p. 150.

39 *Ibid*, pp. 160–3.

40 Ntsu Mokhehle became Prime Minister of Lesotho (formerly Basutoland) in April 1993 following the landslide victory of the Basutoland Congress Party (BCP) in the first free elections since 1970. The 1970 election was suspended, and a state of emergency, declared by

Lesotho's strongman, Chief Leabua Jonathan of the Basutoland National Party, when early returns indicated that the BCP would be victorious.

41 The author was one of the British participants of the Sahara Protest Team (the other being the artist Francis Hoyland) and witnessed the scene.

42 See April Carter, 'The Sahara Protest Team', in A. Paul Hare and Herbert H. Blumberg, *Liberation without Violence*, Rex Collings, London, 1977, pp. 126–56. See also A. J. Muste's account of the project, 'Africa against the Bomb', in Nat Hentoff (ed.), *The Essays of A. J. Muste*, Simon & Schuster, New York, 1967, pp. 394–409.

43 For an account by one of the participant organisers, see Brad Lyttle, *You Come with Naked Hands*, Greenleaf Books, New Hampshire, 1966.

44 For a brief account of the Delhi–Peking Friendship March and an analysis of its strengths and weaknesses, see April Carter, *Peace Movements, op. cit.*, pp. 245–7. This is part of a consideration of 'Transnational Intervention', pp. 245–9.

45 The four clergymen were Rev. Martin Niemöller, the Lutheran clergyman who had spent many years in Nazi concentration camps for his opposition to Nazism, Rt Rev. Ambrose Reeves, former Bishop of Johannesburg and anti-apartheid campaigner,

Rev. A. J. Muste, and Rabbi Abraham Feinburg of Canada. See Rabbi Feinburg's diary of the trip, *Hanoi Diary*, Longman, Ontario, Canada, 1968.

46 See Pat Arrowsmith (ed.), *To Asia in Peace*, Sidgwick & Jackson, London, 1972.

47 See Michael Randle and April Carter (eds), *Support Czechoslovakia*, Peace News, London, 1968.

48 See 'Operation Omega' (from accounts in *Peace News*) in Hare and Blumberg, *op. cit.*, pp. 196–206. See also Carter, *op. cit.*, p. 247.

49 See David McTaggart, *Greenpeace III: Journey into the Bomb*, Collins, London, 1978.

50 Carter, *Peace Movements, op. cit.*, p. 171.

51 *Ibid*, pp. 247–9.

52 *Ibid*, pp. 245–9. The information she provides was corrected and updated by Tim Wallis-Milne of PBI in conversation with the author in 1993.

53 The figures cited are taken from the entry on Chile in Peter Teed, *Dictionary of Twentieth Century History: 1914–1990*, OUP, Oxford, 1992, pp. 89–90. For an account by one of the non-violent activists involved, see Fernando Aliaga Rojas, 'How we won democracy in Chile', in Shelley Anderson and Janet Larmore (eds), *Nonviolent Struggle and Social Defence*, War Resisters International and the Myrtle Solomon Memorial Fund Subcommittee, London, 1991, pp. 51–4.

54 See Sharp, *Civilian-Based Defence, op. cit.*, p. 39.

55 See Sharp, *The Politics of Nonviolent Action, op. cit.*, pp. 90–3.

56 See Pierre Croissant, 'Bolivie 1978: la grève de la faim contre la dictature', in *Alternatives Non Violentes*, No. 39, December 1980, pp. 34–59.

57 See Jean-Marie Muller, 'La non-violence ramène la démocratie', in *Alternatives Non Violentes*, No. 62, December 1986, pp. 26–31.

58 *New York Times*, 12 February 1979. The account of the revolts in the air-force bases at Farahabad and Doshan Tapeh is taken from David Cortright and Max Watts, *Left Face: Soldier Unions and Resistance Movements in Modern Armies*, Greenwood Press, New York, Westport, Connecticut, and London, 1991, pp. 220–1.

59 Enrile was the leader of a reform movement within the armed forces, RAM, and there is evidence that he had been planning to make use of this organisation to seize power himself in a coup against Marcos. His plans were forestalled by Marcos's unexpected announcement of elections, and the victory of Aquino. See Cortright and Watts, *op. cit.*, pp. 225–8.

60 See Adam Roberts, 'Civil Resistance to Military Coups', in *Journal of Peace Research*, Vol. XII, No. 1, 1975, pp. 19–36.

61 See Gene Sharp, 'The Relevance of Civilian-Based Defence for the 1990s', in *Civilian-Based Defence*, Vol. 8, No. 1, October 1992, p. 3. (This journal was previously entitled *Civilian-Based Defence: News and Opinion*, but adopted the shorter title in October 1992.)

62 See the *Guardian*, 21 August 1991.

63 'The collapse of a coup: 56 hours that shook the Soviet Union' in the *Guardian*, 22 August 1991.

64 The majority – about two-thirds of them – were Soviet forces.

65 Zdenek Mylnar, *Night Frost in Prague* (translated by Paul Wilson), C. Hurst, London, 1980, p. 201.

66 *Ibid*, pp. 201–4.

67 Alex P. Schmid (in collaboration with Ellen Berends and Luuk Zonneveld), *Social Defence and Soviet Military Power: An Inquiry into the Relevance of an Alternative Defence Concept*, Centre for the Study of Conflict (COMT), State University of Leiden, 1985, p. 343.

68 Mylnar, *op. cit.*, p. 176.

69 The strike weapon was used in a symbolic fashion during the seven days of open resistance to the invasion, but there was no attempt to call a prolonged general strike since it was considered this would hurt the Czechoslovak people, and their ability to continue the resistance, rather than the occupiers. The primary goals of the invasion were, after all, political, not economic.

70 Mylnar, *op. cit.*, p. 200.

71 *Ibid*, pp. 198–9.

72 *Ibid*, p. 196.
73 *Ibid*, p. 227.
74 Cited in Jean-Marie Muller, *op. cit.*, p. 20.
75 See the interview with Jan Kavan in Michael Randle, *People Power: The Building of a New European Home*, Hawthorn Press, Stroud, 1991, p. 153.

Chapter 4

1 The vote was taken at a meeting on 23 November 1989 following a raid by plain-clothes police on the central TV station and the sacking of its director. Four thousand nine hundred staff voted in favour of the motion, 300 against. See Nigel Hawkes (ed.), *Tearing Down the Curtain*, Hodder & Stoughton, 1990, p. 118. The film of the student demonstration was broadcast the following day – the day on which Jakes and the whole of the Politburo resigned.
2 Richard B. Gregg, *The Power of Non-Violence*, George Routledge & Sons, London, 1935.
3 *Ibid*, p. 26.
4 *Ibid*, p. 36.
5 See the chapter entitled 'Political Jiu-Jitsu' in Gene Sharp, *The Politics of Nonviolent Action, op. cit.*, pp. 657–98. There is a succinct summary of his argument in *Civilian-Based Defence, op. cit.*, pp. 58–9.
6 Sharp, *The Politics of Nonviolent Action, op. cit.*, especially Ch. 13, 'Three ways success may be achieved', pp. 705–76. George Lakey's 1962 MA thesis at Pennsylvania University was entitled 'The Sociological Mechanisms of Nonviolent Action'. A copy of the thesis is housed at the Commonweal Library at Bradford University, W. Yorkshire.
7 Sharp, *Civilian-Based Defence, op. cit.*, pp. 60–5.
8 The distinction is drawn by the Norwegian researcher Johan Galtung in 'On the Meaning of Non-Violence', in *Journal of Peace Research*, Vol. 2, No. 3, 1965, pp. 228–57. See also Boserup and Mack, *War without Weapons*, Frances Pinter, London, 1974, Ch. 1, 'Positive and Negative Conflict Behaviour: Theoretical Problems', pp. 21–36.
9 Boserup and Mack place the Norwegian researcher Arne Naess firmly in the first camp, and Gene Sharp, Adam Roberts, Theodor Ebert, a leading German researcher, and other 'pragmatists' in the second. Galtung attempts to combine both negative and positive approaches, though with an awareness of the problems of employing positive methods in highly polarised situations.
10 I would place Gene Sharp in the first of these two categories since he insists on keeping open the notion that civil resistance and 'civilian-based defence' will be shown by further research to deal with all conflict situations.

Roberts, since the 1970s at least, has clearly placed himself in the second category.

11 See Boserup and Mack on this issue, *op. cit.*, pp. 31–8.

12 Sharp, *The Politics of Nonviolent Action, op. cit.*, Part Two: 'The Methods of Nonviolent Action: Political Jiu-Jitsu at Work'.

13 Boserup and Mack, *op. cit.*, p. 38.

14 See my interview with Elbieta Rawicz-Oledzka in Randle, *People Power, op. cit.*, pp. 167–71.

15 See Jan Zielonka, 'Strengths and Weaknesses of Nonviolent Action: the Polish Case', in *Orbis*, spring 1986, pp. 91–110, especially pp. 103–4.

16 Elbieta Rawicz-Oledzka in Randle, *op. cit.*, p. 169.

Chapter 5

1 Bertrand Russell, 'War and Non-Resistance', in *Atlantic Monthly*, August 1915, pp. 266–74; reprinted in Bertrand Russell, *Justice in War Time*, Open Court, Chicago and London, pp. 38–57.

2 Elihu Burritt, 'Passive Resistance', in Burritt, *Thoughts and Things at Home and Abroad*, Philips Sampson, Boston, 1854, pp. 269–86; reprinted in Staughton Lynd (ed.), *Nonviolence in America*, Bobbs-Merrill, Indianapolis, 1966, pp. 93–108.

3 Clarence Marsh Case, *Non-Violent Coercion: A Study in Methods of Social Pressure*, first published by The Century Co., New York and London, 1923; reprinted by the Garland Publishing Co., New York and London, 1972. See Ch. 2.

4 Richard B. Gregg, *The Power of Non-Violence, op. cit.*

5 Bart de Ligt, *The Conquest of Violence*, George Routledge & Sons, London, 1937, with an introduction by Aldous Huxley; new edition, Pluto Press, London, 1989, with a new introduction by Peter van den Dungen.

6 Krishnalal Shridharani, *War without Violence: A Study of Gandhi's Method and Its Accomplishments*, Harcourt, Brace & Co., New York, 1939; reprinted by the Garland Publishing Co., New York and London, in their 'Garland Library of War and Peace' series, 1972, with an introduction by Gene Sharp.

7 Originally a series of articles, it was published as a pamphlet by the War Resisters League in 1942; an edited version of Hughan's essay is included in Mulford Q. Sibley, *The Quiet Battle, op. cit.*, pp. 317–32.

8 Stephen King-Hall, 'The Small Countries', in *Free Denmark*, Vol. 1, No. 5, August 1942, p. 1.

9 See B. H. Liddell Hart, 'Lessons from Resistance Movements – Guerrilla and Non-Violent', in Adam Roberts (ed.), *The Strategy of Civilian Defence, op. cit.*, pp. 195–211.

10 Gene Sharp, *Tyranny Could Not Quell Them*, Peace News, London, 1959.

11 Commander Sir Stephen King-Hall, *Defence in the Nuclear Age*, Victor Gollancz, London, 1958.

12 Gene Sharp was an Assistant Editor of *Peace News* from 1955 to 1958 and was involved in the Direct Action Committee against Nuclear War in the early period; April Carter became Secretary of the Direct Action Committee in 1958. Adam Roberts was also an Assistant Editor of *Peace News* in the early 1960s and took part in some of the Committee of 100 demonstrations. They went on to become some of the leading researchers in the field. Hugh Brock, as *Peace News* editor in the 1950s and early 1960s, and Chairman of the Direct Action Committee, played an important role in encouraging the exploration of the concept.

13 Bradford Lyttle, *National Defense through Nonviolent Resistance*, Shann-ti Sena, Chicago, 1958.

14 *Preventing World War III: Some Proposals*, Quincy Wright, William M. Evans and Morton Deutsch, (eds), Simon & Schuster, New York, 1962.

15 Adam Roberts (ed.), *Civilian Defence*, Peace News, London, 1964, p. 7.

16 'The purpose of civilian defense is to defend. It is not an exercise in moral speculation, but a practical means of national defense. Its validity depends upon the degree to which it would meet [certain] tests as compared with defense based upon military means.' From *In Place of War: An Inquiry into Nonviolent National Defense*, prepared by a working party of the Peace Education Division, American Friends Service Committee, Grossman, New York, 1967, p. 70. Although this was clearly written from a pacifist position, and the panel included some of the best-known American pacifists, the criteria put forward for judging the efficacy of civilian defence are virtually indistinguishable from that of the 'pragmatic' school.

17 Adam Roberts (ed.), *The Strategy of Civilian Defence, op. cit.* The book was republished by Penguin, Harmondsworth, in 1970 under the title *Civilian Resistance as a National Defence: Nonviolent Action against Aggression*, with a new introduction by Roberts noting the significance of the Czechoslovak resistance to the Soviet-led invasion of 1968.

18 Gene Sharp, *Civilian-Based Defence, op. cit.*

19 The term 'defence by civil resistance' was first proposed by Adam Roberts in *Nations in Arms*, Chatto & Windus (for the International Institute of Strategic Studies), London, 1976, p. 101. It was adopted by the Alternative Defence Commission in Britain (of which Roberts was for a period a member) and employed in its report *Defence without the Bomb*, Taylor & Francis, London and New York, 1983.

20 The disadvantage of the term 'social defence' – which I have myself used on other occasions – is that it strongly suggests civil resistance used for social and economic goals rather than for political freedom or national independence.

21 See the Appendix for a selected list of publications in this field.

22 For developments in Holland in the 1970s, see Hylke Tromp, 'The Dutch Research Project on Civilian Defence, 1974–1978', in *Bulletin of Peace Proposals*, Vol. 9, No. 4, 1978, pp. 301–7.

23 See Hylke Tromp, 'Nouveaux points de vue sur la défense sociale', in *Les Stratégies Civiles de Défense* (Proceedings of the International Colloquium of Strasbourg, 27/28/29 November 1985), ANV-IRNC, Paris, 1987, pp. 198–210, in particular p. 199.

24 Alex P. Schmid, *Social Defence and Soviet Military Power, op. cit.* The book is discussed in the next chapter.

25 For a brief overview of Swiss defence policy, including its non-military dimension, see Dietrich Fischer, 'Invulnerability without Threat: The Swiss Concept of General Defence', in *Journal of Peace Research*, Vol. XIX, No. 3, 1982, pp. 205–25.

26 On the Yugoslav doctrine of General People's Defence, see Adam Roberts, *Nations in Arms, op. cit.*, pp. 172–217. On the role of 'non-military resistance'

within the overall strategy, see pp. 210–13.

27 The original English-language titles of these studies, available, in mimeograph form only, from the Commonweal Library, University of Bradford, Bradford, West Yorkshire, are: *Total Defence and Civil Resistance*, 1972; *The Technique of Civil Resistance*, 1976; and *Occupation, Resistance and Law*, 1980. For a critical review of Swedish postwar defence policy up to 1978, and an assessment of the official interest in civilian defence, see Haken Wiberg, 'Swedish National Security Policy: A Review and Critique', in *Bulletin of Peace Proposals*, Vol. 9, No. 4, 1978, pp. 308–15 and 334.

28 See p. 5 of *Complementary Forms of Resistance: A Summary of the Report of the Swedish Commission on Resistance*, prepared by Lennart Bergfeldt and published in mimeograph form by Swedish Official State Reports, SOU 1984:10.

29 See Bruce Jenkins, 'Civilian-Based Defence Discussed in Moscow and the Baltics', in *Civilian-Based Defence: News and Opinion (CBD)*, Vol. 7, No. 6, August 1992, pp. 2–3 and 18.

30 The full text of the Lithuanian Supreme Council's declaration is published in English in *CBD*, Vol. 7, No. 3, May/July 1991, p. 4. See also, in the same issue, Christopher Kruegler, 'A Bold Initiative in Lithuanian

Defence', p. 1, and Bruce Jenkins, 'Einstein Institution Delegation Discusses Civilian-Based Defence with Lithuanian Officials', pp. 2–3.

31 Bruce Jenkins, in *CBD*, Vol. 7, No. 6, August 1992, pp. 2–3. See also, in the same issue, Steven Huxley, 'Lessons from the Baltics', pp. 6–7.

32 See Roger S. Powers, 'Baltic Defence Officials Consider Civilian-Based Defence at Vilnius Conference', in *CBD*, Vol. 7, No. 6, August 1992, p. 1.

33 Thus Roberts states that 'the core of the idea of civilian defence is a prepared policy for the defence of a society against such violent threats as coups d'état, or foreign invasion or occupation. Many very important instances of civil resistance may not fall within this definition, either because they are directed against different types of threat, *or because the key element of advance preparation is lacking*' (emphasis added). See 'Civilian Defence Twenty Years On', in *Bulletin of Peace Proposals*, Vol. 9, No. 4, 1978, p. 299.

34 Gene Sharp, 'Gandhi as a National Defense Strategist', in *Gandhi Marg*, Vol. XIV, No. 3, July 1970. The essay is reproduced in Sharp, *Gandhi as a Political Strategist, op. cit.*, pp. 171–98. The passage in question appears on p. 172.

35 Jan Zielonka, 'Strengths and Weaknesses of Nonviolent Action: The Polish Case', in *Orbis*, spring 1986, pp. 91–110.

36 See Gustaaf Geeraerts, 'Two Approaches to Civilian Defence: Instrumentalists and Structuralists', in *Bulletin of Peace Proposals*, Vol. 9, No. 4, 1978, pp. 316–20; and, in the same issue, Adam Roberts, 'Civilian Defence Twenty Years On', pp. 293–300, which, in part, vigorously rejects the notion that civilian defence 'is appropriate only in a much re-structured society'. Roberts' article was republished in the French journal *Alternatives Non Violentes*, No. 39, December 1980, together with a short response by me. See pp. 17–28.

37 Roberts, 'Civilian Defence Twenty Years On', *Bulletin of Peace Proposals, op. cit.*, p. 295.

38 Bruce Jenkins, writing in *CBD*, August 1992, speculates that defence officials in Estonia and Latvia may be reluctant to train the large Russian minorities in these countries in civilian forms of resistance because of the fear that they would collaborate in any attempt to re-impose authoritarian, pro-Russian rule. See p. 18 of this issue.

39 See D. J. Goodspeed, 'The Coup d'Etat', in Roberts, *The Strategy of Civilian Defence, op. cit.*, pp. 31–46; Adam Roberts, 'Civil Resistance to Military Coups', in *Journal of Peace Research*, Vol. XXI, No. 1, 1975, pp. 19–36; Vanessa Griffin, 'Social Defence against Coups', in Shelley Anderson and Janet Larmore (eds), *Nonviolent Struggle and*

Social Defence, op. cit., pp. 59–66.

40 Gene Sharp, *Making Europe Unconquerable*, Taylor & Francis, London, and Ballinger, Cambridge, Mass., 1985, p. 146.

Chapter 6

1 Boserup and Mack, *War without Weapons, op. cit.*

2 For a good, accessible edition, see Anatol Rapoport (ed.), *On War*, Karl von Clausewitz (translated by J. J. Graham), Penguin, Harmondsworth, 1968. The book was first published in 1832.

3 Boserup and Mack, *op. cit.*, p. 148.

4 *Ibid*, p. 148.

5 Gandhi's writings and speeches in this area are collected in M. K. Gandhi, *Non-Violence in Peace and War (NVPW), op. cit.*, Vol. I. See especially Ch. 61, 'If I were a Czech', Ch. 64, 'The Jews', Ch. 68, 'Non-Violence and World Crisis', Ch. 84, 'To the Brave Poles', Ch. 114, 'To Every Briton'.

6 See 'The War Resolution' in *NVPW*, from *Harijan*, 26 August 1939, in which Gandhi recounts how his draft resolution based on 'out-and-out non-violence' was rejected in favour of one by Jawaharlal Nehru.

7 See 'Letter to the Generalissimo' (Chiang Kai-shek) dated 14 June 1942 in *NVPW*, pp. 404–7.

8 M. Desai, reporting Gandhi's response to an enquiry, in *Young India*, 31 December 1931. Reprinted in *NVPW* as 'Theory and Practice of Non-Violence', pp. 105–10. The quotation appears on p. 109.

9 *Harijan*, 13 April 1940. See 'Two Questions from America' in *NVPW*, pp. 264–6. The quotation appears on p. 265.

10 *Harijan*, 12 April 1942. See 'Non-Violent Resistance' in *NVPW*, pp. 397–9. The quotation appears on p. 397.

11 Gregg, *op. cit.* A revised and updated edition was published by Navajivan Publishing House, Ahmadabad, in 1960, with an introduction by Martin Luther King. The page references here are to the earlier edition.

12 *Ibid*, p. 93.

13 Walter Lippman, 'The Political Equivalent of War', in *Atlantic Monthly*, August 1928, pp. 181ff. Cited in Gregg, *op. cit.*, pp. 93–4. A slightly condensed version of William James's essay is to be found in Henry Steele Commager, *Living Ideas in America*, Harper & Row, New York, 1951.

14 Gregg, *op. cit.*, p. 94.

15 B. H. Liddell Hart, *The Real War*, Little Brown, Boston, 1930, p. 506. Cited in Gregg, *op. cit.*, pp. 68–9.

16 Gregg, *op. cit.*, p. 94. The quotation, summarising von Clausewitz, is from A. A. Walser, 'Air Power', in *The Nineteenth Century and After*, London, April 1923, p. 598.

17 *Ibid*, p. 84.

18 However, de Ligt, too,

acknowledged that war had played a role historically in bringing people and civilisations together, and, to quote his words, he 'even based the methods of anti-militarist fighting on, amongst others, *La Psychologie du Combat* and *La Psychologie Sociale de la Guerre* by the French Commandant Charles Coste'. (De Ligt, *The Conquest of Violence, op. cit.*, Pluto Press edition, p. 204.)

19 A selection of this correspondence, which appeared originally in *Young India*, is reproduced in *NVPW*, pp. 73–5, 86–8, 99–101, and 416–27. De Ligt met Gandhi in Lausanne and Geneva in 1931 after the latter had attended the Round Table Conference in London, and was critical of the position he had taken at the conference in demanding that India should take control of her own defence forces. De Ligt also wrote to Romain Rolland, with whom Gandhi was staying in Geneva, upbraiding him for remaining silent about Gandhi's 'war propaganda' in the 1914–18 war, and stating: 'We no longer need an infallible Messiah'. See the introduction by Peter van den Dungen to the Pluto Press edition of *The Conquest of Violence, op. cit.*, pp. xxii–xxiii.

20 De Ligt, *op. cit.*, p. 239.

21 *Ibid*, pp. 230–1.

22 *Ibid*, p. 248.

23 'Our own frontiers are not those traced by the diplomatic hand: they are everywhere and nowhere, since we are first men, cosmopolitans, internationalists and then Dutchmen . . . above our country, we put humanity: above our essentially bourgeois nation, the Socialist International . . . The more we act in this way, the more faithful we shall be to the noblest of Dutch traditions.' (*Ibid*, pp. 245–6.)

24 *Ibid*, p. 255.

25 See the abridged version of her essay in Mulford Q. Sibley, *The Quiet Battle, op. cit.*, p. 319.

26 *Ibid*, p. 324.

27 *Ibid*, p. 325.

28 *Ibid*, p. 325.

29 Stephen King-Hall, *Defence in the Nuclear Age, op. cit.*, p. 198.

30 *Ibid*, pp. 198–9. Hughan, however, does observe that: 'Neither army morale nor war fever in the aggressor nation is likely to hold out long against this reversal of all that makes the spirit of a campaign' (*The Quiet Battle, op. cit.*, p. 326). And in a section headed 'Plight of the Enemy Government' she anticipates that the check administered by civil resistance to the enemy's plans will turn 'the prestige of conquest to international ridicule', cause difficulties for the aggressor at home, provide opportunities to his domestic opponents, and swing formally neutral countries against him.

31 *Ibid*, p. 199.

32 *Ibid*, p. 199

33 *Ibid*, p. 200.

34 *Ibid*, p. 147.

35 *Ibid*, p. 147.

36 *Ibid*, p. 167.

37 See Roberts, *The Strategy of Civilian Defence, op. cit.*, p. 240.

38 But like King-Hall, Roberts fails to acknowledge that this tactic is also suggested by Hughan.

39 Theodor Ebert, 'Organisation in Civilian Defence', in Roberts, *op. cit.*, pp. 255–73. The quotation is on pp. 257–8.

40 Theodor Ebert, 'Eléments d'une stratégie de défense civile', in *Les Stratégies Civiles de Défense*, Proceedings of the Strasbourg International Colloquium, November 1985, organised by the Institut de Recherche sur la Résolution Non-Violente des Conflits (IRNC), published as a special number of *Alternatives Non Violentes*, 1987, pp. 36–46. The quotation (translated by Michael Randle) appears on p. 40.

41 Roberts contributed a chapter on 'Civilian Defence Strategy' to *The Strategy of Civilian Defence* which sets out some of the main elements of the Sharp/Roberts approach at that period. For an early exposition of Sharp's approach, see ' "The Political Equivalent of War" – Civilian Defence', in *International Conciliation*, No. 555, November 1965, and reprinted with revisions (including 'civilian-based defence' in the title) in Gene Sharp, *Social Power and Political Freedom, op. cit.*, pp. 195–262. For a more fully worked-out version of Sharp's approach to strategy, see Gene Sharp, *Making Europe Unconquerable, op. cit.*, especially Chs 5 and 6. See also Gene Sharp, *Civilian-Based Defence, op. cit.*, especially Ch. 4.

42 The term was coined by Theodor Ebert in the 1960s.

43 Sharp, *Making Europe Unconquerable, op. cit.*, p. 130.

44 After Jaroslav Hasek's character in *The Good Soldier Schweik* who thwarts all the intentions of his superiors by a show of dumbness and a feigned misunderstanding of orders. See the edition published by Penguin (translated by Cecil Parrott), Harmondsworth, 1973.

45 Adam Roberts, *The Technique of Civil Resistance, op. cit.*, p. 126.

46 In *People Power, op. cit.*, I briefly analyse some of the implications for civil resistance of the struggle in Eastern Europe which culminated in the revolutions of 1989.

47 Boserup and Mack, *op. cit.*, pp. 150–1.

48 Von Clausewitz, *On War*, cited in Boserup and Mack, *op. cit.*, p. 155.

49 Boserup and Mack, *op. cit.*, p. 168.

50 *Ibid*, p. 172.

51 Gene Keyes, 'Strategic Nonviolent Defense: The Construct of an Option', in *Journal of Strategic Studies*, Vol. 4, No. 2, June 1981, pp. 125–51. See also his PhD thesis, 'Strategic Nonviolent Defense in Theory: Denmark in Practice', York University, Toronto, 1978.

52 Roberts, *The Technique of Civil Resistance, op. cit.*, pp. 134–6.

53 *Ibid*, p. 135.

54 *Ibid*, p. 169.

55 Sharp, *Making Europe Unconquerable, op. cit.*, p. 131.

56 Boserup and Mack, *op. cit.*, p. 161.

57 Wolfgang Sternstein in Roberts (ed.), *The Strategy of Civilian Defence, op. cit.*, p. 134.

58 Boserup and Mack, *op. cit.*, p. 162.

59 *Ibid*, pp. 166–7.

60 Roberts, 'Civilian Defence Twenty Years On', in *Bulletin of Peace Proposals, op. cit.*, p. 299.

61 Schmid, *Social Defence and Soviet Military Power, op. cit.*

62 *Ibid*, pp. 27–30.

63 *Ibid*, pp. 27–9.

64 *Ibid*, p. 29.

65 *Ibid*, p. 402.

66 See Sharp, *Making Europe Unconquerable, op. cit.*, pp. 135–7. See also Jacques Semelin, 'La Résistance Civile face au Genocide', Ch. 8 of his major study *Sans Armes face à Hitler*, Editions Payot, Paris, 1989, pp. 179–220. An English translation was published as *Unarmed Against Hitler: Civilian Resistance in Europe 1939–1943*, Praeger, Westport, Connecticut, 1993.

67 In contrast to his earlier work. See especially Sharp, *Gandhi Wields the Weapon of Moral Power*, Navajivan Publishing House, Ahmadabad, 1960. Thus, on p. 3 of this volume, he writes: 'It is important to see this method [i.e. *satyagraha*] of fighting evil in the perspective of Gandhi's whole philosophy, for this weapon is an expression of a way of looking at life and a way of living.'

68 Civil resistance, including strikes and mass demonstrations, did of course play a major part in the struggle for democratic rights within former Yugoslavia, a struggle often inextricably linked to campaigns for national independence by the constituent republics of the federation. Since the outbreak of the war, beginning in Slovenia in mid-1991, there have also been courageous acts of non-violent intervention by citizens' groups, notably those associated with the anti-war movement, in the various formerly constituent Yugoslav republics, sometimes in conjunction with international organisations. Thus far, the struggle within the province of Kosovo has taken non-violent forms. Kosovo's autonomous status was arbitrarily curtailed in 1988 when the Serbian Assembly adopted a new republican constitution and established virtual military rule in the province in face of mass protests; Belgrade formally dissolved Kosovo's provincial assembly and government in July 1990. Whether it will be possible to prevent the spread of war to Kosovo and Macedonia, and a wider Balkan conflict, is a question still in the balance at the time of writing.

69 There is some evidence that UN economic sanctions against Serbia in 1992 had the effect of consolidating Slobodan Milosovic's support within the country; some commentators have also argued that sanctions against Iraq prior to and following the Gulf War of 1991 similarly consolidated support for Saddam Hussein. See also Roberts, 'A Note on International Economic Boycotts', in *The Technique of Civil Resistance, op. cit.*, pp. 101–17, for a discussion of some of the problems and possibilities here. See also Margaret P. Doxey, *International Sanctions in Contemporary Perspective*, Macmillan Press, Basingstoke, 1987.

70 See Liddell Hart's contribution to Roberts (ed.), *The Strategy of Civilian Defence, op. cit.*, p. 208.

71 Roberts, in *The Technique of Civil Resistance, op. cit.*, p. 129, cites in this connection the judgement of one observer that China was deterred from launching an attack on Macao at least in part because its leaders feared that 'any change in Macao would disrupt business in Hongkong from which China earns £500 million a year.' The quote is from David Bonavia reporting from Peking, *The Times*, 23 January 1975.

72 See Roberts, *Nations in Arms, op. cit.*, p. 52.

73 Roberts, *The Technique of Civil Resistance, op. cit.*, pp. 126–7.

74 See Roberts, *Nations in Arms, op. cit.*, pp. 222–5.

75 Sweden's Parliamentary Defence Committee report of 1984 on *Complementary Forms of Resistance* includes in the definition of non-military resistance 'irregular armed resistance by organised civilian groups'. See the summary by Lennart Bergfeldt, *op. cit.*, p. 5.

76 See Jeremy Bennett, 'The Resistance against the German Occupation of Denmark, 1940–45', in Adam Roberts (ed.), *The Strategy of Civilian Defence, op. cit.*, pp. 154–72, and especially pp. 161–4.

77 See B. H. Liddell Hart, 'Lessons from Resistance Movements – Guerrilla and Non-Violent', in Adam Roberts (ed.), *The Strategy of Civilian Defence, op. cit.*, pp. 195–211.

78 Bart de Ligt's classic study *The Conquest of Violence, op. cit.*, not only includes sabotage among the methods of non-violent action but contains an appendix which includes practical suggestions such as cutting telephone wires.

79 See Wolfgang Sternstein, 'The Ruhrkampf of 1923' in Roberts, *op. cit.*, especially the section headed 'Sabotage and its effects', pp. 123–6.

80 Alternative Defence Commission, *Defence without the Bomb, op. cit.*

81 *Ibid*, p. 209.

82 Swedish Commission on Resistance, *Complementary Forms of Resistance, op. cit.*, p. 8.

83 Lithuania's Deputy Defence

Minister at the time, Stankovicius, speaking to the Einstein Institution, Cambridge, Mass., in the summer of 1992. See Bruce Jenkins, 'Civilian-Based Defence Discussed in Moscow and the Baltics', in *CBD*, Vol. 7, No. 6, August 1992, p. 2.

84 *Ibid*, p. 2.

85 See Theodor Ebert, 'Organization in Civilian Defence', in Roberts (ed.), *The Strategy of Civilian Defence, op. cit.*, pp. 255–73, and on the Indian campaigns, p. 263.

86 *Ibid*, p. 266.

87 Boserup and Mack, *op. cit.*, pp. 66–7.

88 April Carter, 'Political Conditions for Civilian Defence', in Roberts (ed.), *The Strategy of Civilian Defence, op. cit.*, pp. 274–90. The passage quoted is on p. 289.

89 *Ibid*, p. 289.

90 Roberts, 'Civilian Defence Twenty Years On', in *Bulletin of Peace Proposals, op. cit.*, p. 298.

91 See the entry under 'Organisation' in Jean-Marie Muller, *Lexique de la Non-Violence*, Institut de Recherche sur la Résolution Non-Violente des Conflits, Saint-Etienne, 1988, pp. 62–3.

92 Muller, 'L'Etat de la Question', in *Les Stratégies Civiles de Défense*, Proceedings of the International Colloqium in Strasbourg, 17/28–29 November 1985, published as a special number of *Alternatives Non Violentes*, 1987.

93 *Ibid*, pp. 16–17. See also Muller,

'Why and How to Work with Governments', in Shelley Anderson and Janet Larmore (eds), *Nonviolent Struggle and Social Defence, op. cit.*, pp. 11–14.

Chapter 7

1 Tilly, Tilly and Tilly, *The Rebellious Century, op. cit.*, shows the role of popular agitation, occasionally violent, but overwhelmingly non-violent, in France, Germany and Italy in securing democratic participation in government. Belgium and Sweden are two other countries where strikes and other forms of civil resistance played a direct role in the achievement of adult suffrage.

2 For an excellent discussion of the issues involved, see April Carter, *Direct Action and Liberal Democracy*, Routledge & Kegan Paul, London, 1973. See also Stanley Alderson, 'When Is Civil Disobedience Justified?', in *The Political Quarterly*, April/June 1974, pp. 206–15.

3 As the historian D. G. Williamson expressed it: 'It was this apparent legality [of Hitler's appointment as Chancellor] that inhibited and confused all but the most clear-sighted opponents of the Nazi regime.' See D. G. Williamson, *The Third Reich*, 'Seminar Studies in History' series, ed. Roger Lockyer, Longman, London, 1988, especially pp. 8–11.

4 See the debate between Allen Skinner and Michael Randle on this issue in *Peace News*, 19 December 1958, and the contribution to the debate by Gene Sharp, *Peace News*, 30 January 1959. See also Michael Randle, 'Non-Violent Direct Action in the 1950s and 1960s', in Richard Taylor and Nigel Young (eds), *Campaigns for Peace: British Peace Movements in the Twentieth Century*, Manchester University Press, 1987.

5 The World Court Project is co-sponsored by the International Peace Bureau, International Physicians for the Prevention of Nuclear War, and the International Association of Lawyers against Nuclear Arms.

6 Michael Quinlan, a senior civil servant in the Ministry of Defence in the early 1980s, presents the most intellectually coherent moral and strategic case for nuclear deterrence and – with certain provisos – the actual use of nuclear weapons from the perspective of a Catholic who accepts the doctrine of just war. See his article, 'Preventing War: Why Deterrence Becomes an Inexorable Policy', in *The Tablet*, 18 July 1981, pp. 688–91, and the subsequent correspondence in that journal during July and August 1981. See also Walter Stein, 'Preventing War', in *The Tablet*, 22 August 1981, pp. 808–9, written in response to Quinlan's article, and his more detailed analysis of

the arguments in a series of three articles in *The Tablet* on 20 and 27 October and 10 November 1984.

Chapter 8

1 See Narayan Desai, 'Intervention in Riots in India', in A. Paul Hare and Herbert H. Blumberg, *Liberation without Violence, op. cit.*, pp. 74–91. and A. Paul Hare and Ellen Wilkinson, 'Cyprus-conflict and its Resolution' in the same volume, pp. 239–247.

2 See, however, Hans Sinn, 'Next: UN Reform?', in *Peace Magazine* (Canada), January/February 1993, pp. 18–22, who discusses the possibilities of unarmed peacekeeping by the UN. Sinn was a founder-member of Peace Brigades International and is a member of the New Democratic Party Task Force on UN Reform. An Australian researcher, Thomas Weber, has also recently completed a PhD thesis at La Trobe University in Healesville, Victoria on unarmed peacekeeping in general and the work of the Shann-ti Sena in particular.

3 See Terry McCarthy, 'Woman of Peace Takes on Military', in the *Independent*, 6 December 1992. See also Alan Clements, *Burma: the next killing fields?*, Odonian Press, Berkeley, California, 1992, with a foreword by the Dalai Lama.

4 Bruce Russett, 'Politics and Alternative Security: Towards a More Democratic, Therefore More Peaceful World', in Burns H. Weston (ed.), *Alternative Security: Living without Nuclear Deterrence*, Westview Press, Boulder, Colorado, 1990, pp. 107–36. The passage cited appears on p. 108.

5 See Susan George *et al.*, *The Debt Boomerang: How Third World Debt Harms Us All*, Pluto Press with the Transnational Institute, London, 1992. See also Susan George, *A Fate Worse than Debt*, Penguin, Harmondsworth, 1988.

6 See Bruce Jenkins, 'Civilian-Based Defence Discussed in Moscow and the Baltics', in *CBD*, Vol. 7, No. 6, August 1992, p. 2.

INDEX

Abernathy, Ralph 83
accomodation theory
    (Lakey/Sharp) 106
Adams, President John 38
Africa
    anti-nuclear protest 56, 81,
        82–3
    civil resistance concept 207
    independence movements
        54–5, 72–3, 76, 83–4, 111
    see also individual countries
Africa Freedom Action 84
African National Congress
    (ANC) xiv, 55, 73–6 *passim*,
    118
Aguirre, Luis Perez 87
Albert Einstein Institute (USA)
    130
Aldermaston March (Britain)
    55, 81, 123
Alexander the Great 154
Alexi, Patriarch 91
Algeria
    anti-nuclear Sahara Protest
        56, 81, 82–3
    war of independence 8, 76,
        191
    generals' attemped coup 56,
        89, 107, 132
Alternative Defence
    Commission (Britain) 128,
    170
Ambedkar, Dr Bhimrao Ramji
    68

America
    17th C. Quaker protest 28
    campaign for and War of
        Independence 37–8, 179–80
    see also Latin America; United
        States of America
Amnesty International 116,
    209
Anabaptists 26–7
Anand Panyarachun 15
anarchist movements 21, 29, 42,
    45, 177
ANC *see* African National
    Congress
Angola, independence 75, 76
Angry Brigade (Britain) 58
anti-nuclear protest *see* nuclear
    weapons
apartheid, campaign againt
    xiv–xv, 4, 60, 73–6, 81, 113,
    117
Aquinas, St Thomas 24–5, 26
Aquino, Benigno 88
Aquino, Corazón 88
Arendt, Hannah 2, 5, 17, 198
Aristide, Jean-Bertrand 60
Aristophanes 19
Aristotle 24
Armenia, civil war xiv
assassination, Tolstoy's
    rejection of 45–6
Attlee, Clement 185
Attwood, Thomas 40
Aung San Suu Kyi 207

241

Modern Essays

Frank Kermode

Frank Kermode is widely regarded as the most distinguished literary critic in the English language. In this collection of some of his best short pieces he considers poets and dancers, obscenity and modernity, and such diverse figures as J. D. Salinger and Muriel Spark, D. H. Lawrence and Samuel Beckett. Kermode consistently demonstrates that criticism of a high order can indeed 'defy the action of time'.

'In almost any review, Professor Kermode comes up with some shining new key to turn in the subject's lock' (*Listener*). He is 'one of the two or three outstanding English critics of his generation' (*Observer*). His reviews 'are definitely among those responsible for sending people into the bookshops and libraries' (*Times Literary Supplement*). In fact, 'there is no better critic writing in English than Kermode at his best' (*New Republic*).

Frank Kermode has been Northcliffe Professor of Modern English Literature at University College London, King Edward VII Professor of English Literature at Cambridge, and Charles Eliot Norton Professor of Poetry at Harvard. He is the General Editor of the Modern Masters and Masterguides series, and of the Oxford Authors. He is a Foreign Honorary Member of the American Academy of Arts and Sciences, an Officer de l'Ordre des Arts et des Sciences, and has received several honorary degrees. He now lives in Cambridge.

ISBN 0 00 686206 3

Fontana Modern Masters
Editor: Frank Kermode

Foucault

J. G. Merquior

'I have never been a Freudian, I have never been a Marxist and I have never been a structuralist.'   Michel Foucault

Michel Foucault wanted to defy categorization; he wanted to institute a new order of learning and thinking. When he died, still in his prime, in June 1984, he had already earned the nickname 'the new Sartre'. By attempting a highly original and daring merger of philosophy and history, he had set out to revitalize Western philosophy with bold, provocative theses on our attitudes to madness, the assumptions of science and language, our systems of punishment and discipline, and our ideas about sex. Finally, he presented new perspectives on the phenomenon of power and its relationship with knowledge.

J. G. Merquior's is an uninhibited critical assessment of Foucault as 'a historian of the present'. Encompassing all his published work and an impressive array of secondary literature about Foucault, it appraises his philosophical history and his debts to previous thinkers such as Bachelard and Kuhn, and sketches his complex relationship to French structuralism. It closes with an outline of Foucault's ideological profile as a Nietzschean master of the neo-anarchist mood, and raises important queries as to the ultimate value and legitimacy of his kind of philosophical rhetoric, with its attendant view of the role of the modern intellectual. As more people come to grapple with what Foucault *means*, with his true worth, Merquior's incisive, sane introduction will become indispensable.

ISBN 0 00 686226 8

Local Knowledge

Further Essays in Interpretive Anthropology

Clifford Geertz

'One of the most original and stimulating anthropologists of his generation.'
Contemporary Sociology

'These essays in cultural anthropology show the sparkle of [the author's] style, a rare enough quantity among social sciences.'
Washington Post

Clifford Geertz is arguably the most distinguished anthropologist of our time. His book *The Interpretation of Cultures* was published in 1973 to instant acclaim and is still considered an enormously influential work in modern social science. The sequel to this classic is *Local Knowledge*: a dazzling collection of essays in which Geertz rejects large abstractions, goes beyond the mere translation of one culture into another, and looks at the underlying, compartmentalized reality. Moving easily between the most exotic and most commonplace cultures, he demonstrates the power of anthropological thought to hold 'local knowledge' in dynamic tension with 'global knowledge'.

'One could celebrate the range of subjects on which he knowledgeably touches . . . the toughness of [his] mind, as well as the acerbity with which he exercises that toughness . . . It's invigorating to stretch one's mind on the Nautilus machine of his prose.'
New York Times

ISBN 0 00 686264 0

Fontana Modern Masters
Series Editor: Frank Kermode

Arendt

David Watson

Hannah Arendt was one of the most controversial figures in Western intellectual life in the period following the end of the Second World War. Again and again, she returned – to the annoyance of some and the enlightenment of many – to a recent past whose painful, complex moral history she obstinately, doggedly excavated, in order to display it to a public often uneasy about the implications of her discoveries. Her subject was totalitarianism – she analysed what it meant, and from where in the human pscyhe it sprang. She sought to clarify how we could begin to make judgement on the perpetrators of unthinkable crimes, how responsibility, punishment and due process might be weighed and measured. Arendt anatomized the lasting political and social impact of regimes which had not only enveloped her own family and friends in Europe, but changed the face of the world which the survivors inhabited. Her books *The Origins of Totalitarianism* and *Eichmann in Jerusalem* were a commercial and critical success, she was widely admired as a popular commentator, and her scholarly reputation soared on publication of her significant contributions to political theory – *The Human Condition* and *On Revolution*.

Though she offered no easy answers, readers turn to her still because she was a true *critic* – someone who could make distinctions, tease out meanings. Watson examines her distinctive approach to the questions of judgement and personal responsibility, and traces the development of her thought from political history and theory towards pure philosophy, culminating in the achievement of her posthumously published *The Life of the Mind*. He argues that in her attempt to make sense of the extraordinary events of her life and times, Arendt articulated fundamental questions which demand our continued attention.

ISBN 0 00 686237 3